MW00824821

Horace Mann's Troubling Legacy

American Political Thought

Wilson Carey McWilliams and Lance Banning

Founding Editors

Horace Mann's Troubling Legacy

The Education of Democratic Citizens

Bob Pepperman Taylor

UNIVERSITY PRESS OF KANSAS

© 2010 by the University Press of Kansas
All rights reserved

Published by the University Press of Kansas (Lawrence, Kansas 66045), which was organized by the Kansas Board of Regents and is operated and funded by Emporia State University, Fort Hays State University, Kansas State University, Pittsburg State University, the University of Kansas, and Wichita State University

Library of Congress Cataloging-in-Publication Data

Taylor, Bob Pepperman.
Horace Mann's troubling legacy : the education of democratic citizens / Bob Pepperman Taylor.
p. cm. — (American political thought)
Includes bibliographical references and index.
ISBN 978-0-7006-1745-6 (cloth : alk. paper)
1. Democracy and education—United States. 2. Mann, Horace, 1796–1859.
I. Title.
LB695.M35T39 2010
370.11'5—dc22

2010009288

British Library Cataloguing-in-Publication Data is available.

Printed in the United States of America

10 9 8 7 6 5 4 3 2 1

The paper used in this publication is recycled and contains 30 percent postconsumer waste. It is acid free and meets the minimum requirements of the American National Standard for Permanence of Paper for Printed Library Materials Z39.48-1992.

I should never have allowed the gates of the town to be opened to people who assert that there are higher considerations than those of decency.

—J. M. Coetzee, *Waiting for the Barbarians*

CONTENTS

PREFACE

Studying Horace Mann's writings has allowed me to think about the two primary duties of my professional life: teaching and studying American political thought and democratic theory. No figure occupies a more central position in American political history in terms of addressing these matters together and examining the deep interconnections and relationships between them. In the twentieth century John Dewey was the towering philosopher of democratic education. He willingly admitted, however, that he built on the inspiration and experience of his great nineteenth-century predecessor. It was in the century of Dewey's birth, rather than the century in which he published his important writings on education, that the common school became the primary institution of political socialization in American life. Although the revolutionary generation spoke of the great need for education in a free republic, it was the generation coming to maturity in the middle of the nineteenth century that solidified the institutional form for meeting this need; Horace Mann and his colleagues cultivated, defined, shaped, and instituted the common schools as the location for this politically necessary education. These public schools would come to be thought of as the single most critical tool for building civic equality and producing responsible, productive, unified, and committed citizens. No figure in the generation of educational founders can match the eloquence, influence, and achievements of Horace Mann; no figure provided a more articulate philosophical or effective political defense of public schooling, and no figure persuaded as many of his fellow Americans that common schools were essential to the health and stability of political democracy. Although our system of public education is much too decentralized for us to speak of a single founder or founding event, to the degree that we can name a spokesperson for the generation that built the common schools, Mann is that person. His legacy ties together the recurring American fear of civic corruption and the American preoccupation with education as the proper antidote to this corruption.

The American common school, as explained and championed by Horace

Mann, was thus developed to serve primarily political ends. It is not surprising, given this political preoccupation, that we find within the common school a tension between its political purposes and its educational values. The aims of an educator, after all, are what we might consider "philosophical," governed by fidelity to knowledge and truth: the task is to guide individual students, to the degree possible, to a true understanding of the world they find themselves in and to help them develop the skills and virtues most likely to allow them, as they grow to maturity, to shape their own lives to best fit, respond to, and at times challenge the realities of that world. The aims of civic education, in contrast, are political: the task is to mold individuals to become responsible members of a particular kind of political community with its unique needs, demands, and obligations. Although we might hope and imagine that in a just and healthy democracy we would find little conflict between these two tasks, we can see that in practice they lead to rather different educational emphases. For the civic educator, the task is to produce a particular kind of citizen; for the educator released from political goals, the end of education is less to shape students than to develop their reason and knowledge to such a degree that they are able to take personal responsibility for shaping themselves as free and independent individuals—thinking through their own views, cultivating their own tastes, developing their own life plans, and becoming unique people. Although it is comforting to think that in a democracy these two projects are complementary (we like to say that democracy is the form of government that values free and autonomous individuals), the open-endedness of the educational process is worrisome from the political perspective; the temptation is to try to produce an education with a known and satisfactory outcome. Free men and women are often a bit too unpredictable for the civic educator's taste.

The theorist of democratic civic education must find a way of resolving, or perhaps just balancing, these tensions, and Horace Mann provided the first great American formulation for thinking through and contending with this problem. I have much to say in the chapters ahead about the relative success of Mann's overall project and the degree to which we continue to struggle with the problems raised by his work and example. For now, it is sufficient to suggest that he pulls us in two different directions. On the one hand, he suggests that the civic work of the schools can be satisfactorily performed primarily by the institutional context and constraints, as opposed to the pedagogical methods and curricular content, of the child's education. In this spirit, Mann emphasizes the civic work that can be accomplished simply by bringing together students from different walks of life in a common educational experience in which they are treated as civic equals despite their disparate backgrounds. On the other hand, Mann's civic project grew to emphasize pedagogy and the content of the curriculum. Although it is impossible to completely and always separate these matters (for example, Mann is quite right to claim that humane elements of his pedagogy have clear implications about the way democratic societies should treat their children), it is nonetheless true that the degree to which we move from the first emphasis to the second is the degree to which the philosophical or intellectual purposes of education begin to be overshadowed by the political. At the end of the day, I suggest, Mann opens the doors for both ways of thinking about the role of civic education in a democratic society, even if he ultimately leans (like many of his followers) toward a more aggressive civic coloring of the overall educational project. I argue that we would do best to resist this temptation and try instead to severely limit the degree to which political rather than intellectual norms govern the methods and content of teaching in our schools (and in our institutions of higher learning as well).

Part of the burden of this book is to explain why and in what ways Mann ultimately overpoliticized his vision of the common school. At least in part, this is because Mann shares with his contemporary Ralph Waldo Emerson a strong sense of the limits and dangers of democratic politics. In his essay "Culture," Emerson writes: "Let us make our education brave and preventative. Politics is an after-work, a poor patching. . . . We shall one day learn to supersede politics by education. What we call our root-and-branch reforms of slavery, war, gambling, intemperance, is only medicating the symptoms. We must begin higher up, namely, in Education." Emerson's assumption is that education must in some important sense help us to transcend politics, that democratic life will not itself generate sufficient citizen virtue or desirable political outcomes. When Mann moves in the direction of shaping democratic citizens, above and beyond merely educating free individuals, it is because he shares the pessimism about democracy that is captured by Emerson's comment, as well as the corresponding inflated hope for education. Ironically, this political pessimism encourages an increasing emphasis on and optimism about an education shaped more by political than philosophical values. Only an education that has itself become fundamentally political, it seems, can rescue and elevate the "poor patching" of democratic politics.

I argue in what follows that we should resist this temptation to think of education as the source of such political salvation, since doing so threatens the philosophical purposes and commitments of the educational process.

Instead, if we take our cue from the less heroic strain in Mann's work, we will focus our political energy on delivering educational opportunities justly and equitably, promoting schools and institutions of higher learning where children and young adults from differing backgrounds can meet on terms of equality and (hopefully) develop relationships that transcend what Mann calls the "alienating competitions of subsequent life." These civic goods are fully compatible with a strict commitment to the philosophical integrity of our pedagogy and curricular content. When we move in this direction, we give up the hope of using the schools to produce a political world in which significant conflict and disagreement disappear. We maintain a commitment, however, to the intellectual veracity of education and a faith in the indirect goods that flow from such academic integrity. As educators, we must trust that, in the end, cultivating the intellectual virtues within just and equitable educational institutions is our best hope for the democratic education of our children and our young men and women. Our desire and goal must not be to transcend politics but to help citizens grow to be as reasonable, knowledgeable, and tolerant of one another as possible. Anything beyond that, and we betray our faith in both education and democracy.

ACKNOWLEDGMENTS

I am especially grateful to Patrick Neal, Fran Pepperman Taylor, and Alex Zakaras for their willingness to read this book in manuscript form, provide me with both comments and encouragement, and tolerate what must have seemed at times like a trying excess of conversation about Horace Mann and civic education. Maris Vinovskis and David Labaree also provided thoughtful and much-appreciated comments on the manuscript. Thanks are owed to my colleagues in the political science department at the University of Vermont for their comments at a departmental seminar. Anne Clark and Caroline Beer were both kind enough to give me frank feedback about a troublesome passage. Patricia Mardeusz of the Bailey/Howe Library supplied me with information and advice beyond the call of duty. The entire staff of the Massachusetts Historical Society was wonderfully helpful and accommodating. The University of Vermont supported this project by granting me administrative and sabbatical leaves. Once again, I am deeply appreciative of Fred Woodward of the University Press of Kansas for his help and guidance.

Horace Mann's Troubling Legacy

Chapter 1

Horace Mann's Legacy

In 1846 Horace Mann, secretary of the Massachusetts Board of Education, wrote in his *Tenth Annual Report* that anyone who, like himself, wishes to provide education to the whole American citizenry faces a difficulty: "It is obvious, that, in a free government, the cause of Popular Education cannot advance, without a corresponding advancement of the people. Hence, he who would improve the schools, must enlighten the public."[1] As an educational leader and promoter, he found himself in the position of having to prepare the citizenry, to "enlighten" them, to accept a good that, had they been fully aware of their own interests, they would have demanded. Sadly, they were not yet demanding the education they (and their children) required; luckily, there were reformers like Mann who were in a position to educate citizens about their own educational needs.

A similar problem presented itself at a general level when Mann considered our political institutions more broadly. In a lecture delivered during his tenure as secretary, Mann observed the following problem:

> Our political institutions are a rich alluvium for the growth of self-esteem; for, while every body knows that there are the greatest differences between men in point of honesty, of ability, of will to do good and to promote right, yet our fundamental laws,—and rightly too,—ordain a political equality. But what is not right is, that the political equality is the fact mainly regarded, while there is a tendency to disregard the intellectual and moral inequalities. And thus a faculty, designed to subserve, and capable of subserving the greatest good, engenders a low ambition, and fills the land with the war-woop of party strife.[2]

Our freedoms, Mann suggests, grow out of the laws that proclaim and establish our political equality. This equality, however, blinds us to other legitimate and natural inequalities between us—inequalities not of political standing but of moral and intellectual character. Thus, our freedoms create a situation in which it is hard to recognize, let alone admit, that some people are upright while others are untrustworthy, that some are capable while others are not, that some live for service to others while some are selfish and self-serving. Our interests, because of their equal political status, are thought of as comparable despite their different moral or intellectual foundations. To the degree that this is the case, it is increasingly difficult to mediate competing interests in any way other than through the use of pure political power, the ongoing struggle between factions and parties. Perversely, freedom threatens to create an environment in which our political life becomes adversarial, self-interested, and unprincipled. Our inclination toward self-esteem has a proper and natural place in a healthy political order. When it is unleashed and unchecked in a free political environment, however, it threatens to corrupt and debase citizens and thereby politics. Something must be done to lead the democratic citizenry in a different direction if political corruption is to be avoided. Mann's message is that democracy must, in significant ways, be saved from itself.

In both the previously quoted passages, Mann is alluding to an old story about democracy and democratic politics. The traditional complaint about democracy is precisely that it is anarchic and unprincipled: people's desires are given free play, and every imaginable human want claims equal standing with every other. For critics of democracy, this looks like a recipe not only for political chaos but also for moral and intellectual chaos. How can one make any reasonable moral or intellectual distinction between this desire and that one, between this interest and some other, if political equality appears to sanction all? It is not surprising that people come to believe that political equality grants their interests a more general equal value, regardless of the actual content and substance of those interests. In the language of Jeremy Bentham, pushpin comes to equal poetry. We may know, in our private lives, that this is an absurd position to hold. It may seem obvious to us in this private context that not all ways of living are equally desirable, not all beliefs equally appealing, nor all human qualities equally admirable; indeed, to think otherwise would threaten the meaning and significance of human action by denying the importance (perhaps even the possibility) of moral and intellectual evaluation and choice. This private insight, however, is difficult to apply to political life without appearing to challenge the equal standing of the full array and diversity of citizens' beliefs, lifestyles, interests, and desires. For critics of democracy, this just proves that democracy moves quickly and necessarily toward nihilism and confusion.

Advocates of democracy have always been acutely aware of these concerns and criticisms. Three options are available to those defending some variant of democracy from its critics. First, we may concede the criticism of the democratic many but deny the conclusion drawn. There may be ways to design a popular government so as to control and channel the energies of the citizenry without requiring citizens to be anything other than the people their critics describe them to be. If, as Publius suggests in *The Federalist Papers*, constitutions can be organized so that ambition may "be made to counteract ambition,"[3] requiring different elements of the government to share powers and provide checks and balances against one another, perhaps the public good can be served through the actions of shortsighted, even morally vicious, citizens. At least on some readings, we find proof of the genius of our founders and the Constitution in the fact that we do not require a virtuous citizenry in order for the American political system to produce desirable outcomes. The founders, on this reading of their achievements, are praised for having built a "machine that would go of itself,"[4] a virtuous polity that does not require the cultivation of virtuous citizens.

In truth, however, the founders were less than fully confident about this solution to the problem of popular government. Scholars have frequently noted that many of the founding generation assumed that at least the governing class in the new nation must achieve some acceptable level of education and political virtue, even if the people themselves were not expected to achieve a very high level of either. Thus, the Senate was expected to ensure that a sensible class of political elites would control and subdue the more unruly and unreasonable popular politicians in the House of Representatives.[5] Likewise, it is suggestive that Thomas Jefferson considered his work in establishing the University of Virginia, created to prepare representatives of the "natural aristocracy" to assume their role as enlightened leaders, one of his greatest contributions to building the new nation.[6] In both these cases, the assumption of the founding generation appears to have been that regardless of the ignorance and lack of virtue in the populace at large, the new nation required a learned and virtuous political elite to keep it stable and secure. Popular government, we might say, had better not become too popular. The attraction of Federalist republicanism, from this perspective, is that it allows a requisite level of political virtue among key elites by limiting the democratic character of the government. This solution to the problems of democracy is neither as confident in constitutional mechanics nor as trustful of the possibilities of popular government as it may first appear.

The founders' own doubts are not the only reasons to be less than fully convinced by this first response to critics of democracy. Most obviously, this understanding of popular constitutionalism requires a kind of magic, or at least a remarkably well-engineered new "science of politics,"[7] about which we might well be skeptical. Is there really reason to believe that a political order can be so ingeniously constructed as to produce excellent outcomes even if none of the political actors are aiming at them? What if the political representatives are not virtuous and choose to flatter and corrupt the many for their own purposes?[8] Or imagine this: could such a political mechanism be successful if the people were actually *more* virtuous, less self-interested, than the constitutional designers assumed?[9] And, perhaps most fundamentally, why would we think of this system as democratic in the first place, if it were not intended to reflect the conscious will of the people themselves?

A second option available to the democrat is to deny the claim on which the first option rests and simply assert to the contrary that "the people" have a kind of natural virtue that will prevent them from succumbing to the "self-esteem" Horace Mann worries about. Jean-Jacques Rousseau presents one of the most powerful expressions of a view that could lead us in this direction. In a famous passage in *Discourse on the Origin of Inequality*, Rousseau contrasts the ethical response of a philosopher, a "man of reason," with that of the "rabble" in the marketplace. A fight breaks out in the street. The philosopher, in his room above the fracas, comfortably closes his window, blocks out the violence, and exercises his reason to explain why the affairs below have no claim on him. "He has merely to place his hands over his ears and argue with himself a little in order to prevent nature, which rebels within him, from identifying him with the man being assassinated."[10] The common women in the market below, however, have not been sufficiently corrupted by reason and the philosophical life to allow them to rationalize indifference, to lose their compassion for and connection with those around them; rather, without hesitation, they intervene to break up the fight, to "prevent decent people from killing one another."[11] For Rousseau (at least in this passage) the more "civilized" individual, the one with greater intellectual cultivation, has the least moral virtue and engagement. The moral instincts of common people are uncorrupted by the abstractions and rationalizations employed by the most sophisticated, learned, and powerful members of society. Although this illustration is not explicitly political, drawing democratic implications about the distribution of virtue and vice is an obvious possibility; democracy would depend on the superior moral instincts of the least refined members of society—the democratic many. For an American example of such a sensibility, consider Henry Thoreau's claim, at the beginning of *Resistance to Civil Government*, that the virtues of the uncorrupted people themselves, rather than the government, had achieved all the good in the United States and that the people would have been able to achieve even more good if the political authorities and elites had not made a habit of interfering with them: "this government never of itself furthered any enterprise, but by the alacrity with which it got out of its way. *It* does not keep the country free. *It* does not settle the West. *It* does not educate. The character inherent in the American people has done all that has been accomplished; and it would have done somewhat more, if the government had not sometimes got in its way."[12] For Thoreau, it appears, the people themselves are naturally energetic, industrious, sensible, and trustworthy.

As attractive and compelling as this populist image may be, there is obviously good reason to be wary of this position. Although it is probably always advisable to resist romanticizing or exaggerating the virtue of social and political elites, it is equally advisable to avoid the same mistakes when evaluating the moral and intellectual virtues of the demos more generally. Thoreau himself, a few pages after praising the accomplishments of the American people, heaps contempt on his fellow citizens for what he takes to be their moral cowardice.[13] Criticizing the vice and ignorance of the many is, of course, a well-worn convention not only in traditional political thinking but in contemporary social science as well.[14] If sound political judgment requires at least a modestly accurate understanding of the facts of political life, even a democratic citizenry half as uninformed and intellectually unsophisticated as they are often portrayed would be real cause for concern. We are faced with a parallel problem when we consider the moral virtues of the many. Whereas traditional political theory inveighs against the dangers of "mobocracy," modern political science often warns us about the lack of political engagement by most citizens, about apathy and political cynicism. Either way, the advocate of democracy is faced with the problem of explaining why and how most democratic citizens, with their all too human intellectual and moral imperfections, should be trusted with democratic power.

Such considerations lead to the third option for the democratic theorist, which is to attempt to develop a realistic and sufficient account of political education for the whole democratic people. Even Rousseau, with his skepticism about the virtue of elites, appears compelled to admit the need for some program of civic education for the many. In *On the Social Contract*, a civil religion, aided by the constitutional framework developed by the somewhat mysterious "Legislator," provides the institutional context and practices for citizens to become educated in the democratic virtues.[15] John Dewey's political theory provides us with an even more explicit tie between education and democracy; Dewey's democratic concerns led him to become the foremost educational theorist of his era, and it would be no exaggeration to describe his democratic theory as being, at its base, a theory of civic education (and his theory of education as being fundamentally civic in character). It is not surprising, in light of the challenges of democratic politics and the imperfections of democratic citizens, that democratic theory has often focused on the possibilities for, the nature of, and the proper approach to the educational development of the demos. From this perspective, as Paul Woodruff writes, "Education is the hope of democracy."[16]

Horace Mann believed that political realities required a profound skepticism about the first option for thinking about democratic government. There was simply too much political warfare and too little focus on the good of the political community as a whole to expect the public good to be served by the cultivation and pursuit of self-interest—regardless of the genius of the constitutional structure of the young republic. Nor was Mann attracted, by temperament or as a result of life experience, to the populist sensibilities of the second democratic option. He was, however, so profoundly committed to the third that he became one of the most influential political figures and advocates for democracy in nineteenth-century America.

This advocacy presents a dilemma, or perhaps even a paradox, for democratic theory and practice. Of the three options presented, only the second takes the democratic populace as it finds it and assumes that the citizenry already possesses the requisite intelligence or virtue to wield political power responsibly. Both the first and third options assume the need for citizen leaders with exceptional insight and ability to cultivate a more desirable political practice than could be expected in a democracy without their intervention. Only the third option intends to actually change and shape the character of the people themselves. We might see Mann's comments as reflecting a strong sense of "optimistic realism" about the nature of his fellow citizens; there is no romantic notion about people as he finds them, but he has great hope about their capacity for improvement. We also might find the perspective of his claims to be disquieting; although democracy is the only form of government committed to equal respect for the interests, political standing, and participation of all citizens, here we have the seemingly odd (and possibly disturbing) claim that it is legitimate to develop a program to make citizens worthy of the political respect we seem to owe them in the first place. Who is qualified to make such a claim against (and for) the demos? What is the source of his or her legitimacy? Is it the social standing of such individuals that allows them to make such claims, and if so, how did they gain such an unequal standing in a democracy? Or is it the content of their teaching that gives them authority, and if so, how are we to judge that this teaching is either appropriate or necessary for citizens? Why should citizens accept this program of education in the first place? The paradox of democratic education is found in the claim that a program of educational improvement will make the democratic citizenry worthy of the political respect due them simply by virtue of their equal political standing.

In Mann's comments presented at the outset, we see this problem writ small and writ large. In the most immediate context, Mann's role as the secretary of the Board of Education put him in the position of promoting public education to the sometimes unwilling (or at least unenthusiastic) beneficiaries of that education in the state of Massachusetts. In the larger context, he believed that public education would address a general problem facing American democracy: it would give citizens the knowledge and skills politically required of them, and it would promote what he took to be the moral character requisite for democratic citizens. Mann's task, as he saw it, was to recognize the democratic paradox and confront it honestly with an ambitious plan of civic education for the citizens of his own state and, eventually, for all citizens of the United States.

It would be impossible to overestimate the ambition of Mann's project. He thought of himself as engaged in completing the unfinished work of the American founding. In much the same spirit as the lecture quoted earlier, we find in the *Ninth Annual Report* the critical observation that "the freedom of our institutions gives full play to all the passions of the human heart."[17] Although the founding generation had fought to establish our freedoms, they had done nothing to prevent this freedom from unleashing the worst (or at least the least admirable) elements of our human nature. Mann referred to the careful and thoughtful education of our children as the most "neglected and forgotten" of our duties,[18] and he believed that only the performance of this duty could prevent the nation's original founding from being incomplete and, ultimately, self-defeating. Mann's task was to show us how (and cajole us) to fulfill our educational obligations, thus finishing the work begun by the founders. On his own terms, Mann viewed his work as foundational; it was required to complete the work of the American Revolution.

All this, of course, conveys a breathtaking level of chutzpah. Just who was Horace Mann, and why did he believe that he was qualified to play such a momentous role in American political and social life? Why should we take his ambitions seriously?

Although Mann's legacy in American history is tied to the common school, which evolved into our system of public schools, it is most accurate to think of him broadly as a nineteenth-century reformer and statesman rather than as only an educator. Born on a modest farm in Franklin, Massachusetts (named for Benjamin Franklin), Mann found his way to Brown University and then studied law at Judge Tapping Reeve's famous law school in Litchfield, Connecticut. He quickly established himself as a legal talent and orator and turned to a political career. Mann was first elected to the Massachusetts Assembly in 1827 at age thirty-one. By 1836 he was serving as president of the Massachusetts State Senate. During the development of his political career, Mann became visible statewide as a Whig reformer. He was identified, unsurprisingly, with the temperance movement; more important, he was the driving force behind the establishment of America's first state lunatic hospital (the hospital in Worcester accepted its first patients in 1833). Although politically involved with educational issues, he was not deeply identified with the growing movement to reform, expand, and improve the common schools until he joined forces with James Carter, a widely known and respected educator and politician, on a bill to establish a Massachusetts State Board of Education, an advisory body to be appointed by the governor and answerable to the legislature. This bill was passed into law in 1837. In a move that would annoy many Massachusetts educators, the professional politician and lawyer Mann, rather than the highly regarded educator Carter, was asked to serve as the board's first secretary—a position with the extremely modest salary of $1,500, no administrative budget or support personnel, and little legal power outside the charge to educate the public about the common schools and to report annually to the legislature about the conditions in and development of these institutions. Against the advice of friends, who were convinced that the job was a dead end that would destroy his promising political career, Mann resolved to give the state "more than $1,500 worth of good" and accepted the position.[19]

During the next twelve years, from 1837 to 1848, Mann worked seemingly endless hours; traveled the state over and over; wrote twelve lengthy, widely read, and influential annual reports (as well as countless articles, pamphlets, and letters on education); gave a steady stream of public lectures; and established himself as by far the most visible, important, and influential educator in America. In 1848 he was elected to the seat in the U.S. House of Representatives made vacant by the death of John Quincy Adams (Mann served his final year as secretary and completed Adams's term in Congress simultaneously). He was then elected to two full terms in Congress and played a significant role in the debate surrounding the Compromise of 1850 (he was a strong opponent of it and fiercely attacked the senior member of the Massachusetts congressional delegation, Senator Daniel Webster, for supporting it). He left Congress in 1852 to run as the Free-Soil candidate for governor of Massachusetts. After his defeat at the hands of the Whigs (with whom he had broken over the issue of slavery and the Fugitive Slave Act), he agreed to become the first president of Antioch College, serving during the school's tumultuous early years until his death in 1859.

Despite the range of his career, Mann's legacy is as an educator and, most importantly, as the greatest nineteenth-century advocate of the common school. The inscription on the pedestal supporting his statue that stands before the Massachusetts Statehouse in Boston proclaims him the "Father of the American Public School System." The great historian of New England intellectual history, Perry Miller, referred to Mann as the "prophet of the American system" of education,[20] and John Dewey, perhaps the most important twentieth-century figure in American public education, called Mann "the greatest of the American prophets of education in and for democracy."[21] For all his importance, however, Mann is not a widely known or studied figure in the development of American democratic theory or practice. More than 100 years after they were written, the Horace Mann League and the Hugh Birch–Horace Mann Fund of the National Education Association reprinted the twelve annual reports prepared by Mann between 1837 and 1848. A number of these reprinted volumes contain a brief biographical sketch inside the front cover to help the reader locate Mann in American history. The heading for this sketch is "Little-Known Builders of America." The presumption behind the publishing project is obviously that these reports and their author represent something fundamental to an understanding of the American political order; the presumption behind the heading for the biography is that regardless of this great importance, there is no reason to assume that Americans will be familiar with Horace Mann or his work as an educator and politician.

The more one studies Horace Mann's legacy, the more revealing this heading appears. Mann was clearly a leading statesman in the politics of nineteenth-century America. Francis Parker, writing in 1896, suggests that

Mann achieved his ambition of becoming an American founder comparable in importance to Washington and Lincoln,[22] and as already noted, John Dewey thought Mann played a crucial role in the development of American democracy. For many, Mann is an American hero, and his work in promoting the common school was fundamental to the evolution of our democratic political community.[23] Even commentators who are critical of Mann are critical precisely because they believe in his centrality to American political history.[24]

In contrast to these views is the almost deafening silence about Mann in the literature investigating American political and democratic theory. Although he has been the subject of a number of biographies, the most recent and by far the most distinguished of these, by Jonathan Messerli, was published a generation ago.[25] For students of American political thought, Mann is truly one of the "Little-Known Builders of America." Although there are still schools that bear his name (ironically, at least one of these is a prestigious private college preparatory academy), and we can find (often superficial) obligatory praise for him in histories of American education, the intellectual assessment of his ideas and legacy has been extremely, even shockingly, modest. Despite what we know about his historic role in establishing our public school system, and despite our recognition of the importance of public schooling in the American democratic experience, Mann has received almost no significant attention as a democratic thinker.

How can we explain such a lack of interest in Mann's intellectual legacy? Even among Mann's admirers, we find the surprising view that there is not much of an intellectual legacy to discover. B. A. Hinsdale, writing more than 100 years ago, expresses what might be called a conventional wisdom about Mann: "The first thing to grasp is that Mr. Mann was not a theorist, philosopher, or scientific pedagogist. His writings show no trace of speculative talents. In all his work, he was devoted to the practical or useful."[26] Although Mann spent the central years of his career developing and articulating an argument about the role of public education in a democracy, Messerli claims that there is a "dearth of philosophical content in his writings."[27] Mann has been thought of mainly as an institution builder, a savvy and energetic but fundamentally practical and unphilosophical politician, rather than a theorist or inventor.

It is certainly true that Mann built his own career, both institutional and philosophical, on the shoulders of others. Institutionally, Mann was just one of many during his generation to strongly believe in the need to improve the systems and traditions of public education in the young republic.[28]

Philosophically, he thought of himself as the inheritor of an educational tradition running from John Locke (Mann referred to Locke's *Thoughts on Education* as "by far better than any thing which had ever then been written" on the topic[29]) to his contemporary and friend George Combe, a Scottish phrenologist. His relationship with Combe was the source of some embarrassment concerning Mann's philosophical commitments. Although I investigate Combe's views (and Mann's adoption of them) in detail in chapter 2, for now it is sufficient to suggest that Mann's close relationship with and profound admiration for Combe raises the question of whether Mann was merely an intellectual faddist (or worse). Combe's *The Constitution of Man* was a best-selling phrenological study and work of moral philosophy, and Mann was deeply influenced by it.[30] Mann's wife, Mary Peabody Mann, claimed her husband was intellectually independent of Combe, but in truth, he often acted more like a disciple than a critical reader.[31] Admirers sometimes try to separate Mann's acceptance of Combe's moral philosophy from his acceptance of Combe's beliefs regarding head shapes and cranial bumps,[32] but the evidence suggests that he was persuaded by and concerned with both elements of Combe's "science."[33] Thinking about the influences on Mann's intellectual life, we might fear that his views are purely derivative or, worse, that they border on the crackpot.

In addition to these intellectual issues, there are qualities of Mann's character that can be offputting; to be honest, it is not obvious where to begin with these matters. Mann's prose conveys the highest intensity of Victorian moralism and cannot help but seem disingenuous or, at the very least, morally hysterical to many contemporary readers.[34] Mann was a moralist to the very depths of his being, and it is impossible not to find him a bit of a philistine and a prig.[35] Mann vilified his political opponents, thinking it unimaginable that people of good faith could disagree with him on issues so morally clear to his mind as public education and slavery.[36] His biographer notes (with some exasperation), "There was . . . little humility in the man,"[37] and Mann's lack of self-doubt made him impatient with and sometimes downright distrustful of democratic institutions such as town meetings and political parties.[38] Perhaps less important, but nonetheless potentially annoying to the contemporary reader, is Mann's tendency to present himself in heroic terms, such as in the opening passage of his (final) *Twelfth Annual Report*. There he observes that when he accepted the position of secretary, he could have flattered the citizens of Massachusetts and had an easy go of it. However, he chose to honestly address the real problems facing the common school, although this path was "imminently perilous." He continues:

"But duty left no option. The only way to end prosperously, was to begin righteously."[39] Mann was nothing if not sure of his own righteousness.

These intellectual and character flaws are real, and they have disturbed the most honest and sensitive of Mann's readers.[40] But they are also largely beside the point. As an educator, Mann may have seemed a humorless Puritan at times, but more often he is distinctive for his humanity and his sympathy for children. For instance, he hated corporal punishment, and he insisted that young children require frequent physical play for physiological health, happiness, and learning. He attacked the pedagogical use of recitation as an intellectually deadening and counterproductive educational technique. He insisted, contrary to contemporary practice, that the meaning of words and ideas must be the aim and end of reading, spelling, and other language arts. He also insisted that teachers must cultivate a kind of friendship with their students, making education not a coercive or combative struggle between pupil and instructor but rather a pleasure and a communion. He scolded his fellow citizens for caring more about the beauty and comfort of other public buildings above that of the schoolhouse, and he demanded that we recognize children's right to humane, comfortable, productive, and happy school environments. He strongly opposed all practices that would create intellectual or moral competition among and between students. In short, he was an overwhelmingly humane and progressive educator, and he was justly praised for these sensibilities in his own lifetime and deserves to be praised in ours as well. Each time we notice Mann's arrogance or his lack of humor or his overpowering moralism, we should remind ourselves of his profound contribution to the development of educational sensibilities and practices aimed at cultivating happy and autonomous students.

For our purposes, however, Mann has even stronger claims to our attention. Quite simply, he believed that adequate public education was essential for the success of any democratic political community. That is, quality public education is not only a humane good for children; it is also a democratic necessity. This belief has become a core element of the American democratic experience and commitment, and we can thank Mann for providing its first great articulation and defense. It is a view that is receiving increased and sophisticated attention from today's political philosophers.[41] Mann's view is informed by a coherent (if ultimately unpersuasive) understanding of human nature, civic education, political obligation, and the relation between ethical and political life. It is true that Mann's democratic theory is recognizably Lockean in some ways (but not in others) and that he draws heavily on Combe's work for his moral psychology. This should not prevent us from appreciating that Mann's unique contribution was to articulate these views into a clear and popular "public philosophy."[42] If this did not require philosophical genius, it certainly required the genius of what might be called a "philosophical statesman." Taking Mann's own ambitions as a founder as our cue, and recognizing his extraordinary success in championing the common school, it becomes clear that Mann demands serious attention and must be reckoned with not just as an institutional force but as an intellectual and theoretical one as well. His was the defining voice in the American understanding of the relationship between public schooling and civic education in the nineteenth century—that is, when these ideas were first systematically formulated and advocated in a form that would become the standard model in the American political experience. Mann thought highly of his own position in American society for good reason: he was, in fact, engaged in work that would become central to our understanding of the purposes and benefits of the democratic community and our conception of how to negotiate the democratic paradox. Mann set the historic agenda for civic education in American society.

It is tempting to dwell on his obvious intellectual and personal weaknesses in developing a critique of Mann and perhaps even a justification of why we need not take him seriously as a political thinker. But I believe this would be a mistake, partly because of his obvious significance as a historical figure in building our public school system, but even more importantly because of his arguments about the role of democracy and education in the service of this institution building. By taking Mann seriously as a contributor to American political thought, by considering Mann's influence as a thinker and a theorist of civic education, we find both his greatest strengths and his most significant weaknesses, and these are different from the traits that have attracted the attention of many of his interpreters.

I argue in what follows that Mann has had a defining impact, for both better and worse, on the way we think about education and its relation to civic life. Like John Dewey who followed him, Mann was profoundly committed to democratic equality and a rich, participatory civic life. And like Dewey, Mann's deep faith in modern science reflects the limitations of both his educational theory and the democratic theory on which it is built; his hope is that moral life can be transformed by a new moral science, just as material life has been transformed by modern physical science.[43] This dream is for a civic life in which moral certainty and consensus replace doubt and political disagreement. Mann's program of civic education promises to dissolve political disputes, to make them impossible or, perhaps, unimaginable. Rather than thinking of education as a way to promote the civic virtues required to tolerate and manage political controversy, Mann ultimately hoped and aimed for a political life without any significant controversy at all. This is an impossible hope, and it partially derails our proper educational goals and purposes. We are in danger of being left with both an incomplete understanding of the aims of education and a hopelessly pious and platitudinous understanding of civic life. Ironically, the deep civic conviction driving Mann's democratic education ends up threatening the intellectual qualities and moral development necessary for a more modest, but more democratically helpful, educational program.

I hope to demonstrate that when we look closely at Mann's educational writings, we see that his vision of the civic nature of education is so overwhelming that it threatens to drown out both private concerns and more conventional intellectual and aesthetic values. Like Mann, contemporary American political theorists often ask, first, what democracy requires of its citizens; then they contemplate how to design schools to produce these desirable civic results. According to Miller, such a perspective grows from Mann's "profoundly democratic conviction that the schools should be so conducted as automatically to produce exactly what America wants."[44] I argue that by placing the civic requirements of education first, we are in danger of promoting an overpoliticized and underintellectualized educational program. We are in danger, in short, of corrupting the (essential) intellectual content of education. Understanding Mann's role in formulating the American concern with civic education will help us see the temptations, dangers, and limitations of this distinctly American project.

In his magisterial *Anti-Intellectualism in American Life*, Richard Hofstadter famously roots American anti-intellectualism in the populist religious rebellions against those most fiercely intellectual of founders—the Puritan oligarchs.[45] Studying the thought and work of Horace Mann, we find another root of anti-intellectualism sunk deep into the heart of our educational system. To the degree that we, like Mann, think of the education of children and young adults as required, first and foremost, by the pathologies, failures, and dangers of democratic society, we will be constantly tempted to define, structure, and evaluate education by political rather than intellectual standards. The American experience with mass education has been and continues to be importantly shaped by the kind of democratic anxiety that drove Mann to work so tirelessly as secretary of the Massachusetts Board of Education and then as president of Antioch College. This kind of anxiety has encouraged the democratization of education from Mann's time to our own; it has also politically perverted and distorted this education from time to time in the past, threatens to do so in the present, and will likely continue to do so in the future as well.

At the end of the day, Horace Mann can tell us a great deal about the very best in our educational tradition, as well as some of our worst educational mistakes and weaknesses, and he can show us how to look at both these extremes in our current public schools and systems of higher education. I believe, and hope to show, that coming to terms with these strengths and weaknesses is necessary for properly formulating the civic mission—indeed, the overall educational mission—of our public schools. I also argue that we find in contemporary higher education a movement toward a civic conception of purpose similar to that promoted by Mann, and that this threatens both the intellectual and the civic integrity of the undergraduate missions of our colleges and universities. I argue, overall, that some elements of civic education are unavoidable at all levels of our educational system. I also suggest, however, that the influential model for thinking about this education that we have inherited, as Horace Mann's children, is not as helpful as an alternative, less ideological, more conventionally academic and intellectual model. The democratic paradox described earlier cannot be completely avoided, and Mann is right to alert us to it honestly and clearly. The level of his alarm about the dangers facing democracy, however, led him to place too much emphasis on moral and civic education and too little on the values and benefits of a seemingly less ambitious, more intellectually focused liberal education. By defining our educational mission in fundamentally civic terms, Mann has provided us with a model that creates significant tension with intellectual integrity; paradoxically, it also appears to provide a less effective civic education for democratic citizens than we should desire and expect from our schools.

In the chapters that follow, I begin (in chapter 2) by looking at Mann's criticism of the democratic society he found emerging around him. He believed in the unprecedented potential of that society, but also in the grave (internal) dangers it faced. In chapter 3 I look at the educational program of the common school and why Mann believed this would be the central political institution in America, allowing us to reap the promises and avoid the dangers of democracy. Chapter 4 turns to Mann's presidency of Antioch College, how he translated his own theory of democratic education to fit higher education, and how his experiences at Antioch relate to certain key developments in higher education in our own time. The final chapter reassesses Mann's theory of civic education in light of contemporary debates on this topic.

Chapter 2

The Need for Common Schooling

Emerson announced in his 1837 Phi Beta Kappa lecture, "The American Scholar," that America's "day of dependence, our long apprenticeship to the learning of other lands, draws to a close."[1] The time had come for Americans to forge a new and unique identity. Even the revolutionary generation had failed to break from the intellectual bonds of the past; only now, in the first half of the nineteenth century, were we in a position to develop our true intellectual and cultural independence. Horace Mann was present at Emerson's lecture, and he shared the sense that his generation stood at the edge of a new world, distinct even from that of the revolutionary generation.[2] In a lecture delivered two years after Emerson's, Mann emphasized the political elements of this break from the past:

> Even the last generation in this country,—the generation that moulded our institutions into their present form,—were born and educated under other institutions, and they brought into active life strong hereditary and traditional feelings of respect for established authority, merely because it was established,—of veneration for law, simply because it was law,—and of deference both to secular and ecclesiastical rank, because they had been accustomed to revere rank. But scarcely any vestige of this reverence for the past, now remains. The momentum of hereditary opinion is spent.[3]

The founding generation unknowingly unleashed an unprecedented democratic order in which heredity and convention would no longer rule, in which the simple will of democratic citizens would determine the nature of law and political obligation.[4] The Revolution, of course, had been a dramatic turning point in our history, but Mann's generation was the first to confront the full implications of what the revolutionaries could only imperfectly understand and almost certainly would not have approved of.[5] New forces, for both good and evil, were vigorously competing for the soul of the republic. Mann was certain that social and political decisions made during his lifetime would have profound implications for the health and definition, if not the very survival, of the nation. While Emerson asked that we voluntarily develop a unique American idiom, Mann saw that, for better or worse, a new political world was already upon us.[6]

Mann was certainly not the only member of his generation to believe that the new nation was facing a critical and defining moment in its young life. He was, however, a particularly articulate, nervous, and influential representative of this view. As noted at the outset of the previous chapter, Mann worried that a free society might unleash profoundly undesirable human impulses. "It is a truism," he writes in another lecture, "that free institutions multiply human energies."[7] The danger is that these energies can be focused just as easily on ignoble purposes as on noble ones—perhaps even more easily. "Our institutions furnish as great facilities for wicked men, in all departments of wickedness, as phosphorus and Lucifer matches furnish to the incendiary."[8] Freedom, for Mann, is a dangerous proposition.

This danger was clear to Mann wherever he looked in American public life. In many of his pronouncements, from the annual reports to his lectures and elsewhere, his anxiety about these matters is palpable. The history of republics, he reminds us, is a "splendid yet mournful train" of liberatory promises followed by anarchy and despotism.[9] American politics was, he thought, already showing signs of decadence. The government's generation of revenue from lotteries and alcohol sales, for example, was unjustly regressive and promoted vice, suggesting a kind of republican sickness and corruption.[10] The love of office, reputation, and power was clearly becoming the driving force of politics, promoting crassly self-interested "convulsions of party strife."[11] We are beginning to suffer "insane illusions of martial glory,"[12] and an ostentatious love of wealth and material gain was becoming the norm. "Compared with our fathers, we have become a most mercenary race," and Mars and mammon have become our greatest gods.[13] Our extremes of wealth and poverty were beginning to rival those in Europe, and "vast and overshadowing private fortunes are among the greatest dangers to which the happiness of the people in a republic can be subjected."[14] These inequalities are enforced not by the sword of the state but by the economic domination of the rich over the poor, the rising industrialists over the growing class of industrial workers; he warns, the "feudalism of Capital is not a whit less formidable than the feudalism of Force."[15] When Mann surveyed the American political community in Massachusetts and beyond, he saw increasingly selfish, unequal, and morally repugnant qualities emerging with force.

The diseases of freedom are found not only in political and social life for Mann; they infect private life as well. There are occasional comments in his writings suggesting a prudish disgust with popular culture,[16] but the most striking illustration of this sensibility is found in his attack on popular literature. Mann distrusted and was befuddled by Nathaniel Hawthorne's work and was unwilling to make his brother-in-law's stories available to schoolchildren.[17] This was symptomatic of Mann's more general hostility toward literature. In the *Third Annual Report*, and again in a lecture, he delivers a truly remarkable screed against fiction.[18] The indictment is broad. First, fiction seduces the young, whose "minds are immature and unbalanced, and have no touchstone, whereby they can distinguish between what is extravagant, marvelous and supernatural, and what, from its accordance to the standard of nature, is simple, instructive and elevating."[19] Bringing the young reader under its spell, literature makes it impossible for him or (more likely) her to tell the difference between truth and fancy, right and wrong. Such readers will likely feel a real connection with the characters in these stories, but Mann is convinced that such sympathy is misplaced for two reasons. First, it is simply the result of artistic manipulation by the author and may not represent an appropriate emotion toward the type of person the character represents. Second, and more important, such feelings are a distraction from the concern we owe to real, rather than fictional, individuals. In fact, concern for fictional characters can perversely harden us to the needs of flesh-and-blood individuals. "It will be found that those, who squander their sympathies most prodigally over distresses that were never felt, are the firmest stoics over calamities actually suffered."[20]

The reason for this perverse outcome is that literature appeals to our most primitive, least cultivated feelings. Rather than teaching us anything important, fiction merely excites our passions, flatters and manipulates us. Mann is so distressed by stories' power to rob us of our moral freedom by manipulating our instincts that he even refers to a French study establishing a supposed link between mental illness and the reading of romances.[21] The problem here is not just that "*light reading makes light minds*."[22] That is, Mann is not condemning only *bad* literature. To Mann, even literature produced by the hand of a master, such as Charles Dickens, produces nothing more than a self-referential catharsis for the reader. All we experience is the loss of our own self-control to the art of the writer.[23] Never can we be taken beyond the make-believe world of the fiction itself. The relationship between reader and writer becomes insular, self-referential, and removed from any external reality: "The prevalence of novel-reading creates a host of novel-writers; and the readers and writers, by action and reaction, increase the numbers of each other."[24] Now we are in a position to appreciate how terrible this indulgence truly is from Mann's perspective: it robs us of the ability to understand our obligations as free individuals. "Hence great capacities for usefulness are lost to the world, and the most important of human duties remain unperformed."[25] In the final analysis, fiction distracts us from the knowledge we need to perform the duties demanded of us. Fiction is an art for a society like that in Great Britain—a society with a decadent and self-indulgent ruling class and a servile and degraded working class.[26] The popularity of fiction in American society is not simply a sign that we are distracted by mindless entertainments. The news is far worse; this art subverts the virtues required by republican citizens and thereby promotes moral and political degeneracy.[27]

Mann was annoyed by his inability to find a clear or important meaning in Hawthorne's *The Wedding Knell*, and he declared his preference for being a social reformer to being the author of *Hamlet*.[28] Nevertheless, Mann's concern about the reading of literature, and his objection to fiction on principle, reflects not merely a philistine inability to understand or appreciate literary art (although it certainly does reflect that shortcoming to some degree).[29] It also grows from what today's reader might find to be an old-fashioned, almost quaint understanding of republican virtue. Literature may invoke pity for a character in distress, but this response is "but human; to relieve it is godlike."[30] Literature can never teach us how to relieve human suffering and can only indulge our pity in a most unproductive, even counterproductive, manner. Mann believes we need "godlike" individuals committed to promoting the public good. That our citizens are infatuated with literature is not surprising; it is all of a piece with the symptoms of selfishness, greed, and self-indulgence that he also finds in contemporary political and social life. Indeed, to Mann, the moral corruption of individuals is the heart of the problem facing the political community at this critical moment in American history.

Mann's theoretical understanding of these dangers was borrowed, in general form, from George Combe's *The Constitution of Man*. Although it is easy today to lampoon phrenology's study of cranial shapes, bumps, and irregularities, it was, as Megan Marshall points out, "the most widely credited science of the mind" of the mid-nineteenth century. This point is clearly illustrated by the facts that phrenology was incorporated into the Harvard Medical School curriculum in 1832 and that Combe himself was offered the chair of Mental and Moral Philosophy at the University of Michigan.[31] Although their science turned out to be false, insofar as skull shape, for example, has no bearing on moral or intellectual qualities, the more general claim of phrenologists was that the physical study of the brain was the key to understanding not only intellectual experience but the moral life as well. This "naturalist" approach to mind and consciousness has, of course, become the scientific foundation of modern psychology. The brain is the location of the mind or, rather, it *is* (at least a significant element of) the mind; it is an organ, and like other organs, it shapes our nature and in turn is shaped by the environment in which it functions.

This physiological presupposition allowed Combe to argue that there can be a science of both intellect and morality.[32] He identified thirty-five human mental faculties, divided into two orders: "Feelings" and "Intellectual Faculties." The first of these orders includes "propensities," such as sexual attraction ("Amativeness"), self-interestedness, and other qualities that humans share with other animals, as well as sentiments unique to humans (for example, hope, conscientiousness, and wonder). The "Intellectual Faculties" include our ability to make distinctions between objects; understand number, time, and language; make comparisons between things; and the like. The key point for Combe is that each of these faculties is attached to a physical location in a particular part of the brain, and he thought of these locations as independent organs.[33] When the entire human organism is healthy, the different impulses, desires, personality traits, and other qualities of mind and personality function in harmony, just as the organs of any other healthy physiological system do.

To understand this idea of harmony, we can think of people as being governed by three sets of natural laws: the physical (governing basic physical relationships between objects), the organic (governing living objects), and the moral and intellectual (governing understanding and normative affairs).[34] Although the concepts of the first two natural laws—the physical and the organic—seem unexceptional and obvious to us today, the idea of natural laws governing moral life no longer has the intuitive appeal it once did in Western culture (even the idea of the lawfulness of reason and intellectual life has lost its appeal in some contemporary circles). For Combe, however, moral experience is as grounded in material nature as any other element of the physical and organic world; to say that our moral life is in some way independent of the laws of nature, while located in the physical "organs" of the brain, would be incoherent. Although we know that the details of the different "organs" of moral and intellectual experience are wrong, we can see here the profoundly modern understanding that the human mind is to be studied and understood in physiological terms.

At the same time, Combe's overall psychology is obviously pre-Darwinian and therefore does not depend on a theory of evolutionary development. On this matter, his presuppositions are decidedly theological and prescientific. God has created the human body for the purpose of enjoying the world. Since we are moral and intellectual creatures, it is obvious that our moral and intellectual capacities are designed to allow for this enjoyment, just as our other systems produce enjoyment when they are in harmony with the natural world. The physical, organic, and moral laws function independently of one another (it is possible to obey one set but not the others), but individuals are likely to achieve happiness only when all three sets of laws are obeyed (we can think of them as the laws governing safety, health, and moral happiness). These laws also function in a hierarchy, from the lowest (physical) to the highest (moral), with the inferior rightly governed by the superior. All our impulses, from physical appetite to love for another, are natural and good in themselves, but a happy human being is one who governs the former according to the dictates of the latter: "the world is really arranged on the principle of the supremacy of the moral and intellectual faculties."[35] To enjoy the world, we must discover and obey its natural laws.[36] These laws suggest that all our faculties—both higher and lower—are useful and potentially good, but only when functioning in proper relation to one another.

Combe claims that our highest moral propensities incline us to want not only what is good for us but also what is good for others. Indeed, he is convinced that our highest human development leads to the disinterested service of others.[37] "The law of our constitution which has established the supremacy of the moral sentiments, renders it impossible for individuals to attain the full enjoyment of their rational nature, until they have rendered their fellow men virtuous and happy."[38] The fact that so many people do not understand their own investment in the well-being of others is evidence of the degree to which we live in violation of the natural law. This is no more surprising than the fact that so many people live physically unhealthy and shortened lives as a result of their violation of physical and organic laws.[39] Combe's entire moral philosophy and psychology are aimed to satisfy his "hope that man will yet be found in harmony with himself and with the condition in which he is placed."[40] For this to be so, our bodies must be capable of living healthily and happily in the natural environment. Likewise, if we begin to understand our moral nature, we will see that our interests do not naturally conflict with those of our fellows; rather, we are capable of the highest harmonious sympathy with all those around us.

A number of points about Combe's moral philosophy need to be stressed. The first is that there is a significant tension in the doctrine between a kind of intellectual and moral determinism, on the one hand, and an environmentalism that would allow for training, education, and change in our moral and intellectual development, on the other. Combe makes it clear that we inherit our various moral propensities from our parents; thus he strongly recommends that certain types of people either should not marry or should be careful not to marry particular types of mates.[41] Likewise, we can use phrenology to determine who might be a trustworthy (or untrustworthy) servant, the implication being that such character issues are basically hardwired in people's physiology.[42] Although he suggests that (what he sees as obvious) differences in intellectual and moral capacities between racial groups can gradually erode over time, he is unclear about whether this evolution results from environmental changes (education) or the dissolution of racial distinction itself (intermarriage).[43] In contrast to these elements of biological determinism, Combe suggests that the faculties, as organs, can be altered and shaped by use, like a muscle.[44] A person may inherit a certain undesirable balance between different human propensities, but education can exercise and develop higher moral qualities through simple encouragement and use. The brain appears to be most malleable and receptive to this kind of development when an individual is young.[45] Combe never clearly explains the relationship between the degree to which our biology creates us and the degree to which we may be able to shape and reshape that biology to become increasingly healthy (by the standard of natural law).

Second, although this tension in *The Constitution of Man* is real and unresolved, it is apparently not recognized as such by Combe. In fact, he is very clear in his own mind that rather than suggesting that we are enslaved by our biological inheritance, phrenology's greatest message is about our freedom to understand and live in greater conformity with nature. "The present work," he concludes, "may be regarded as, in one sense, an introduction to an essay on education."[46] If his science is right, people can learn not only what they need to bring their lives into closer harmony with nature but also how to train themselves to do so. "If the laws of the Creator be really what are here represented, it is obvious that, were they taught as elementary truths to every class of the community, and were the sentiment of Veneration called in to enforce obedience to them, a set of new motives and principles would be brought into play."[47] Education can teach us the truth about nature, and it can develop our full range of moral impulses and train each of us to set these impulses in the proper hierarchical relationship with one another. We can learn, as a matter of habit, to become altruistic and governed by the highest sense of duty.[48]

Third, this perspective is not to be confused with a conventional Lockean educational doctrine. For Combe, an individual is not a tabula rasa on which the environment writes. Rather, the individual has a full set of impulses and propensities, a complex human nature that acts on the world. These faculties are all, in and of themselves, natural and good; that is, they are all elements of any good human life. What makes them function well or poorly in a particular individual's life is their proper ordering in relationship to one another. "Every faculty is good in itself, but all are liable to abuse."[49] Mann makes it clear that he is impressed with Locke's educational writings but not his epistemology.[50] The educational theory he finds in Combe's work is in some ways oddly premodern, even classical, in its insistence on a complex and unchanging human nature, its claim that the task of philosophy is to understand the proper ordering of these elements of human nature, and its understanding of education as the training or enforcement of this proper ordering.[51] There is a strong environmental and educational element in this theory, but it is not a conventional Lockean environmentalism by any means.

Finally, this doctrine contains a deep quality that can only be described as profoundly wishful thinking. Combe's is a vision of a world beyond tragedy. He wants to prove that "every action which is morally wrong in reference to a future life, is equally wrong and inexpedient with relation to this world."[52] If it appears that we must choose between our interests and what is right, it is merely that we have misunderstood what our true interests are, what will truly make us happy. Indeed, if we simply follow the organic and physical laws of nature, we are unlikely to experience either significant pain or anxiety concerning death.[53] Combe's dream is that moral life will be as law-governed and potentially harmonious as physical nature.[54] Indeed, the claim is that moral education will make moral criticism and perhaps even politics itself unnecessary, through the voluntary virtue of well-educated citizens: "If the views now expounded be correct, this race of moralists and politicians will in time become extinct, because progression being the law of our nature, the proper education of the people will render the desire for improvement universal."[55] The beauty of Combe's theory is its vision of a perfectly harmonious nature that encompasses both physical and moral nature. Mann called *The Constitution of Man* "the greatest book that has been written for centuries," destined, he thought, to "work the same change in metaphysical science that Lord Bacon wrought in the natural."[56] This beautiful vision of moral science and harmony is also, of course, the strain on the theory's credibility.

In the light of *The Constitution of Man*, Horace Mann's understanding of the danger and the potential presented by democracy becomes clearer. The American Revolution produced a republic of unprecedented scale and scope, ushering in a "new era" of human liberty.[57] We have seen some of the pathologies Mann believed this produced, from political viciousness to individual decadence. These pathologies, in Mann's view, grow from the disordered and ungoverned passions and "propensities" unleashed by democratic liberty. The selfish elements of our nature, in and of themselves, are "deaf to the voice of God, reckless of the welfare of men, blind, remorseless, atheistic;—each one of the whole pack being supremely bent upon its own indulgence, and ready to barter earth and heaven to win it."[58] Although the highest development of human beings is for the moral and intellectual capacities to govern the sensual impulses, there is no reason to think that the bulk of people in any given society will achieve this level of self-governance without a great deal of encouragement and training. What we can expect from the sudden and untutored liberation of large numbers of people, in fact, is exactly what we find in American society—a great deal of material and sensual self-preoccupation. Ultimately, this threatens not only the relationship between individuals but also the health of individuals themselves. "The unrestrained passions of men are not only homicidal, but suicidal; and a community without a conscience would soon extinguish itself."[59] Mann's view is not that the sensual, "lower" impulses and desires are evil or ought to be completely annihilated. To attempt such a thing would be to attempt the impossible: "They must be governed; they cannot be destroyed."[60] Even if we could completely defeat the lower elements of our makeup, such suppression would violate an appropriate appreciation of the natural goods that come from them. "As servants," Mann explains, our prerational impulses and propensities "are indispensable; as masters, they torture as well as tyrannize."[61] When unleashed, they divide us from others through their creation of a prison of self-regard, and tyrannize us through their unending demands and insatiable appetites. "We are created and brought into life with a set of innate, organic dispositions or propensities, which a free government rouses and invigorates, and which, if not bridled and tamed, by our actually seeing the eternal laws of justice, as plainly as we can see the sun in the heavens,—and by our actually feeling the sovereign sentiment of duty, as plainly as we feel the earth beneath our feet,—will hurry us forward into regions populous with every form of evil."[62] Once released from a political master or tyrant, republican citizens are in danger of becoming enslaved to and defeated by their own impulses.

For all his patriotism, which is intense, Mann is more than willing to lay significant blame for the problems of American political society at the feet of the founders. The Revolution and the constitutional era brought about a new and unique political situation, but whatever insight the founders had about this new turn in human affairs was inadequate to the realities. Most important, these "events, it is true, did not change human nature, but they placed that nature in circumstances so different from any it had ever before occupied, that we must expect a new series of developments in human character and conduct."[63] This "new series of developments in human character and conduct," however, was exactly what the founders had failed to expect or plan for. While American citizens found themselves with unprecedented personal and political freedom, they were not prepared to govern their own selfish impulses that emerged under these circumstances. In short, although the citizens were liberated, there were no provisions to educate them.

> On what grounds of reason or of hope, it may well be asked, did the framers of our National and State Constitutions expect, that the future citizens of this Republic would be able to sustain the institutions, or to enjoy the blessings, provided for them? And has not all our subsequent history shown the calamitous consequences of their failing to make provision for the educational wants of the nation? . . . They did not reflect that, in the common course of nature, all the learned and the wise and the virtuous are swept from the stage of action, almost as soon as they become learned and wise and virtuous; and that they are succeeded by a generation who come into the world wholly devoid of learning and wisdom and virtue.[64]

Our founders were guilty of a dangerous, politically destabilizing, and morally costly lack of attention to matters of civic education. By not attending to this education, "selfish and profligate men" are given access to the political stage, driving out the "intelligent and conscientious men" and pandering to "those whom ignorance and imbecility have prepared to become slaves, until, by a transition so gradual and stealthy, as to excite no alarm, the nominal republic may become an actual oligarchy . . . not however, the selected best, but the selected worst."[65] The founders were apparently unaware of the dangerous vices threatening to be unleashed by their own revolution, or at least the degree to which these vices would be impossible to contain.

Consider that James Madison had famously argued in *Federalist* 51 that the genius of the new Constitution was located in its acceptance of the fact that citizens and politicians would never be "angels": "If men were angels, no government would be necessary. If angels were to govern men, neither external nor internal controls on government would be necessary." Given the tyrannical impulses we can expect to find in both the governing and the governed, the founders pursued the "policy of supplying, by opposite and rival interests, the defect of better motives." Thus, through shared and separated powers that function as checks on one another, "the private interest of every individual may be a sentinel over the public rights."[66] To the degree the founders in fact pursued this policy of controlling and channeling, rather than reforming and educating, citizens' tyrannical inclinations, they were, from Mann's perspective, unrealistically optimistic about their own constitutional powers and unnecessarily pessimistic about reforming the negative elements of human nature.

The founders' failure to address this fundamental political problem need not be the end of the story, however. The optimistic element of Mann's (and Combe's) phrenology suggests that although unruly by nature, the sensual and egoistic impulses are also potentially subject to control by our higher nature. In a democratic society, "reason, conscience, benevolence, and a reverence for all that is sacred, must supply the place of force and fear."[67] The bad news, of course, is that it is by no means inevitable that this will happen. The good news is that there is no reason to think that all normal people cannot achieve this level of moral development. If it is true that "from our very constitution . . . there is a downward gravitation forever to be overcome,"[68] it is also true that overcoming this gravitation is a realistic possibility. This belief constitutes the heart of Mann's democratic faith. Our moral and intellectual lives are governed by laws just as real and knowable as those governing our bodies; we need only learn, acknowledge, and submit to them in order to bring order and freedom to the world created by political liberty.

> My proposition . . . is simply this:—If republican institutions do wake up unexampled energies in the whole mass of a people, and

> give them implements of unexampled power wherewith to work out their will; then these same institutions ought also to confer upon that people unexampled wisdom and rectitude. If these institutions give greater scope and impulse to the lower order of faculties belonging to the human mind, then, they must also give more authoritative control, and more skilful guidance to the higher ones. If they multiply temptations, they must fortify against them.[69]

The founders only began the process of building republican institutions, and they woefully neglected to address the problem of preparing citizens to manage the freedom granted them.

This brings us to an important point that is not always sufficiently understood by Mann's readers. Mary Peabody Mann was persuaded that a foundational element of her husband's thought was a faith in human progress,[70] and commentators have often taken their cue from Mrs. Mann. It is certainly true that we find a conception of human progress in Mann's ideas,[71] and much of this concept he shares with Combe. Combe, in fact, argues in the opening pages of his book that the "constitution of this world . . . appears to be arranged in all its departments on the principle of slow and progressive improvement."[72] Mann certainly agreed (as discussed in more detail in chapter 3) that the development of democratic polities opens the door for an unprecedented level of human happiness (built on an unprecedented level of human moral development). But this point is sometimes misrepresented to imply that Mann was in some way sanguine about human progress or believed that this progress was in some way inevitable.[73] We can see from his moral theory, however, that Mann was in no way complacent about political freedom leading to all good things. On the contrary, the experience of history suggests that republican governments are famously self-defeating. The early experience of the American republic presents us with reasons to be nervous about our own future. "If we maintain institutions, which bring us within the action of new and unheard-of powers, without taking any corresponding measures for the government of these powers, we shall perish by the very instruments prepared for our happiness."[74] Far from having an abiding faith in the intellectual and moral development of humankind under republican government, Mann was deeply alarmed by the potential for moral and political disaster.

Rather than exhibiting a rationalist complacency about historical progress, Mann's view is more accurately described as Manichaean. Human history is sadly littered with illustrations of unrestrained tyrants imposing their selfish wills on the weak. In a democratic society the potential for tyranny is almost infinitely greater. "A few men, whom we call tyrants and monsters, having got the mastery, have prevented thousands of others from being tyrants and monsters like themselves."[75] When the kings and autocrats have been defeated, however, the potential for unleashing tyrannical impulses among the populace at large becomes a dangerous reality. "Should all selfish desires at once burst their confines, and swell to the extent of their capacity, it would be as though each drop of the morning dew were suddenly enlarged into an ocean."[76] Just as democracy's promise is for a fully free life for all citizens, so its failure would mean not just the submission to a new tyrant but also the corruption of the citizenry at large into tyrants themselves. If democracy's promise is the greatest opportunity for humankind, it also presents the gravest dangers for not only our political corruption but our general moral corruption as well. Mann's message is about the dramatic struggle between the greatest good and the greatest evil, rather than about the necessary or inevitable triumph of republican liberty. As he writes in his *Twelfth Annual Report*, "It may be an easy thing to make a Republic; but it is a very laborious thing to make Republicans; and woe to the republic that rests upon no better foundations than ignorance, selfishness, and passion."[77]

To "make Republicans" is therefore an educational task of the highest order. Indeed, in light of his moral and political psychology, it is not surprising that for Mann, "the work of education" is "always paramount" to all other political work.[78] What is perhaps a bit surprising is that he believes this educational work is most appropriately aimed at children. Mann notes that previous generations of New Englanders, including the revolutionary generation, hoped the college-educated clergy would provide the citizenry with a moral education sufficient to promote a vigorous and widely dispersed civic virtue. His observation is that, overall, this approach to the problem has failed. "Our ancestors seem to have had great faith that the alumni of our colleges would diffuse a higher order of intelligence through the whole mass of the people, and would imbue them with a love of sobriety and a reverence for justice. But either the leaven has lost its virtue, or the lump has become too large; for, surely, in our day, the mass is not all leavened."[79] The clergy are admirable, but they fail simply because they work with adults, who are too set in their habits and inclinations to be very educable.

> The same Almighty power which implants in our nature the germs of these terrible propensities, has endowed us also, with reason and

> conscience and a sense of responsibility to Him; and, in his providence, he has opened a way by which these nobler faculties can be elevated into dominion and supremacy over the appetites and passions. But if this is ever done, it must be mainly done, during the docile and teachable years of childhood. I repeat it, my friends, *if this is ever done, it must be mainly done, during the docile and teachable years of childhood.*[80]

Human nature allows a limited period in which the moral and intellectual virtues can be developed, after which time such work becomes increasingly unlikely. In the *Twelfth Annual Report* Mann bluntly suggests that children, "the materials upon which" education "operates[,] are so pliant and ductile as to be susceptible of assuming a greater variety of forms than any other earthly work of the Creator."[81] Children are malleable, plastic in a way that adults are not: "Education addresses itself specially to the young, because the young are always ductile and mouldable."[82] Elsewhere, Mann puts it this way: "Men are cast-iron; but children are wax."[83]

It is important to note the overwhelmingly pragmatic nature of this argument. Civic education is required if people are to become good republican citizens; this education is likely to be successful only with children, since it turns out to be a fact of human nature that only children are unformed enough to respond to the appropriate teaching and encouragement. Mann is not arguing here that children have a right to education or that subjecting children to paternalistic civic education allows us to avoid a less desirable and defensible paternalistic education of adult citizens. Although we may assume, on the grounds of his moral theory, that Mann believes an appropriate civic and moral education will help children grow to live better and freer lives than they would without this education, it is striking that his own explanation for the focus on children stresses almost entirely political consequences. If there is a paternalistic educational good for the child, this claim is significantly underdeveloped. The overwhelming thrust of Mann's case for the civic education of children is that democratic society faces a profound crisis, and only children are capable of being shaped into the kind of citizens required for a successful and virtuous democracy.

Mann is convinced, then, that "the world is to be rescued through physical, intellectual, moral and religious action upon the young."[84] He warns of inevitable disappointment if we expect adult citizens to learn civic virtues without receiving a civic education while young. "In order that men may be prepared for self-government, their apprenticeship must commence in childhood. The great moral attribute of self-government cannot be born and matured in a day; and if school-children are not trained to it, we only prepare ourselves for disappointment, if we expect it from grown men."[85] Our greatest political hopes and energies, therefore, should be focused on the civic education of children. Without such an education, the prospects for the American republic are not very bright.

Mann recognizes that, despite the founders' lack of attention to education, there is an important educational tradition, especially in New England, that is responsible for whatever degree of civic education there is in the United States. He argues that the tradition of free schools in the New England colonies is the main reason that the America Revolution avoided the excesses suffered by the French. "Such an event as the French Revolution never would have happened with free schools; any more than the American Revolution would have happened without them. The mobs, the riots, the burnings, the lynchings, perpetrated by the *men* of the present day, are perpetrated, because of their vicious or defective education, when children."[86] What he fears, however, is that our educational inheritance is insufficient to address, and may in fact be diminished by, current political conditions.

When Mann assumed his position as secretary of the Massachusetts Board of Education in 1837, he was particularly concerned about the role of elite private schools in the mix of public and private institutions providing primary education to Massachusetts' children.[87] He considered this to be a major problem for two general reasons. First, it was simply inefficient and wasteful. He makes this point early on, and it constitutes a strong political element in his promotion of the common school.[88] This is an empirical claim, of course, emphasizing the redundancies in such a system; that is, multiple buildings, teachers, and other resources were supplied to a locality that could be served by a single school and teacher. Mann hoped to score strong political points by emphasizing the economic efficiencies (indeed, the overall low cost) of tax-supported public schooling, but as a normative issue, this argument is of interest only indirectly, to the degree that a waste of resources naturally weighs more heavily on the poor than on the rich.

Of greater moral significance is Mann's second argument—that private schooling threatens democratic cohesion and equality. Cohesion is threatened, first, by the religious sectarianism we can expect from private schools.[89] Even more troubling, perhaps, is the production and exacerbation of social inequality, for where there are private schools, "the foundation of the greatest social inequalities is laid."[90] This inequality takes many forms, from intellectual stratification to more obvious forms of economic inequality. Without government involvement in education, many poor children would simply be abandoned to "hopeless and inevitable ignorance."[91] Even when there is public education, private schools tend to drain intellectual talent, among both students and teachers, away from the common schools.[92] In short, without a dominant common school system, we are in danger of creating an intellectually privileged class that is out of touch with and out of reach for less affluent Americans.[93] And finally, Mann fears that this intellectual class will consist of an economically advantaged group that becomes corrupted by its own social privilege and "stand[s] as a barrier against improvements" for the rest of society.[94] In all these ways, private education "tends strongly to a perversion of the social feelings of the children,—to envy on the one side, and to an assumption of superiority on the other."[95] Lack of opportunity and the anger this can generate are obvious disadvantages for the poor. But Mann believes that the privileged also suffer from moral arrogance and false pretense as a result of these inequalities.[96] Above and beyond the obvious suffering caused by economic inequality and injustice, the fracturing of the democratic community prevents an appropriate fraternity from developing and thereby distorts the moral life of all its members.

The challenges facing the common school, from Mann's perspective, were multiple and significant, and they would all have to be addressed if common schools were to replace the mixed public-private system of educating Massachusetts' children. Mann was appalled by the infrastructure of the common school, from the poor condition and architecture of the buildings to the limited availability of teaching tools such as blackboards, maps, and libraries. Teachers were underpaid and underemployed over the course of the year, making it difficult to attract and retain talent in the profession.[97] Resources to remedy all these situations were scarce. Student attendance was spotty, and discipline was scandalous, with a significant number of teachers being driven from their posts each year by rebellious students.[98]

Whatever else we may think of these problems, they were, for Mann, profound intellectual and moral failings on the part of various key constituencies and the public as a whole. Intellectually, for example, taxpayers frequently fail to recognize their obligation to support the education of all children. "I believe that this amazing dereliction from duty . . . originates more in the false notions which men entertain *respecting the nature of their right to property*, than in anything else."[99] In a particularly testy passage in the *Tenth Annual Report*, Mann charges the "ignorant and uneducated voters" with being a major obstacle to building effective common schools.

> This shows, in a striking manner, how dangerous it is to suffer a class of ignorant people to grow up in a community. They are like movable ballast in a ship, always on the wrong side, and always most dangerous in the greatest crisis of danger. When a man contemns or neglects the means of education, he has become so ignorant that he does not know how ignorant he is. Such men are not merely their own enemies, but they are the natural enemies of all who love knowledge.[100]

Mann has comparably critical comments about what he takes to be widespread parental ignorance in the raising of children.[101]

By far the greatest obstacles to creating effective common schools, however, are moral rather than intellectual. Greed drives businesses (particularly smaller businesses) to refuse child employees the opportunity to leave work to attend school.[102] A comparable greed drives citizens to rebel against paying the taxes needed to sustain the common school. "The complainers are the wrong-doers. The cry, 'Stop thief,' comes from the thief himself."[103] School committees, the bodies of local citizens charged with governing and overseeing the common school, suffer both from a lack of trust and support from their fellow citizens and, in many cases, from a lack of integrity in their own right.[104] But perhaps the group receiving the greatest scolding from Mann is parents themselves. He questions the competence of a great many parents, but even worse is what he takes to be the perverse moral education provided to children by their corrupt parents. Writing of the difficulty in getting some parents to take school attendance seriously, he refers to the "fearful and wide-spread epidemic" of "*parental indifference*" to the "enormous evil of absence."[105] If Mann is right about the kind of moral degeneracy found among the citizenry as a whole, it is only to be expected that parents would be infected as much as any other social group.

> Were children born with perfect natures, we might expect that they would gradually purify themselves from the vices and corruptions, which are now almost enforced upon them, by the examples of the world. But the same nature by which the parents sunk into error and sin, preadapts the children to follow in the course of ancestral degeneracy.[106]

The problems facing the common school, in short, grow from the same pathologies found in the political community as a whole.

The long and short of it is that we have failed to develop the full power and science of education. "Education has never yet been brought to bear with one hundredth part of its potential force, upon the natures of children, and, through them, upon the character of men, and of the race."[107] This failure both reflects our political failures and threatens to exacerbate them. Our potential for improving the common schools also holds the key to addressing the whole array of political pathologies threatening the political community. "In order to preserve our republican institutions, must not our Common Schools be elevated in character and increased in efficiency?"[108] It would be impossible to exaggerate the degree to which Mann tied the fate of democracy to the fate of the common school.

> Common Schools derive their value from the fact, that they are an instrument, more extensively applicable to the whole mass of the children, than any other instrument ever yet devised. They are an instrument, by which the good men in society can send redeeming influences to those children, who suffer under the calamity of vicious parentage and evil domestic associations. . . . They are the only civil institution, capable of extending its beneficent arms to embrace and to cultivate in all parts of its nature, every child that comes into the world. Nor can it be forgotten, that there is no other instrumentality, which has done or can do so much, to inspire that universal reverence for knowledge, which incites to its acquisition.[109]

The egalitarian reach and redemptive program of common schools make them the single most significant institution for the promotion of political education and civic virtue in a free society. For Mann, this makes them "*the greatest discovery ever made by man*."[110] Even accounting for Mann's all too frequent hyperbole, we can appreciate the logic that leads him to place his greatest political faith in public education. Only here, in the common school, do we find the means to break the degenerative cycles endemic to republican government. Although Mann suggests that education is "one of the inalienable rights of a republican,"[111] his emphasis, as we have seen, is generally less on children's right to an education than on the political community's need for educated citizens. And by educated citizens, he means above all else moral and virtuous citizens. In this emphasis, Mann is not unique; he is, however, the most articulate and sophisticated theoretician and spokesperson for this program.[112]

In a lecture entitled "Special Preparation, a Pre-Requisite to Teaching," delivered in 1838, we can see the degree to which Mann's moral and educational theory looks in many respects less modern and liberal than classical. Discussing the need for specialists in education, he seems to borrow Plato's argument that teachers do for the soul what doctors do for the human body or trainers do to produce excellent animals. We need skilled professionals to mold our young.[113] The art of the teacher is not simply to convey information effectively or to train the intellect. Although there is certainly intellectual work to be done, the greatest task of the teacher is to understand the different qualities of human nature and to produce within the student a proper balancing and relationship among them. Without this balancing, without the higher mastering and controlling the lower, the soul will be at war with itself. By achieving a proper ordering, students become free, able to tame and govern their potentially rebellious appetites, and able to embrace their obligations to the common good—indeed, to understand their own good in relationship to the good of others.[114] The heart of Mann's moral theory, borrowed from Combe's phrenology, provides him with the tools to explain our republican and educational pathologies, as well as their solutions.

Jonathan Messerli has a particularly jaundiced view of Mann's commitment to the moral education of citizens. He points out that in the mid-1830s, Mann debated issues of moral freedom with Elizabeth Peabody (his future wife's older sister, and a distinguished educator herself). Whereas Peabody held a restrained view of moral education, thinking that educators should refrain from being very aggressive on moral issues, Mann strongly objected and insisted, in Messerli's words, on the need for a "controlled and supervised environment which would coerce men to lead virtuous lives."[115] Messerli is clearly uncomfortable with the paternalism of Mann's position. "The common man, at least for the present then, required guidance by enlightened men of good will and needed to be educated by an institution which taught him to live within existing legal restraints while paradoxically finding an expanding personal freedom. Mann considered himself just such a leader and the public school which he advanced just such an institution."[116] It is certainly true that, for better or worse, Mann believed that the public schools, led by people such as himself, had the primary and supremely important mission of creating individuals virtuous enough to govern their "lower" (more selfish) natures by their "higher" (altruistic and self-sacrificing) human "propensities." Only then would people be free to understand and pursue their true, communal interests; only then would the political community become harmonious and fraternal. For Mann, an aggressive education of Americans' character was the only possible path to achieving this desirable republican outcome.

We know from Mann's exchange with Elizabeth Peabody that it was possible for thoughtful, experienced, and successful educators in the nineteenth century to take a more low-key, relaxed attitude toward moral and civic education than that taken by Mann. But Mann's goal of making normative civic education the primary and highest purpose of the common school reflected more than his own democratic views and commitments; this goal was reflected in the legislative history of Massachusetts as well. When Mann served as secretary, an 1827 school law was part of the legal structure defining the context, responsibilities, and governance structure of the common schools. This legislation had borrowed and reenacted a passage from a 1789 statute.

> It shall be, and it hereby is, made the duty of the President, Professors, and Tutors, of the University at Cambridge, and of the several Colleges in this Commonwealth, Preceptors and Teachers of Academies, and all other Instructors of Youth, to take diligent care, and to exert their best endeavors to impress on the minds of children, and youth, committed to their care and instruction, the principles of piety, justice, and sacred regard to truth, love to their country, humanity, and universal benevolence, sobriety, industry, and frugality, chastity, moderation, and temperance, and those other virtues, which are the ornament of human society, and the basis upon which the Republican Constitution is founded. And it shall be the duty of such Instructors, to endeavor to lead those under their care, as their ages and capacities will admit, into a particular understanding of the tendency of the above mentioned virtues, to preserve and perfect a Republican Constitution, and to secure the blessings of Liberty, as well as to promote their future happiness, and the tendency of the opposite vices to slavery and ruin.[117]

Although Mann's theory of human nature and psychology differed significantly from that most likely held by the more orthodox Congregationalists responsible for this legislation, his moral and civic concerns were obviously reflected in the New England educational mainstream as a whole. His genius was to translate this concern into a theory and language for a more deeply democratic society than that imagined by previous generations.

Once again we see the extraordinary ambition of Mann's educational program. For Mann, as for earlier generations of Massachusetts educators, education is the moral shaping of the soul of the (immature) student. The project has intellectual elements, but it is ethical and civic above all else. Intellectual life properly serves, and is governed by, moral life. As Lawrence Cremin writes, "Here . . . was a total faith in the beneficent power of education to shape the future of the young republic—a kind of nineteenth-century version of ancient Athenian *paideia*."[118] For Mann, the failures in American political culture grow in large part from a lagging commitment to the vigorous undertaking of this project, and these failures will continue to grow in number and intensity until we understand the nature of their remedy. Only the common school can cure what ails us.

Chapter 3

The Ends of Common Schooling

Horace Mann's increasingly successful consolidation of political power and authority as secretary of the Board of Education is illustrated by the fact that he was invited to deliver the July Fourth oration to the city of Boston in 1842—an honor conferred on Massachusetts' most influential and eloquent citizens. His thesis, unsurprisingly, was "that our existing means for the promotion of intelligence and virtue are wholly inadequate to the support of a Republican government."[1] He warned that under our untried form of government, "where all are rulers, all must be wise and good, or we must suffer the alternative of debasement and misery."[2] He brought down thunderous applause with his final charge to the audience to "collect whatever of talent, or erudition, or eloquence, or authority, the broad land can supply, *and go forth*, AND TEACH THIS PEOPLE."[3] Twenty thousand free copies of the speech were distributed. In Messerli's judgment, the *Christian Examiner* captured a widely felt sentiment when its correspondent, William Ware, wrote that Mann's oration was "the most valuable discourse ever delivered on a fourth of July."[4] Mann's authority as the foremost educational leader in Massachusetts—indeed, in the nation at large—was clear.

Mann emphasized from the beginning of his tenure as secretary that there were three critical elements—intellectual, moral, and political—to his educational program. As early as the *First Annual Report* he wrote that Massachusetts law aimed to establish common schools where students "may be well instructed in the rudiments of knowledge, formed to propriety of demeanor, and imbued with the principles of duty."[5] Despite Mann's political skills and popularity, however, he encountered resistance on all three fronts during his tenure. These conflicts forced him to develop, articulate, and defend his views.

A central fight over both the intellectual and moral content of common schooling took the form of a nasty pamphlet war between Mann and a group of disgruntled Boston schoolmasters. During the summer of 1843, one year after his triumphant July Fourth oration, Mann toured Europe, visiting schools in Great Britain, Holland, France, and Germany. His *Sev-*

enth Annual Report provided a detailed discussion of his findings and, most important, a lengthy and positive assessment of the Prussian schools. Mann had been predisposed, through the influence of Combe and other friends, to admire the Prussian educational system. The enthusiastic portrait of that system in the *Seventh Annual Report* insulted some teachers at home in Massachusetts, however, and Mann found himself embroiled in conflict with some Boston teachers.

Building to his discussion of the Prussian schools in the *Seventh Annual Report*, Mann is careful to acknowledge that regardless of the strength of their educational program, schools in Prussia were employed in the service of an authoritarian state. His claim, however, is that such schools would be all the more appropriate in a free, democratic society.[6] He is also careful to praise our own tradition of common schools and to emphasize their egalitarian structure.[7] "Massachusetts has the honor of establishing the first system of Free Schools in the world. . . . Our system, too, is one and the same for both rich and poor; for, as all human beings, in regard to their natural rights, stand upon a footing of equality before God, so, in this respect, the human has been copied from the divine plan of government, by placing all citizens on the same footing of equality before the law of the land."[8] Once these points are established, Mann presents the Prussian pedagogy and curriculum as a model from which we should learn. Not in Prussia alone, but throughout Europe, the books used for reading instruction are "practical and didactic," whereas those used in Massachusetts tend to present overly "oratorical, sentimental, or poetical pieces." Mann is convinced that the European emphasis on "science and the useful arts" is significantly more educative and appealing to children than our own stress on literature and belles lettres.[9] Mann strongly criticizes the practice of teaching students to read by first teaching them letters rather than whole words, and he notes that the Prussians do not make this mistake.[10] He also strongly criticizes the recitations common in Massachusetts schools and contrasts them with the Prussian practice of teaching more "from the head" than "from the book."[11] Prussian teachers are expected to engage their students intellectually, in conversation,[12] not merely require them to memorize and repeat what they have found in a book. They engage the whole intellectual world of the student, making sure that any given lesson draws on material from a wide range of disciplines and skills.[13] An example of the practical application of knowledge to problem solving is the Prussian practice of teaching drawing, which, if taught in Massachusetts in the same way, could greatly stimulate the "inventive genius of our people."[14] Mann's praise of the Prussian curriculum is a response to its overall practicality, and his praise of the pedagogy is due to its emphasis on conceptual understanding, communication, and problem solving. All these elements stand in contrast to the general educational practices he observes at home.

Mann's enthusiasm for Prussian schoolmasters is even more exuberant when he considers the moral context of the school. Many elements of the curriculum, such as the way music is taught, are very effective at promoting moral ends.[15] Above all, however, the professional demeanor of Prussian teachers promotes enthusiasm among students and friendship between students and teachers. These schoolmasters teach while standing, rather than sitting, and they generate a strong sense of excitement about the material and engagement with the class. Their enthusiasm wins their students' attention and interest.[16] Students appear to be happy, to enjoy school, and to be well behaved.[17] Teachers are so capable and professional that their manner is actually "better than parental, for it had a parent's tenderness and vigilance, without the foolish dotings or indulgences to which parental affection is prone."[18] These teachers are free from arrogance and pretension, in contrast to the "overbearing manners" and "dogmatism in the statement of his opinions" common to English and American teachers.[19] Although Mann had often expressed the view that women are better suited than men to teach very young children (and would promote that view again in the future), he is impressed that men do extremely well with small children in Prussia.[20] In all, Prussian teachers combine competence and enthusiasm with the proper blend of gentleness and firmness. The result is a well-ordered and extraordinarily effective school. Mann suggests that, in all honesty, the Massachusetts schools fail to measure up to these standards: "I mean no disparagement of our own teachers by the remark I am about to make. . . . But it was impossible to put down the questionings of my own mind,—whether a visitor could spend six weeks in our own schools without ever hearing an angry word spoken, or seeing a blow struck, or witnessing the flow of tears."[21] The moral universe of the Prussian school is efficient, humane, productive, and happy.

Mann's evaluation is not without a few critical elements. Although the Prussians are not as guilty of abusing "emulation" (competition and comparisons between students, the uses of prizes, and so forth) as the English and Scottish, they still rely on this technique more than educators should.[22] Likewise, although their use of the Bible in the daily curriculum is appropriately nonsectarian, the schools are required to teach either the Lutheran or Catholic catechisms, depending on the student populations being served.[23] Teachers and school officials, therefore, are sometimes placed in the position of having to teach doctrine they do not believe in, and Mann views this as illustrative of the danger of the state being in the business of defending particular religious denominations.[24] Overall, however, despite these few critical comments, Prussian schools and educators measure up most favorably in comparison with Massachusetts schools and teachers. Mann's praise is so enthusiastic that some dubbed him "the Prussian" after the appearance of the *Seventh Annual Report*.[25]

Mann's arguments about the proper intellectual and moral content of schooling in the *Seventh Annual Report* are very much in keeping with the perspective we find throughout his educational writings. As early as the *Second Annual Report* he includes, not surprisingly, a great deal of advice about curricular and pedagogical issues: we should teach reading comprehension by interesting students in the meaning of words, rather than through dry recitations; we should teach spelling through the comprehension of words, rather than through the memorization of letters alone; we should use age-specific materials; we should think of language arts as verbal, rather than as purely rational and mechanical, in nature; we should have a curriculum that is well integrated.[26] The assumption is that a science of pedagogy can help us find the most natural and effective ways of teaching, and when this is achieved, learning will be a great pleasure for students.[27] Poor teaching and curricular materials make schooling miserable and the relationship between student and teacher combative. Good teaching promotes the common interest between student and teacher and makes their relationship fruitful and affectionate. "Knowledge cannot be poured into a child's mind, like fluid from one vessel into another. . . . He is not a passive recipient, but an active, voluntary agent. He must do more than admit or welcome; he must reach out, and grasp, and bring home."[28] Good teachers promote this natural process, allowing every student to "think with his own mind, as every singer, in a choir, must sing with his own voice."[29] Mann's view in this report is sensible, modern, humane, and very much compatible with what he writes about the Prussian schools five years later.

The same can be said of the claim in the *Third Annual Report* that we should design our curriculum around the rule that the practical is much more important than the beautiful or the artistic, that "by the ordinations of Providence, utility outranks elegance."[30] Likewise, Mann believes that physiology, the study of "bodily structure" and the impact of this knowledge on human health, is useful knowledge that should be integrated into the curriculum of the common schools.[31] Similar sensibilities drive the praise in the *Eighth Annual Report* (as discussed later) for vocal music and music instruction. In the *Ninth Annual Report* Mann claims that educators have now come to understand that the "*exhibitory*, *explanatory*, and *inductive* method" is superior to its opposite, the "*dogmatic*."[32] And throughout his career, Mann argues that recitations are pedagogically disastrous, having the ability to destroy the "capacity of wonder . . . in a day."[33] In all these cases and many more, Mann defends an understanding of the intellectual content of common schooling very much in keeping with the arguments of the *Seventh Annual Report*. This is also true of the moral claims in that report. Mann consistently criticizes pedagogies that promote emulation or student competition.[34] He consistently criticizes the use of corporal punishment and demands that methods be found to produce a more friendly and productive relationship between students and teachers.[35] He consistently promotes cooperation and friendship in the classroom.[36] And he consistently promotes a curriculum and pedagogy that will produce "harmony with external nature," such as his extensive discussion of health education in the *Sixth Annual Report*.[37]

If Mann's overall perspective has not changed significantly in the *Seventh Annual Report*, his message to Massachusetts teachers is decidedly pointed and provocative, and it hit a very raw nerve. In a 144-page pamphlet entitled "Remarks on the Seventh Annual Report of the Hon. Horace Mann, Secretary of the Massachusetts Board of Education," thirty-one Boston schoolmasters strenuously objected to that report.[38] The rhetoric of the pamphlet is sometimes driven more by passion and outrage than by reason or prudence, especially the early pages (written by a different author than the later sections). Mann is accused of having declared current teachers in Massachusetts unfit for their position,[39] of being unqualified to serve as secretary,[40] of subscribing to untested educational fads such as phrenology and to a belief in the need for normal schools,[41] and of knowing comparatively little about the Boston common schools. The authors score at least a minor debater's point in accusing Mann of hypocrisy in his criticism of emulation, given his enthusiastic willingness to compare the educational performance of various towns, by name, in his annual reports: "Is not here a strong appeal to the principle of emulation in putting 'head' in such antithesis with 'foot' and 'bottom,' and in placing such emphasis on 'Brighton,' at the expense of poor 'Dana' and 'Pawtucket'?"[42] More convincingly, and in more measured tones, Mann is accused (correctly) of drawing extraordinary conclusions from a very quick and superficial tour of European schools.[43] There are, it is rightly pointed out, real and honest disagreements about teaching methods, and Mann does not do full service to the complexity of the issues involved.[44] Without a lot of experience on Mann's side of the argument, it would be imprudent to jump too quickly in his direction.[45] And when we consider Mann's promotion of the teaching of words before individual letters, he provides no evidence to support his claim that this method produces quicker and superior results.[46]

These elements of the schoolmasters' response range from the ad hominem to the reasonable. But when we move to their response to the moral elements of Mann's presentation in the *Seventh Annual Report*, we see the full extent of the gulf between Mann and his interlocutors. They are deeply offended by Mann's views about how to promote intellectual development, and they believe these differences of opinion reflect a deeper moral error on Mann's part. In a word, they are offended by Mann's moral theory, especially its suggestion of a (potential) harmonious natural relationship between student and learning, student and teacher. Mann is simply wrong, they think, to emphasize the pleasure of the student in the educational process: "*let it be suggested, that the mere promotion of a child's pleasure should never form the basis of any system of education*."[47] Mann's "grand mistake lies in the *rank* assigned to pleasure."[48] To focus on the students' pleasure would be to abdicate responsibility for teaching appropriate discipline and respect for authority. "As the fear of the Lord is the beginning of divine wisdom, so is the fear of the law, the beginning of political wisdom. He who would command even, must first learn to obey."[49] To the schoolmasters, the idea that affection should be the first relationship between student and teacher confuses the true order of the learning process: duty first, and only later (if at all) is affection desirable. "Kindness cannot supply the place of authority, nor gratitude that of submission."[50] Quite simply, Mann misunderstands the nature of children and underestimates their need to be controlled by fear and austere discipline.

The psychology informing the schoolmasters' position rejects Mann's phrenological belief that self-interest properly educated and encouraged will willingly (even enthusiastically) submit to rightful authority. Fear, not affection, is the tool most required to subdue children into submission: "The fear of doing wrong is compatible with, if not inseparable from, the most dauntless courage to do right. Since, then, fear is most predominant in childhood, being the natural concomitant of weakness and dependence, we should take advantage of it, and make it subservient to good ends."[51] Mann's doctrine is insidious, in their view, because it implies that discipline must be pleasurable and voluntary in order to be natural and just. Indeed,

Mann's moral theory, if put into practice, would lead not to the creation of good citizens but to lawlessness and rebellion. "Those who know not how to be governed, are surely incapable of that self-government which is the very essence of freedom. If children are brought up with the notion that they are never to be restrained by force, they are in great danger of becoming the victims of lawless and ungovernable passions."[52] Mann's confusion about training the intellect reflects a deeper confusion about educating the moral sense. This deeper confusion will lead to moral and, ultimately, political disaster.

Mann's response to this pamphlet, "Reply to the Remarks of Thirty-one Boston Schoolmasters on the Seventh Annual Report of the Secretary of the Massachusetts Board of Education," is an even longer work (176 pages) than that produced by the schoolmasters, and it is classic Mann.[53] He plays the aggrieved party to the hilt, beginning by noting his "astonishment and grief"[54] upon first reading the "Remarks" and ending with complaints about his suffering and self-sacrifice as secretary. "The office which it has been my lot, for the last seven years, to fill, has been one of unexampled trials and difficulties."[55] "The laboriousness of my duties, the scantiness of my pay, after deducting necessary expenses, (and every dollar of my salary from the beginning, has been devoted to the cause,) and the thankless nature of the services rendered, have repelled all from competition with me. Some men, it is true, have tried to get me out, but nobody has tried to get in."[56] In between these complaints, he denies that he disparaged the Boston schools,[57] defends his educational experience and qualifications to hold the office of secretary,[58] and hammers away at the schoolmasters as aggressively and opportunistically as any defense attorney has ever defended a client. Although he promises not to "be vindictive, but vindicatory,"[59] the schoolmasters have at least some grounds for complaint when they later claim that Mann's response was "severe."[60] Louise Hall Tharp's observation that "Mann gave his enemies battle with more of his strength than they deserved" is certainly to the point in this pamphlet war.[61]

In the midst of Mann's impassioned rhetoric, however, there are two key points to note. First, he never sufficiently defends his curricular and pedagogical views from the (not unreasonable) observation that they were not sufficiently defended on empirical grounds in the *Seventh Annual Report*. This side of the dispute is simply ignored by Mann, presumably because he thinks the argument is unworthy of response or does not believe it is the true source of the disagreement. Instead, he saves his strongest ammunition to attack the moral and political claims of his opponents. Here he scores significant points, if only by drawing attention to the radical differences between himself and the schoolmasters. The view of authority in the "Remarks," Mann claims, is despotic rather than democratic.[62] In response to their understanding of discipline, Mann writes, "Rather would I say, Accursed is that community to whose children, outward 'law,' and 'authority' are made the rule of life, instead of conscience and a pure heart, and the reverence of God for His moral attributes rather than for His omnipotence."[63] Instead of helping children learn to love knowledge, cultivate self-discipline, and become integrated into a loving and affectionate community, the schoolmasters treat children as natural rebels to be suppressed. "Authority, Force, Fear, Pain! These are the four cornerstones of 'School Discipline.' Not Duty, Affection, Love of Knowledge, and Love of Truth; but Power, Violence, Terror, Suffering!"[64] These teachers have confessed their own inadequacies as educators in their appeal to fear and power. "What a damning sentence does a teacher pronounce upon himself, when he affirms that he has no resources in his own attainments, his own deportment, his own skill, his own character; but only in the cowhide and birch, and in the strong arm that wields them!"[65] If we can look beyond the exclamation points for a moment, it is certainly true that Mann's conception of educational psychology and his hope for educational outcomes are significantly different from those found in the "Remarks."

This dispute between Mann and the Boston schoolmasters produced another round of pamphlets (only twenty-nine teachers signed the next pamphlet; Mann's final response was a 124-page effort), but little additional light was shed on the issues. Years later, after Mann's death, Theodore Parker commented about the controversy: "How he [Mann] did work! How he did fight! How he licked the schoolmasters! If one of the little mosquitoes bit him, Mann thought he had never taken quite notice enough of the creature till he had smashed it to pieces with a 48-pound cannon-shot which rung throughout the land."[66] Parker is certainly right that Mann produced an extraordinary, overly zealous, and almost certainly unnecessary response to this attack; Mann significantly overestimated his vulnerability to the charges made against him and was personally much more sensitive to criticism than he needed to be (or probably should have been).[67] But it is also true that Mann was correct in thinking that the different approaches to the intellectual elements of schooling reflected deeper, more significant differences in moral worldview and that the case for the common school required the defeat of what he took to be entrenched, less humane, and undemocratic perspectives.

Others have observed that there is more than meets the eye in the battle over the *Seventh Annual Report*. Raymond Culver notes that the schoolmasters' "Remarks" represented more than pedagogical and curricular conservatism and wounded vanity—although they certainly represented these as well. In addition, "religious prejudice" appears to have played a significant role in the affair.[68] The moral differences between Mann and the authors of the "Remarks" were grounded in significantly different theologies, the clash between an orthodox Congregationalism and Mann's liberal Unitarianism. The fight between Mann and the schoolmasters was much more about their views of the ends of education, and how these grew from different understandings of human nature, than it was about pedagogical differences concerning the most effective way to teach spelling. Although the curricular and pedagogical differences were real enough, they were symptomatic of more profound moral and religious differences rather than being the fundamental source of the conflict.

Mann had already been engaged in a significant public argument about the role of religion in the schools prior to the outbreak of the pamphlet war over the *Seventh Annual Report*. Culver, Messerli, and others have told the story of these arguments in detail, but it is helpful to review some of the basic elements of the conflict here in order to evaluate their moral and political content.

Even before looking at Mann's disagreement with religious conservatives over the curriculum of the common schools, however, it is important to understand his ambivalent (at best) relationship with the New England Calvinist tradition. When Mann was a child, the Reverend Nathanael Emmons, a man cut from the old Calvinist cloth, served his hometown of Franklin. When Mann was fourteen years old, his older brother, Stephen, chose to go swimming rather than attend Sabbath services, and he drowned. Officiating at the funeral, Emmons refused any comfort to the family, instead taking the opportunity to assure the congregation that Stephen had died unconverted, had knowingly violated the Sabbath, and was certainly destined for eternal punishment. Mann recalled that his mother, a recent widow, moaned upon hearing that message.[69] Many years later, this terrible experience at least partly informed his judgment, as he wrote in a letter to a friend:

> I feel constantly, and more and more deeply, what an unspeakable calamity a Calvinist education is. What a dreadful thing it was to me! If it did not succeed in making me that horrible thing, a Calvinist,

> it did succeed in depriving me of that filial love for God, that tenderness, that sweetness, that intimacy, that desiring, nestling love, which I say it is natural the child should feel towards a Father who combines all excellence.[70]

Mann's adult religious life would be strongly influenced by the Unitarianism of his friend William Channing and by his own humanistic inclinations, illustrated by his comment to Combe that "to go about doing good is religion."[71] He could never accept what he viewed as the mean-spirited dogma of human depravity, which he believed conflicted with the scientific naturalism of his phrenology and moral theory.[72] Along with this hostility toward orthodox Congregational theology, Mann brought a lifelong Puritan moralism and asceticism to both his private and public lives. His demeanor was as conventionally and intensely Puritan as one was likely to find in nineteenth-century Massachusetts, but his intellectual and religious commitments were at war with those older religious commitments. As Hinsdale observes, Mann "was a Puritan without the theology."[73]

Mann's own religious views and inclinations aside, he was bound in his capacity as secretary to respect the law regarding religious instruction in the schools. This 1827 law made two demands relevant to this discussion. First, as already noted (in chapter 2), it reenacted language from a 1789 law requiring moral instruction, including instruction in "piety" as well as less religious virtues such as love of country, sobriety, industry, "universal benevolence," moderation, and so forth, in the public schools. Second, a new feature was added to the legislation, requiring that school committees "shall never direct any school books to be purchased or used, in any of the schools under their superintendence, which are calculated to favor any particular religious sect or tenet."[74] This law was in effect in 1837 when the Massachusetts Board of Education and its secretaryship were established.

In the first years of Mann's tenure as secretary, the board determined that appropriate books were lacking for teaching moral and religious principles in the schools. It was decided that the board would sponsor the creation of a library for such use, with the understanding that all the board members would approve each volume selected for inclusion in the collection. Since the board consisted of a political mix of Whigs and Democrats and a religious mix of Unitarians, Congregationalists, and Episcopalians, this process was designed to ensure that the library reflected a broad consensus and thus complied with the law prohibiting the promotion of sectarian doctrine. One member of the board, a conservative Episcopalian from

Pittsfield named Edward Newton, had been lukewarm at best about the democratizing tendencies of the common school project. He resigned from the board in 1838 to protest this library policy, presumably because it was too ecumenical for his taste.

Against this political background, Frederick Packard, a representative of the American Sunday School Union's publications program, approached Mann about having a series of the Union's volumes adopted by the Massachusetts common school library. Mann rejected Packard's request on the ground that the books in question were too obviously sectarian to be appropriate for the schools. Packard was a hard man to discourage, and he doggedly pursued his goal by making the matter public and casting it as a question of protecting the religious integrity of public education. Once the issue was ignited, Mann faced a general attack by some religious conservatives on what was portrayed as his program for secularizing the educational system. (Packard bitterly pursued the issue for many years, writing an anonymous review of the *Life of Horace Mann* in the *Princeton Review* seven years after Mann's death in which he continued to claim that Mann's career was best understood as a crusade against religious orthodoxy.[75])

These issues festered over the next few years, and Mann found himself on the defensive, explaining in his annual reports and elsewhere what he took to be the appropriate role of religion in the common schools. Two pamphlet wars are of particular interest in probing Mann's views about more conventionally orthodox Protestants. The first exchange grew from an (initially anonymous) attack on the Board of Education and Mann in 1844 by Newton (probably aided and encouraged by Packard)[76] and the editor of the *Christian Witness*; the second was an exchange of pamphlets with the Reverend Matthew Hale Smith three years later. Although students of these exchanges are in general agreement that Mann never faced any serious political danger over religious matters (indeed, as noted earlier, his own board included religious conservatives), two points are important to remember. First, Mann was deeply troubled by any charge that he disrespected religion or wished to banish it from the schools. Second, the disputes with religious conservatives go a long way in clarifying Mann's own views about the role of morality and religion in public education.

The *Christian Witness* published an editorial charging Mann and the board with undermining religion in the schools. Mann responded with a letter that provoked Newton and others, and the argument spilled over into other publications.[77] Mann's response to the initial editorial concluded that we must not allow the schools to become the focal point for conflict between different religious views. On the contrary, the schools should be designed precisely as a protected social space in which our common beliefs, rather than our differences of opinion, are emphasized. Promoting common values is actually one of the primary (and most necessary) contributions of the common school. "We believe," Mann wrote, that "if the day ever arrives when the school room shall become a cauldron for the fermentation of all the hot and virulent opinions, in politics and religion, that now agitate our community, that day the fate of our glorious public school system will be sealed, and speedy ruin will overwhelm it."[78] The public schools are valuable precisely because they do *not* represent the beliefs of only one group in society.

The editor and Newton were both put off by the aggressiveness and tone of Mann's defense; in truth, Mann was never able, in this or any other controversy, to assume good faith on the part of his opponents or to think of opposing views as anything other than personal affronts to himself.[79] Regardless of the sympathy we might have for Mann's public opponents on this score, however, three arguments marshaled against Mann are more to the theoretical point. First, the *Christian Witness* editor claims that the Protestantism they wish to have taught and promoted in the common schools is not merely a set of views held by one group in a pluralist society. On the contrary, "Our appeal is not to a 'sect,' but to the great body of believers in this Commonwealth."[80] Quite simply, the majority of believers in Massachusetts are, in Newton's language, "sons of the Puritans,"[81] and it is contrary to an appropriate respect for the community's historical legacy to exclude Puritan religion from public schooling. What is required is not just respect for majority viewpoints but deeper respect for the political community's roots and traditions. Second, Newton points out that if religious acceptability is taken to be what everyone would agree to, we are in danger of diluting our religious education to little beyond a tepid "natural religion."

> The idea of a religion to be *permitted* to be taught in our schools, in which all are at present agreed, is a mockery. There is really no such thing except it be what is termed natural religion. There is not a point in the *Christian* scheme, deemed important, and of a *doctrinal* character, that is not disputed, or disallowed by some. As to the "*precepts*," perhaps, there may be a pretty general agreement, and that this is one *great* branch of the Christian scheme we allow. But is this all—all that the sons of the Puritans are willing to have taught in their schools?[82]

Mann's shared religion, in short, is either a vacuous natural theology, presumably derived from rather than informing our observation of nature, or a watered-down Christianity unworthy of the Christian tradition in Massachusetts. Newton makes an additional political argument, premised on the assumption that the schools in Massachusetts were in fine shape prior to the establishment of the board and the appointment of the secretary.[83] This being the case, the creation of a state Board of Education was a political rather than an educational decision, one designed to build and consolidate the power of the state. "We do not need this central, all-absorbing power; it is anti-republican in all its bearings, well adapted, perhaps, to Prussia, and other European despotisms, but not wanted here."[84] This reference to Prussia, of course, is intended to remind the reader of Mann's praise of Prussian schools in the *Seventh Annual Report* released earlier that year.

Mann's later exchange, in 1847, with the Reverend Matthew Hale Smith fills out the case against Mann's view of religion and religious instruction in the schools. This particular pamphlet war was sparked by a sermon published by Smith in which he claimed that Mann was subverting religion in the schools. The dispute reached impressive depths of slander and viciousness, with charges and countercharges concerning honesty and personal conduct. Mann ended up gathering evidence, in a lawyerly program of character assassination, to prove that Smith had hypocritically bowled ten pins recreationally while preaching from the pulpit about the sinfulness of such amusements.[85] Smith found the experience of crossing swords with Mann so enraging that he concludes, "I consider Mr. Mann officially a bad man—bad in his theory and unscrupulous in the modes by which it is extended."[86] Aside from these very public fireworks, however, Smith made the reasonable enough charge that Mann's own conception of religious instruction had a sectarian nature.

> I have not accused Mr. Mann with being opposed to what *he calls* religion in the schools. On the contrary, I charge him with being a dogmatist—a sectarian, zealous and confident, as all sectarians are. I have accused him, and do accuse him, of deciding what those "principles of piety" are, which the Constitution demands to be taught in schools, and of deciding what may be taught in schools, and what shall not.[87]

Although Smith has confused the statute of 1827 with the Massachusetts Constitution, his point remains: we have reason to be skeptical of Mann's pretension to be offering a truly universal understanding of religion, in contrast to sectarian doctrines offered by others. Smith asks, "If I may not teach native depravity in schools, because the Constitution forbids it, may you teach native holiness?"[88] Both require a normative commitment, and Smith sees no reason to think that Mann has successfully claimed a high moral ground transcending dogma and representing universally shared views.

Mann's response to this series of charges from religious conservatives is telling. His strongest answer concerns the simple claim that orthodoxy represents the community's true views, or at least the historic community's views, and thus should be the doctrine taught in schools. Mann correctly points out that Massachusetts is significantly more heterogeneous in its religious opinions than his opponents admit, and it is becoming more so all the time.[89] His reply to Newton and the editor of the *Christian Witness* strains credibility, however, when he claims that in response to the increased pluralism of contemporary religious society in Massachusetts, the Puritans would favor his policy of toleration were they alive today.[90]

In response to the claim that he is undermining real religious teaching, Mann has little to say other than that he is committed to religious instruction in the schools and believes it would be a travesty to remove religion from the curriculum.[91] As for the political charge that the board represents a power grab by the state and is unnecessary to address the true needs of the schools, Mann wins a point by noting that it is the authoritarian Prussian state that enforces religious orthodoxy, not the democratic state in Massachusetts.[92] By winning this point, however, he avoids the deeper charge that his policies represent a significant growth in the centralized power of the state. This may seem an insignificant claim when we compare the almost powerless board and its secretary from the 1840s with the legally and fiscally powerful states of the twenty-first century. It is not without some merit, however, to view Mann's office and ideology as leading toward greater state power and control over education, at the expense of local control.[93]

Looking back over this series of disputes during Mann's career as secretary, we see writ small the content of Mann's views about the proper ends of common schooling, and, in the context of the debates between him and his opponents, we begin to see what was politically and theoretically at stake in the minds of the participants. We know that Mann's understanding of the intellectual content of education and the methods required to cultivate it stresses a number of elements that have become, since his time, conventional wisdom among educators: students are to be understood as active agents in their own education, rather than passive vessels into which knowledge is poured by the teacher; practical skills and applied knowledge are to be emphasized over drill and abstractions; teachers should emphasize induction rather than dogma; good teaching taps into and channels children's natural curiosity so that learning is more a pleasure than a discipline. The key elements here are, first, that nature provides the proper intellectual content of education. Children naturally want to understand the world as they experience it, and we know this is being achieved by the pleasure it brings children and the degree to which they enthusiastically pursue this understanding. Second, this natural content of education is more practical and utilitarian than aesthetic or intellectual. As noted earlier, for Mann, "by the ordinations of Providence, utility outranks elegance."[94] Third, Mann stresses that the intellectual content of education has a foundational but strictly subordinate instrumental importance to our moral goals. He is consistently careful to speak of schools as institutions that cultivate both intelligence and morality,[95] with the final emphasis always on the moral. Intellectual goods have no intrinsic value; they are instrumental to the higher moral goods in whose service they should be employed.

This last point is very important. Mann is under no illusion that education alone produces virtue. He even suggests, contrary to Jefferson's faith in the intellect, that intellectual education is dangerous unless accompanied by strict moral instruction; in the *First Annual Report* he cites a French study that correlates crime rates with increasing levels of education.[96] His claim is not only that intellect without morality is dangerous, however. He also believes that poor or ineffectual cultivation of the intellect stunts the development of moral knowledge. In a remarkable passage from the *Second Annual Report*, Mann argues that by teaching reading poorly, we open the door to the reading of poor (and morally corrupting) literature—what he calls "despicable 'love and murder' books":

> What else, then, can reasonably be expected, than that the graduates of our school rooms, who, by acquiring a knowledge of the coarser and more sensual parts of our language, possess a key to that kind of reading, which is mainly conversant with the lower propensities of human nature, should use the key with which they have been furnished, to satisfy desires, which nature has imparted. But, having no key, wherewith to open the treasures of the intellect, of taste, of that humane literature, which is purified from the dross of base passions, they turn away from these elevating themes, in weariness and

> disgust, and thus stifle the better aspirations of their nature. These treasures are locked up in a language they do not understand.[97]

Until we teach our students to read with much deeper comprehension, they will be readers of books that appeal to (and reinforce) their baser instincts. The intellectual content of our curriculum, from reading to physiology, will be judged effective only to the degree to which it leads us to live in greater harmony with our higher natures.[98]

Mann's battles over the intellectual ends of education, therefore, grew out of and reflected not just intellectual differences with his opponents but profound moral differences as well. The Boston schoolmasters are in full agreement with Mann about the subordination of intellectual to moral ends; there is no reason to think they would object to his claim that "the loftiest powers of the intellect are but ministerial and executive, in relation to the social, benevolent, and moral attributes."[99] In agreement with Mann's religious opponents, however, they deeply disagree with Mann about how we are to understand the nature of these moral ends. Although there are valid disagreements about the empirical effectiveness of various pedagogies, these are not the true source of conflict. Rather, the moral lessons the schoolmasters are interested in reinforcing through the intellectual content of schooling are primarily about subordination, respect for established authority, and learning to repress natural impulses in the interest of moral and religious values. For Mann, the end sought is not subordination and respect for authority; rather, it is the encouragement of our higher natural interests and insights and the creation of self-governing individuals. Understanding is more important to Mann than acceptance; self-determination rather than submission is the goal to be achieved. The intellectual content and methods Mann champions reflect these deeper moral differences between his humanism and his opponents' Calvinist insistence on human depravity and sinfulness.

That Mann understands the nature of this conflict is clear from a letter he wrote to Combe in 1839. In it he brags of a young teacher who asked him for advice about which books to read to help him develop professionally as an educator. Mann recommended *The Constitution of Man*, and after the young man read it, he was distressed by what he feared were conflicts between the views defended in the book and his own orthodox Christianity. Mann tells Combe how he succeeded in convincing this individual to become a "convert beyond the danger of apostasy," how the young teacher abandoned his own orthodoxy and adopted Combe's and Mann's phrenological humanism:

> I spent an entire evening with him, and endeavored to explain to him that your system contained all there is of truth in orthodoxy; that the animal nature is first developed; that, if it continues to be the active and the only guiding power *through life*, it causes depravity enough to satisfy any one; but if the moral nature, in due time, puts forth its energies, obtains ascendancy, and controls and administers all the actions of life in obedience to the highest laws, there will be righteousness enough to satisfy any one; that, if he chose, he might call the point, where the sentiments prevailed over the propensities, the hour of regeneration.[100]

Mann is obviously well aware that his views are in significant tension with a more conventional and conservative Protestantism, that these views have significant implications for how we approach the educational project, and that he is in the position of promoting his own moral project against what he understands to be orthodoxy.

Mann is insistent that education is ultimately "soul-culture."[101] "Arithmetic, grammar, and the other rudiments, as they are called, comprise but a small part of the teachings in a school. The rudiments of feeling are taught not less than the rudiments of thinking. The sentiments and passions get more lessons than the intellect."[102] It is therefore essential that this most important educational project be well planned and vigorously pursued. The content of Mann's moral program for the schools can be divided into two parts—the didactic and the structural. The former includes the overt moral curriculum, the explicit content of moral instruction; the latter relates to the institutional, curricular, and pedagogical contexts of schooling. Both are essential to the success of moral education.

The structural elements can be promoted through both curricular and noncurricular methods. For example, the *Eighth Annual Report* contains a long passage promoting the teaching of vocal music in the schools. Part of the case for this curriculum is simply aesthetic pleasure—music is beautiful and therefore good in itself.[103] The health of the students is also promoted through this exercise of the lungs (no small issue in a society ravaged by tuberculosis).[104] And part of the argument is didactic, focusing on the moral sentiments promoted by song lyrics.[105] But the most important reason to promote vocal music is subtler, Mann believes, and has to do with the literal blending of voices in song. The "social and moral influences of music far transcend, in value, all its physical or intellectual utilities. It holds a natural relationship or affinity with peace, hope, affection, generosity, charity, devotion. There is also a natural repugnance between music, and fear, envy, malevolence, misanthropy."[106] Mann regrets that, on balance, New Englanders are not a musical people and observes, "No hereditary taste for the art has descended to us" from our stern, unmusical Puritan forebears.[107] But we can cultivate these social goods simply by singing good songs with children. Although a song's lyrics may be important and helpful to moral education, the greatest good comes from the sociability of singing. Presumably a great many curricular activities can promote sociability and community, just as vocal music does.

A second great structural requirement for appropriate moral education is the rejection of what Mann calls "emulation." Students should not be encouraged to compare their educational attainments to those of others. They should not be explicitly ranked or be motivated by external forms of recognition, such as prizes and competitions. Emulation is a potential "depraver of the social affections,"[108] and it replaces the intrinsic pleasures of learning with extrinsic rewards and recognitions. This cannot help but make learning superficial and inflame the egoistic instincts moral education is aiming to repress.[109] We are encouraged, through such methods, to care more for reputation than for knowledge itself.[110] Emulation, in short, works to subvert the moral content of education. By removing competitive teaching techniques and the whole universe of external rewards for learning, we make it more likely that the teacher and student will find the right reasons to study and become more receptive to the proper lessons presented by the didactic curriculum.

In addition to curricula that promote cooperation and community and pedagogy that prevents competition and external rewards, the final key element of the structural preconditions for moral education concerns the leadership of the teacher. Mann is insistent that only individuals of the highest moral character should be encouraged to enter the teaching profession. With characteristic hyperbole, Mann argues that no one should ever be allowed to teach "who is not clothed, from the crown of his head to the sole of his foot, in garments of virtue."[111] We know from the *Seventh Annual Report* that Mann admires not just the scope of the Prussian schoolmasters' intellectual knowledge but also their friendly relationship with their students (a kind of friendship that Mann believes is superior in some regards to parental love). Mann opposes a set of clear, tightly proscriptive rules that define proper behavior in schools, on the grounds that this promotes a narrow legalism among students.[112] A teacher must have both moral authority and students' affection to encourage them not only to aspire to obey the rules of the school but also to understand the spirit of those rules and cultivate the desire to live in harmony with that spirit. One of Mann's most cherished projects was the establishment of three normal schools to train schoolteachers, and he did much to encourage the growth of an increasingly professional teacher corps, from publishing the *Common School Journal* to offering teacher training workshops with master teachers. But Mann's conception of the teaching profession is more of a "calling" than the modern understanding of a professional "career." For Mann, there is no private life to be sheltered from the moral demands of being a teacher; the teacher's character must be excellent in its entirety. Only then, Mann believes, are teachers qualified to provide the kind of moral role model and guidance their students require.[113]

In his final year as secretary, a correspondent asked Mann if Catholics should be allowed to teach in Massachusetts common schools. He answered in the affirmative, noting that there is no reason to disqualify Catholics, since what is required is an excellent character, and Catholics are just as capable of achieving this excellence as Protestants. Mann then observes that his correspondent did not ask about "Jews, Mahometans, [or] Pagans" and assumes the writer had "no such cases in hand." It is not clear from this comment whether Mann thinks individuals with non-Christian beliefs should be disqualified from the teaching profession or whether he thinks these different beliefs would potentially create only political, rather than moral, problems for a hiring committee. He does suggest that Catholic teachers should use a Protestant, rather than a Catholic, Bible in the classroom.[114] The ambiguities in this letter make it difficult to understand exactly what Mann thinks about evaluating the moral and religious beliefs of potential teachers, but at the very least, there is reason to think that, in his view, teachers need not be Protestant (with the proviso that they respect the Protestant Bible as a school text). It is also clear that, just as he brags about his own nonpartisanship during his tenure as secretary,[115] he expects everyone connected with the schools—from state officials like himself, to local school committees, to teachers—to be politically nonpartisan and religiously nonsectarian in their demeanor.

We will see that there is a great deal more to be said with regard to Mann's thought about dogma and partisanship in relation to moral (and political) education. For now, it is sufficient to understand that a significant element of students' moral education consists simply in being taught by individuals with high principles who clearly stand above the political and religious frays Mann finds so distasteful and threatening in American society. Mann's belief in the moral influence of such teachers is virtually limitless: with a morally upright teaching corps, even the obscenities, graffiti, petty meanness, and other mundane childlike immorality would disappear from the schools.[116]

The didactic elements of moral education include a range of subjects that relate directly to moral conduct, in the literature studied and the writing assignments completed as well as the examples used in seemingly non-moral subjects such as mathematics.[117] Two mistakes, Mann suggests, are common in the schools. First, a greater emphasis is placed on intellectual than moral training, which misleads children to believe that intellectual goods are superior to all others. Schools are guilty of the "elevation of the subordinate" and the "casting down of the supreme, in the education of children," thereby confusing students about the greater importance of moral goods.[118] Second, the wrong substantive moral messages are often sent in the teaching materials used. For example, history texts chronicle primarily warfare and destruction rather than more noble and humane behavior. "The inference which children would legitimately draw from reading like this, would be, that the tribes and nations of men had been created only for mutual slaughter, and that they deserved the homage of posterity for the terrible fidelity with which their mission had been fulfilled."[119] One perverse consequence of this emphasis on military exploits is the almost complete absence of mention of the contributions of women to the human experience.[120] These histories need to be rewritten to include "at least . . . some recognition of the great truth, that, among nations as among individuals, the highest welfare of all can only be effected by securing the individual welfare of each."[121] Likewise, Mann believes that appropriately inspiring biographies of great individuals are "one of the most efficient of all influences in forming the character of children,"[122] and these biographies should stress lives of "benevolence, of probity, of devotion to truth"[123] rather than martial themes. The essays assigned to children should not focus on abstractions they do not care about or fail to clearly understand; rather, they should address moral issues with direct relevance to students' experience and within their ability to grasp.[124] Mann is confident that the "natural conscience needs training, in order to discern the distinctions between right and wrong, in the same manner that the intellect needs training,"[125] and if we provide appropriate reading materials and classroom assignments stressing the highest moral principles, children will become habituated to being guided by these principles. A book well designed to teach the "obligations arising from social relationships" is capable, he believes, of "supplying children, at an early age, with simple and elementary notions of right and wrong in feeling and in conduct, so that the appetites and passions, as they spring up in the mind, may, by a natural process, be conformed to the principles, instead of the principles being made to conform to the passions and appetites."[126]

Among the moral lessons to be taught, Mann includes the "laws of forbearance under injury, of sympathy with misfortune, of impartiality in our judgments of men, of love and fidelity to truth; of the ever-during relations of men, in the domestic circle, in the organized government, and of stranger to stranger."[127] The assumption growing from Combe's phrenology, recall, is that children have moral natures to be cultivated. The educator is not involved in repressing natural desires and replacing them with moral civilization; instead, the higher natures are encouraged to develop and take their rightful place in governing the lower impulses. Thus, for Mann, it is not just wishful thinking to argue that in a democratic society each individual can be taught to understand the welfare of broader communities—from the domestic, to the local, to the political, and beyond—as natural spheres of moral concern. Learning our duties is not properly understood as learning to deny our own interests and thereby submitting to the interests of others. Rather, it is learning to understand our true interests as they extend within and among these broader human relationships. "It becomes then, a momentous question, whether the children in our schools are educated in reference to themselves and their private interests only, or with a regard to the great social duties and prerogatives that await them in after-life."[128] Among the highest goals is to teach children to be self-governing, so they will freely choose to exercise "self control" and "a voluntary compliance with the laws of reason and duty."[129] In one lecture, Mann summarizes the very concept of education as "such a culture of our moral affections and religious susceptibilities, as, in the course of Nature and Providence, shall lead to a subjection or conformity of all our appetites, propensities and sentiments to the will of Heaven."[130] The morality of private, public, and religious life can be effectively taught by clearly explaining to students, through their studies of appropriate historical, religious, biographical, and fictional literature, the nature of our duties and the way reason explains these duties to us.[131] This project, like that of teaching children the facts of physiology and care for the body, is part of the overall instruction in how to live in harmony with nature.

The most difficult political problems Mann faced concerning the didactic curriculum relate to the role of religion in the schools. In his final annual report in 1848, Mann spends most of his energy defending his conception of the religious instruction appropriate to the common school. Pulling out all the rhetorical stops against those who accuse him of trying to remove religion from the schools, he declares, "I could not avoid regarding the man, who should oppose the religious education of the young, as an insane man."[132] Mann is second to none, he wants us to believe, in his commitment to religion, his belief in the need to cultivate religion as the moral compass for any decent society. "Devoid of religious principles and religious affections, the race can never fall so low but that it may sink still lower; animated and sanctified by them, it can never rise so high but that it may ascend still higher."[133] He also understands, however, that we no longer live in a religiously homogeneous society, and we need to practice religious tolerance on the ground of each individual's imperfect knowledge.[134] We need to find a way to support religion while avoiding ecclesiastical tyranny, on the one hand, and the "greater evils of atheism," on the other.[135] Luckily, despite our increasing religious pluralism, there is still a more or less universal set of shared Christian beliefs and a universal respect for the Bible. It is both legally and morally wrong to use public funds to teach principles that are repugnant to the parents of students, so doctrines unique to particular sects should be barred from being taught in the common school.[136] But, Mann argues, there is no disagreement about having the Bible in the schools: "This Bible is in our Common Schools, by common consent."[137] In the public schools, the Bible is "allowed to speak for itself," and all "children can kneel at a common altar, and feel that they have a common Father and where the services of religion tend to create brothers, and not Ishmaelites."[138] There is no public opinion in favor of a completely secular school system, free from religious instruction.[139] Because it is possible to present religion in a way that emphasizes the shared values of all Massachusetts citizens, Mann implies that his system for religious instruction will actually produce freethinking and responsible Christian adults, rather than the doctrinally submissive or rebellious adults likely to be produced by a more sectarian religious education.[140]

Mann's proposal is, of course, historically unstable: the religious pluralism he defends is clearly restricted to various forms of Protestantism, and this alone fails to fully account, in his own day, for the Catholic presence in (especially) Boston. Taking a wider reading of his claim, and (probably unrealistically) assuming it could be made to work for Catholics (along the lines of his discussion of Catholic teachers mentioned earlier), it would still require a broad Christian consensus. Even during his own time, however, we can see the strains on such a consensus. The easiest claim to make against Mann, the one made by the Reverend Smith and by other interpreters since then, is that Mann's position is itself "sectarian," his protests to the contrary notwithstanding.[141] His version of Christianity is at one with science and stresses works over grace. It is easy to see how a more traditional Calvinist would view Mann's religion as not sufficiently appreciative of the fallen state of the world. Mann is, of course, well aware of this. He appears to hold a more conventionally Greek than Christian view that false moral beliefs are based on mistakes of the intellect rather than perversions of the will.[142] He does pull back a bit from the full implications of his view at times, and in the following passage he waffles on the matter:

> We are not among those who hold that knowledge is a sovereign cure for all the ills of mankind. Men *do* less well than they *know*. The whirlwinds of passion often obscure the brightest sunshine of knowledge. But on the other hand, we are disposed strenuously to maintain, that many errors and transgressions which have been charged to perversity of disposition, are wholly referable to a deficiency in intelligence.[143]

Overall, children can be trained so that their "kindly feelings may be kept uppermost," and this training has the "double blessing of bestowing happiness on the possessor and on the race."[144] Although Mann makes a small occasional nod in the direction of the "whirlwinds of passion," his ultimate claim is that an educated individual understands the laws of God and nature and "voluntarily and lovingly" obeys them.[145] Education, in fact, enables us to "adapt ourselves to the benign and wonderful laws of the system in which we are placed."[146] Although Mann understands the need to make public professions of a belief in sin, it is clear that his own views about sinfulness are very different from those who have less liberal theological dispositions.

Mann was actually very successful in developing and articulating a *political* position concerning religion in the schools, partly because he was clearly acting within the parameters of the law, and partly because the law itself reflected a more general public opinion. Later commentators agree that the extent of political disagreement over this issue was exaggerated in Mann's mind.[147] He was wrong, however, to view his political settlement as theoretically stable or persuasive. It was just a matter of time before the facts of religious pluralism (and moral pluralism more generally) would burst the bubble of a seeming religious consensus. The moral ends Mann promotes are dangerously liberal and humanist from the perspective of New England religious orthodoxy, on the one hand, and wed too closely to religious homogeneity for an increasingly pluralist New England society, on the other.[148]

Mann's confidence in the moral power of education is seemingly unbounded. In the *Eleventh Annual Report* he reprints a long circular letter he wrote to eight distinguished teachers, seeking their opinion about the impact of a proper common school education on the moral development of children. The letter is a far cry from a scientific instrument; Mann leads his correspondents to understand what he already believes, and what he hopes they will confirm, about "the moral power of education in reforming the world."[149] Likewise, his correspondents were obviously handpicked to reflect sympathy with Mann's optimism about these matters. Mann understands the need to stress that all the respondents are Christians who believe in the "*depravity of the natural heart*," so their answers do not violate religious orthodoxy or grow from a utopian humanism.[150] Unscientifically gathered, the information he receives from these teachers reflects more hope and conjecture than proof about the subject. One writes, for example: "My belief is that, under the conditions mentioned in the question, not more than two per cent. [of common school graduates] would be irreclaimable nuisances to society, and that ninety-five per cent. would be supporters of the welfare of the community in which they reside."[151] The significance of this little survey is less the persuasive power of the material for readers today than the tremendous optimism it reflects about the moral ends of common schooling. Mann is clear that he expects the common school to eradicate, almost completely, all forms of childhood and adolescent rebelliousness, delinquency in its petty and more serious forms, and ultimately criminality in the society at large. If taught sensibly about intellectual and moral matters by teachers of the highest intellectual and moral integrity, all children can learn to view their own well-being as tied directly to the well-being of the various communities to which they belong.

Indeed, just as the intellectual ends of schooling are subordinate to the moral, for Mann, the moral ends are subordinate to the greater political ends; at the end of the day, the entire project has grown from Mann's fear of the disorders of democratic politics and society, as surveyed in the previous chapter. So, what are the political ends of the common school?

Unsurprisingly, Mann expects the schools to instill students with civic knowledge. This civic knowledge includes both a practical understanding of American government and political history and a normative understanding of the duties of citizenship. Although most of his energy is focused on the second of these, the first obviously includes the information citizens need to satisfy their duties as jurors and voters, to "qualify each citizen for the civil and social duties he will be called to discharge."[152] Without the schools providing this civic information, children are likely to learn about politics from "angry political discussions, or from party newspapers; from caucus speeches, or Fourth of July orations,—the Apocrypha of Apocrypha."[153] As children grow to adulthood, they are achieving political sovereignty; the schools "must prepare our citizens to become municipal officers, intelligent jurors, honest witnesses, legislators, or competent judges of legislation,—in fine, to fill all the manifold relations of life."[154] Mann's experience as both a politician and a Fourth of July orator makes him acutely aware of the passionate distortions and partisanship endemic to both activities, and he believes the schools have the ability and the duty to bring basic, accurate, nonideological political information to all future citizens. "Shall not accurate views of the nature of government precede the authority to govern?"[155]

We are already well acquainted with the normative elements of civic knowledge, which include the entirety of the moral education that teaches citizens not only to understand but also to embrace their political duties as a form of self-fulfillment. This requires learning to transcend partisanship and crass self-interest in political life, to be impartial in evaluating the demands of justice in the political community. "We want a generation of men above deciding great and eternal principles, upon narrow and selfish grounds."[156] Mann is convinced that this "greatest of all human powers,—the power of impartial thought," is the key to producing citizens who can deal with the great political questions before the nation without the turmoil, partisanship, and political warfare found in contemporary American political life.[157] What is striking about Mann's hopes for this civic education is, again, how profoundly ambitious it is. It is not enough that we raise a generation of citizens knowledgeable about and committed to democratic politics. Such a generation must be so morally upright, so far immune to self-interest as to be almost unrecognizable by contemporary political standards: "We want godlike men who can tame the madness of the times."[158] Because a "partisan cannot be an honest man,"[159] a primary political aim of public schooling is to cultivate citizens for whom partisanship and narrow self-interest are morally repugnant, for whom these are simply not tempting options. Mann's program of moral education is foundational to the civic purposes of the common school. Only this moral education can produce a political culture that, in Mann's view, is acceptably civic in its orientation.

A second grand political end of common schooling, the creation of civic unity, grows from and reflects this moral political culture. Although Mann argues that morally educated citizens will be independent and freethinking,[160] this independence will also luckily and seemingly paradoxically produce a significant civic consensus. Schools must take care not to touch on theological or political topics that are controversial, as we are not yet at "the happy day . . . when all men shall 'see eye to eye.'"[161] Yet he is confident that despite our differences, it is possible to teach about our political system and history in such a manner as to capture "those articles in the creed of republicanism, which are accepted by all, believed in by all, and which form the common basis of our political faith."[162] Just as he argues that our various religious sects share a basic set of Christian beliefs, so there is a set of political commitments common to the full range of political groups and perspectives. It would be a disaster if our schools became politically partisan,[163] and Mann is nervous about the "intolerant zealots" who have no doubt about their own righteousness or the error of their opponents.[164] Nonetheless, he is confident that regardless of the passion animating our political disputes, a political consensus can be identified, taught in the schools, and thereby reinforced and strengthened over time.[165] Mann starkly contrasts the "partisan" with the "patriot," and only the latter looks toward the greater public good.[166] The moral education provided by the common schools should allow students to develop the political perspective of patriots and thereby establish a "cooperation and unity of purpose" in the citizenry during peacetime comparable to that of soldiers during war.[167]

The civic unity promoted by the common school is reflected not only in ideological consensus, however. Just as important, common schooling promotes a fraternal bond between students. In the *First Annual Report*, Mann writes, "It is on this common platform [of the common school], that a general acquaintanceship should be formed between the children of the same neighborhood. It is here, that the affinities of a common nature should unite them together so as to give the advantages of pre-occupancy and a stable possession to fraternal feelings, against the alienating competitions of subsequent life."[168] Mann is fully aware, as we have seen, that the freedom of American society produces competing interests, perspectives, and experiences, all of which can be more divisive than unifying. With proper common schooling, however, these "alienating competitions of subsequent life" can be mitigated by cultivating, during childhood, a fraternal experience of our common humanity. This bond, built in the locality, is the first step toward understanding a more general human brotherhood.[169] It is also required of citizens if they are to be expected to care for the interests of others when engaged in public life.

> Above all others, must the children of a Republic be fitted for society, as well as for themselves. As each citizen is to participate in the power of governing others, it is an essential preliminary, that he should be imbued with a feeling for the wants, and a sense of the rights, of those whom he is to govern; because the power of governing others, if guided by no higher motive than our own gratification, is the distinctive attribute of oppression;—an attribute whose nature and whose wickedness are the same, whether exercised by one who calls himself a republican, or by one born an irresponsible despot.[170]

The fraternity promoted by the common school generates sympathy with others' wants, rights, and interests.[171]

Closely related to this end of social unity, consensus, and fraternity is the third great end of common schooling for Mann—the promotion of equality. The common school is the only truly republican institution for educating the young, since it brings them "together, under the same roof, on the same seats, with the same encouragements, rewards, punishments, and to the exclusion of adventitious and artificial distinctions."[172] Unlike in Europe, where class distinctions are firm, republican Massachusetts promotes "an equal chance for earning, and equal security in the enjoyment of what they earn," to all citizens.[173] Without the common school teaching a common curriculum to all and treating all within its institutional reach equally, this equality of opportunity would be impossible. With the universal education provided by the common school, however, the "tendency to the domination of capital and the servility of labor" can be overcome.[174] Public education, "beyond all other devices of human origin, is the great equalizer of the conditions of men,—the balance-wheel of the social machinery."[175] It achieves equality by giving to each individual the means "by which he can resist the selfishness of other men."[176] That is, it gives each the means by which to become economically independent and therefore beyond the control of representatives of any social class. The theory informing Mann's claims on this matter is a fairly conventional nineteenth-century American agrarianism. Both masters and laborers must work in America and are therefore united in their interest: "The master and the laborer are one."[177] Most make their living as farmers, mechanics, or (small-scale) manufacturers, and in all these realms, intelligence and diligence, rather than social class or status, determine one's success.

A critical element of the equality produced by the common school, then, is an equality of economic opportunity that overcomes rigid and traditional class distinctions. This form of economic equality is premised on a kind of corporate or communal understanding of the ultimate right or title to the resources and wealth of the world. Mann argues that this wealth was created "for the race, collectively," for each generation in succession, and "no one man, nor any one generation of men has any such title to, or ownership in, these ingredients and substantials of all wealth, that his right is invaded when a portion of them is taken for the benefit of posterity."[178] Each individual has the equal right to produce wealth from the resources found in nature, but this claim must always be subordinated to the more general claims of the public and the ongoing good of the community. The dissolution of European social classes in Massachusetts does not translate into the individual right of each citizen to the absolute control of private property. Rather, the message is one of equality of opportunity to pursue independence and self-improvement within the context of the overall good of the (present and future) community.

In addition to this economic equality, the common schools promote even deeper forms of equality. All children are assumed to have roughly the same capacities and interests in education. "By the ordinance of nature, the human faculties are substantially the same all over the world, and hence the best means for their development and growth in one place, must be substantially the best for their development and growth every where."[179] The common schools are therefore poised to bring "the common blessings of heaven, to encompass all," by which Mann means intellectual and moral blessings above economic ones.[180] Mann's commitment to equal access to these goods is illustrated by his strong opposition to the practice of keeping common schools open for private subscription after completion of the public terms; he roundly condemns the practice on the grounds that it constitutes an unjust insult to the poor by failing to respect their equal right to the benefits of schooling.[181] In the final analysis, the common school teaches our "common destiny," as well as the insidiousness of all claims to superiority derived from the "casual and accidental distinctions of wealth, or parentage, or rank."[182] Not only the poor but the affluent too need the experience of the common school if they are to overcome the pernicious effects of social and economic distinction.[183] In Mann's view, "equal educational privileges" are greater than "all other means ever devised" to "approximate the idea of a Republican government."[184] Civic and natural equality is the presumption of the common school, and the lessons taught reflect this equality while promoting republican forms of economic equality as well.

A fourth significant political outcome of public schooling predicted by Mann is the creation of economic affluence. Although claims about how common schools promote economic well-being are scattered throughout Mann's writings, he develops the idea most fully in the *Fifth Annual Report*. With an observation that sounds strange to the modern ear, Mann notes that "rarely if ever" have the defenders of education "descended to so humble a duty as to demonstrate its pecuniary value, both to individuals and to society."[185] He is very clear that the economic benefits of education may "be justly regarded as the lowest" goods produced by schools.[186] Yet he aims to convince families that education is an excellent investment for the economic well-being of their children and to convince capitalists that education will dramatically benefit their businesses.[187] He has "novel and striking evidence," he claims, "to prove that education is convertible into houses and lands, as well as into power and virtue."[188] Mann wrote a circular letter to capitalists to inquire about the differences they observed between laborers with common school educations and those without. The responses overwhelmingly support Mann's claim about education's economic productivity. He concludes from this survey that common schooling "is not only the most honest and honorable, but the surest means of amassing property."[189]

Educational historian Maris Vinovskis has studied the *Fifth Annual Report* in some detail and explains the profound methodological problems in Mann's approach to proving his point. Just as with his later circular letter concerning moral education, presented in the *Eleventh Annual Report*, Mann's letter to capitalists prompts his respondents for the correct answers. In addition, the respondents were handpicked to ensure that Mann would receive the answers he sought, and he spoke with at least some of them about the matter prior to presenting them with the survey. In short, Mann's collection of data is nowhere near scientific or objective. Nonetheless, for all its shortcomings, the report was warmly received. "Although Mann's estimate of the value of antebellum education is clearly exaggerated and based on faulty data and reasoning, it appeared scientific and plausible to his contemporaries."[190] In fact, this report was very widely read and cemented Mann's position as a successful champion for the common school in the United States.[191]

Vinovskis points out that Mann was initially reluctant to appeal directly to material interests when defending the common school, since such an appeal could end up exacerbating qualities in American life (such as materialism) that he hoped the common schools would battle. By the time of the *Fifth Annual Report*, however, Mann had had two close calls with the Massachusetts legislature; in both 1840 and 1841, movements to abolish the Board of Education, and therefore his position as secretary, had proved to be real threats. In addition, the depression of 1839–1843 made spending on common schooling look extravagant. In light of these challenges to his project, Mann decided to pursue the argument that schooling can produce economic abundance. This decision presents a real problem, however. Though protesting that material gain is the least of the arguments for education and the common school, Mann is willing to appeal to "inferior motives" in the hope that families will educate their children, who, "when educated, will feel its higher and nobler affinities."[192] Likewise, critics in the community may be silenced by appealing to the wealth that can be generated by education, in the hope that once children are in the schools, they will find the higher purposes of education.[193] Mann's own psychology, however, claims that we cannot get to moral truths and laws through the cultivation of "lower" impulses. Rather, material goods, though real and not to be shunned, must be subordinated to and governed by higher intellectual and moral goods. To cultivate the material appears to threaten to unleash a materialism not in keeping with either Mann's educational values or his overall political purposes. Regardless, Mann's *Fifth Annual Report* was a tremendous success. He protests, at the end of the report, that "to my own mind, this tribute to its [education's] worth . . . is still the faintest note of praise which can be uttered, in honor of so noble a theme," and that wealth "dwindles into insignificance when compared with those loftier and more sacred attributes of the cause, which have the power of converting material wealth into spiritual well-being, and of giving to its possessor lordship and sovereignty, alike over the temptations of adversity, and the still more dangerous seducements of prosperity."[194] One wonders, however, if he oversold the material benefits of the common school to the detriment of his greater political purposes, just as he had feared.

There is one more important political purpose we can glean from Mann's defense of the common school. Making his case for the material benefits of common schooling, Mann comments, "The instructed and talented man enters the rich domains of nature, not as an intruder, but, as it were, a proprietor, and makes her riches his own."[195] When we are properly educated, we reap the benefits of nature by working in harmony with her. This is true not only of our economic life; Mann's belief is that education is the harmonizing of our behavior and beliefs with the material, intellectual, and moral laws of nature. Just as educated individuals understand the laws governing health and wealth, so they understand and submit to the laws governing moral life. Properly instituted, the common school promises to produce citizens who pursue a political life in harmony with the laws of nature. The democratic polity can produce the most pathological of all politics, one in which all become petty tyrants. It can also produce, with successful common schooling, a politics in which the entire citizenry promotes a political harmony that brings out the greatest potential of nature. The common school can prevent the worst and create the best imaginable political community.

When we look at the battles Mann fought over pedagogy and the curriculum, it is clear that the most serious issues at stake are actually about morality and religion. When we look more closely at the moral and religious debates, however, we see that there are important political issues in play as well—most important, how to negotiate the nature of schooling in an increasingly democratic and pluralistic America. Mann's program aims for increased tolerance and openness to ideological difference, as well as the expansion of state control of public education. Orestes Brownson, editor of the *Boston Quarterly Review*, attacks Mann and the Board of Education precisely on these latter grounds, just as the governor and the legislature respond to what they view as a threat to Democratic localism by Whig centralization and (liberal) ideological imposition.

The occasion of Brownson's assault on Mann's educational project is the publication of the *Second Annual Report*.[196] Brownson, annoyed by the heavily pedagogical and curricular focus of the report, claims that the board and its secretary have not given serious thought to the true problems of education, that is, to issues concerning religion and politics.[197] On the first of these counts, Mann and the board are proposing and defending a program of religious instruction that is simply vacuous. Brownson agrees with other critics of Mann's nonsectarianism, viewing it as so general that it "means nothing at all." In truth, he says, "There is . . . no common ground between all the various religious denominations in this country, on which an educator may plant himself."[198] The same is true of politics; the values of Democrats and Whigs are absolutely opposed, and the hope of finding some common goals and beliefs reduces political commitments to a meaninglessly vague set of platitudes. In reality, Whigs are committed to "Hobbism" and deny the "internal light" available to all men. Democrats, in contrast, have faith in the character and religious sensibility of the common people.[199] These differences are fundamental, and they lead Whigs to an overbearing authoritarianism and Democrats to a respect for the rights and freedom of the people.

This brings us to the heart of Brownson's critique. His most significant charge is that the fundamental assumption driving the board and Mann is that the government has the right to educate the people in a democracy. Five years prior to the publication of the *Seventh Annual Report*, Brownson accuses the board of emulating Prussia. In the United States, he claims, the citizens should be presumed to be wiser than the government. "To entrust . . . the government with the power of determining the education which our children shall receive, is entrusting our servant with the power to be our master."[200] Although there is Democratic representation on the board, Brownson is unimpressed; the thrust of the board's action is based on what he takes to be a Whiggish denial of this basic democratic principle.[201] By assuming the right to determine the library materials to be used in the common schools, and by assuming the right to educate teachers in normal schools, the board and Mann are establishing a Prussian-style tyranny over the people at large. "In the view of this respectable Board, education is merely a brand of general police, and schoolmasters are only a better sort of constables."[202] Brownson does not deny that there is a role for the state government in public education, but he would confine this to raising revenue. When it comes to curriculum and teacher selection, power should be left in the hands of the parents in their local districts. "To confide our Common Schools to the Board, is like taking the children from their parents, and entrusting them to strangers."[203] To allow the board and the secretary the power to shape and direct public education is to allow a political power that is altogether undemocratic. The province of democratic government "is to reflect, not to lead, nor to create the general will."[204]

Brownson's argument suffers from both exaggeration and a lack of analytic precision. The exaggeration is seen in his claims about the power held by Mann and the board. Joy Elmer Morgan underestimates the degree to which Mann is, in fact, bent on establishing centralized responsibility for public education when she writes, "The Massachusetts Board of Education was carefully set up to preserve the traditions of local self-government."[205] But Brownson, too, grossly overstates localities' loss of autonomy with the establishment of the board. Mann, after all, has no staff, and his only real authority is to persuade and report on conditions in the common schools.

The lack of analytic precision in Brownson's critique is seen in his unjustified and dramatic contrast between local- and state-level political power: he assumes that local power is obviously and purely democratic and that state power is obviously not. This assumption, of course, is not at all obvious, and he makes no attempt to justify it.[206]

Despite these weaknesses, Brownson's attack goes straight to the "democratic paradox" in Mann's position: the claim that democratic citizens require preparation before they deserve respect and can assume the responsibility growing out of their presumed democratic sovereignty. Brownson's position is simply to deny the legitimacy of the paradox itself; government must be the servant and not the teacher of the people. But by the end of the essay, it is clear that Brownson himself is not as free from the paradox of democratic education as he might wish. Arguing that children are actually educated by the "spirit of the age," he identifies the problem as one of educating adults to behave in such a way as to properly socialize children into responsible adulthood. Brownson, too, therefore assumes the need for democratic education. His differences with Mann are that he locates this education in institutions of civil society—the lyceum movement, the Christian ministry, the press—rather than the government, and he directs his primary attention to the education of adults rather than children.[207] Despite his fierce objection to the state's involvement in education, however, he does not avoid the more general problems raised by the paradox of democratic education.

As we have seen, Mann had reasons to prefer his approach to education over Brownson's. He believed that the moral and political education of adults is ineffective. He believed that only common schools could generate sufficient democratic equality to allow the cultivation of democratic virtues and the resources required (appropriate conditions of equality and prosperity, for example) for the practice of democratic citizenship. Despite these reasons and potential answers, Brownson raised questions of democratic concern that went to the heart of Mann's project, and it is striking that Mann never felt compelled to engage them in any way approaching the seriousness with which he responded to the Boston schoolmasters or his religious critics. The criticism most deeply driven by democratic considerations is the criticism Mann felt least threatened by. To him, this criticism did not represent a truly principled objection to his work. We know Mann considered his legislative critics to be deeply unprincipled and that he dismissed the appeal to local control as crass partisanship.[208] There is no evidence that he found Brownson's criticism theoretically compelling or significant enough to require a serious and thoughtful answer.[209] In retrospect, though, Brownson raised critical political issues of parental and local control that continue to haunt American public education today.

Mann's educational crusade faced serious challenges on pedagogical, religious, and political grounds. His achievement was to repel all three attacks by building a case for the common school on the foundation of a humanist pedagogy; an increasingly tolerant, if still primarily Protestant and unstable, moral consensus; and a paternalistic,[210] increasingly centralizing democratic politics.

The Reverend Smith's charge that Mann was disingenuous about his own partisanship was at least partly true. Mann's moral, religious, and political program for the common school was not above partisanship; however, contrary to Smith's suspicion about Mann's hypocrisy, Mann was probably convinced that it was. At the very least, Mann's arrogance and self-righteousness blinded him to his own partisanship, and his critics are certainly justified in raising this issue. It must also be admitted, however, that even if Mann was not above the partisan battles, and even if his political coalition was not as inclusive as he insisted, Mann *did* forge political alliances across religious affiliations and political parties, and he *did* promote common schools that were liberal, open, and tolerant of ideological difference to the extent possible in the context of mid-nineteenth-century Massachusetts politics.

The more interesting point concerns the nature of Mann's partisanship, the substantive content of his views. As has become clear, Mann's natural religion was, in many ways, more Greek than Christian, emphasizing the liberating quality of moral knowledge rather than the need to manage and contain the intractable fact of human sinfulness. Mann had hope for moral progress, but this hope was lodged in a Manichaean view of our possibilities; we would find our democracy either deteriorating into the most degraded and tyrannical of societies or evolving into the most perfect, harmonious, just, and upright polity imaginable. The moral stakes were obviously extreme, requiring a level of educational success approaching perfection. This hope for moral perfection reflected Mann's extraordinary anxiety about and fear for democracy. Significant moral and political disagreement and conflict signified for him the corruptions of self-interest, and these threatened the basic stability of democratic society. The ultimate political goal of the common school was to produce a level of moral, religious, and political consensus that would make disagreement about the fundamental principles and goods of society impossible.[211] Learning to overcome partisanship, virtuous citizens would certainly disagree about the pragmatics of public life, but never about its basic values and purposes.

Unlike his orthodox opponents, and contrary to Brownson's polemic, Mann accepted and embraced the developing American democracy. His fear of the potential chaos and tyranny resulting from this democracy grew from the old Puritan tradition emphasizing social agreement and conformity of belief. Mann rejected Calvinist theology, but he could not escape the Puritan vision of religious consensus. This drove him to seek a moral and civic form of consensus to replace the greater religious unity of historic Massachusetts.[212] If the faith of earlier generations was no longer possible (or even desirable) in the contemporary world, given the inhumanity of Calvinist teachings, we needed some comparable faith to bind society together. For Mann, this was the natural religion and humanist morality he found in Combe's phrenology. The science of morality would be the cement of a democratic society, just as Calvinist theology had sustained the old Puritan social order.

Mann's fear of democratic conflict, then, was the driving force in his plan for the common school. His hope to use the schools to overcome deep disagreement led, however, to a noticeably unbalanced and politicized educational program. Mann's attraction to science and practical knowledge was due at least in part to the ability to find single and demonstrable answers to the questions raised in these domains; his distrust of the arts and literature grew from their need to be interpreted, their ambiguity, the imprecision of the knowledge they generate. Mann's deepest wishful thinking, and the point at which he became an ideological partisan (his own protests to the contrary notwithstanding), was his hope of transferring the kind of intellectual certainty found in science and practical affairs to those elements of life, such as our moral and political disagreements or our experience of the arts and humanities, that are not subject to such consensus and that lack such clear and demonstrably certain answers. Mann's educational vision stressed the production of substantive agreement and consensus and, through these shared values, the subsequent promotion of fraternity and universal respect for duty. An intolerance for substantive ambiguity, debate, and disagreement haunted Mann's common schools, and his fear of these potentially divisive forces led him to place his faith in what he saw as a law-bound moral and political theory. The result was an educational program heavy on the practical, utilitarian, and scientific and weak on the aesthetic, narrative, and interpretive. His program may be one that we (at least partially) approve of today, but it is not one, as he claimed and wished, that has abolished the need for ongoing debate about our deepest moral and political commitments. Nor is it one that does everything possible to prepare citizens for a democratic political practice where real substantive disagreement exists on these matters.

When Mann exhorted his fellow citizens, on 4 July 1842, to "*go forth*, AND TEACH THIS PEOPLE," what he ultimately had in mind was an education in the moral foundations of citizenship. His conception of how to approach this education, however, offered both more and less than he intended. It offered a more politically (and morally) contentious content than he claimed or admitted (either publicly or to himself). It offered less in terms of the skills required for the negotiation of disagreement, interpretation, and the democratic process. Because Mann aimed to promote an education that would eliminate significant democratic disagreement, he failed to plan for precisely the kind of skills required by democratic citizens in a real democratic society—the society referred to by Hawthorne as "our tongue-governed democracy"[213]—in which citizens have profound disagreements and need to learn the arts of persuasion, civility, critical evaluation, and self-doubt.

Chapter 4

Higher Education

In October 1853, in his "Dedicatory and Inaugural Address" at Antioch College, Horace Mann made his first public appearance as the founding president of this unique nonsectarian (within the confines of Christianity) coeducational institution of higher learning. The speech he gave that day was among his most eloquent, skillfully developed, and powerful, even if it offered few surprises for those familiar with the ethical, political, and educational ideas of his earlier career. Mann had brought his reforming educational program to the world of higher education. The fundamental problem for colleges, he told the crowd of more than 3,000 curious and enthusiastic Ohioans, is to properly understand and answer the question, "what do youth need in order to become ministers of good to the world?"[1]

The answers Mann provides to this question are urgent, to his mind, for reasons we can now anticipate. What is at stake is not merely the salvation of individual souls but the integrity of our collective life as a nation. "For magnitude, for tenacious vitality, there are no crimes like national crimes. Individuals can debase individuals, but governments can brutalize a race."[2] Our greatest threats may be collective, but "no limits can be affixed to the influences which the humblest institution or the humblest individual may exert."[3] With proper encouragement and training, honorable graduates of even new and small colleges like Antioch will be able to help reform and heal our nation and lay the foundation for the development of a virtuous consensus in American democratic society.

Not surprisingly, Mann suggests to his audience that the vast majority of the problems in the world around us "proceed immediately from the bodily appetites and propensities."[4] The body thus presents the first great set of educational challenges. Glossing Combe, Mann argues that God originally created our bodies to live harmoniously with nature: "I hold it to be morally impossible for God to have created, in the beginning, such men and women as we find the human race in their physical condition now to be."[5] After providing a long and horrifying litany of human debauchery, Mann concludes that our physical suffering from diseases and other bodily troubles is the result of releasing our lowest animal impulses from their original control by our intellectual and moral capacities. "Awful and unspeakable violations of God's laws have done this dreadful work," he argues, but we can be restored to health by returning to a condition in which our natural bodily needs are governed by principles higher than themselves.[6] If "it took successive ages of outrageous excess and debauchery, to drain off his [man's] electric energies and make him even accessible to disease,"[7] we can likewise look forward to a time when "men will speak of Christian and un-Christian health, as they do now of Christian and un-Christian character."[8] The temptations of the body were responsible for the human fall from the Eden of nature. This fall has produced a human body that continually and progressively grows alienated from and threatened by nature. We have inappropriately promoted bodily desires from their natural position as the least of the human goods to a commanding position as the greatest of human wants. Moral reform requires, first, the disciplining of these desires and the subsequent living of healthy lives. Education must therefore begin with this project of physical discipline.

The second "grand want" of human beings is the development of the intellect. The primary task here is to discover and understand the natural laws that govern the world we inhabit. The "intelligence of man is yet to pervade the earth as it now pervades the body, and to command the forces of nature as it now commands its own limbs."[9] Mann suggests, in language that should bring a nod of approval from many present-day environmentalists, that our rebellion from nature has corrupted our intellect, thereby handicapping our effective and appropriate interaction with nature. "Anglo-Saxon egotism" has conceived of nature as something to be enslaved rather than understood, worked with, and lived in harmony with. "We boast of conquering and subduing the forces of nature. What the ancients worshipped as gods, we speak of as captives and slaves. In our self-complacency, we talk of imprisoning the elements to make them do our bidding. We boast of turning the lightning into an errand-boy; of using gravitation as our pile-driver; of tasking rivers and winds to grind our mills."[10] This attitude is a corruption of the truly Christian understanding of the intellect's role: "How different from all this is the view of the Christian philosopher!"[11] Mann suggests, optimistically, that "the soul of man is feeling its way outward, beyond his own body, into the body of nature."[12] This is necessary if we are to learn to live in accord with, rather than in constant antagonism against, the world around us.

The educational implications of this analysis are profound. Because the world is governed by natural laws that never vary across time and space, the type of training required by the intellect is historically constant and unchanging. For Mann, "All heathen lands are to be civilized and Christianized; and what we now call civilization and Christianity are to be purified and elevated into forms indefinitely higher than at present prevail."[13] Just as the bodily propensities need to be disciplined to assume their appropriate place in the hierarchy of human goods and knowledge, so must the intellect focus on its proper objects and purposes. These educational demands are historically constant and universal, even if we are only beginning to fully understand them in the modern, democratic world.

The taming of the appetites and the proper focusing of the intellect, of course, depend on the successful governance of the third element of our nature—our moral capacities. "To render the cultivation of the intellectual nature beneficial or even safe, nay, to save it from being baneful, it must be accompanied by moral education."[14] Our current civilization suffers from an imbalance between our intellectual and our moral development. Intellectually, we are becoming increasingly successful at manipulating and enslaving nature, but we fail to understand how to properly use our scientific knowledge to live harmoniously with nature. This failure has implications beyond our relationship with the nonhuman world. Our scientific prowess has not freed us from "caste" and the social divisions produced by selfishness, nor has it been used to challenge the dogma that produces religious and moral intolerance. At present, clearly, it is "in the sphere of the intellect alone that men are becoming truly civilized."[15] According to Mann, this is a more dangerous imbalance in our human world than is generally recognized. "The more I see of our present civilization and of the only remedies for its evils, the more I dread intellectual eminence when separated from virtue. We are in a sick world, for whose maladies the knowledge of truth and obedience to it are the only healing."[16] The human relations with nature, and the social relations among humans themselves, are distorted by our imbalanced intellect. Only the moral law can properly guide both our intellect and our body.

Mann makes two key claims in this speech about the nature of moral law. First, he contends that it is knowable and demonstrable. "God created the universe upon the principle of the supremacy of the moral law, and it would be easier for mankind to walk on their heads or breathe in vacuity than to subvert this moral order of creation. And all these propositions are as capable of demonstration as any theorem in mathematics."[17] Given the obvious truth (for Mann) that God could have created the universe only to be harmonious and good, the conclusion is that moral laws can be thought of as propositions that, if abided by, can eliminate suffering and conflict and generate in their place health, cooperation, and human communion. Poor health, conflict, contentiousness of all sorts can only be caused by the violation of moral law. The misery produced by these troubles is proof of this violation; anything that mitigates or eliminates these ills must likewise be in accord with the moral law given by nature.

Second, Mann claims that this demonstrable moral law can be taught and learned and incorporated into human life just as any other form of true knowledge can be. Moral education consists, he implies, in both the understanding of these moral laws and the training of the conscience to adhere to them.[18] His assumption appears to be that there are such obvious good blessings to be gained by living according to the dictates of moral law, both for the individual and for the society she or he is a part of, that once moral law is properly exposed, all individuals will voluntarily and happily submit to it. Our suffering and conflict are a result of ignorance rather than of perverse will. "At the judgment day even Satan himself, all concreted into falsehood as he will be, will be seen to be still more of a fool than a liar!"[19]

As suggested earlier, there is a sense in which none of this discussion is surprising, insofar as it is very much in keeping with the ideas Mann consistently promoted in the service of the common school. What is important for our purposes, beyond the recognition of this address as one of Mann's most accomplished performances, is the degree to which Mann believes his educational and moral theory requires that we approach higher education in more or less the same way we approach the primary educational project of the common school. First and most importantly, college education must be as committed to moral (including physical) education as it is to any more narrowly construed intellectual instruction. It would be a gross dereliction of educational duty to allow students to become morally corrupted while stimulating their intellectual capacities.[20] This means a strict attention to the physical and social habits cultivated during the college years. A college must be as committed to teaching students to govern their health, their physical appetites, and their passions as it is to guiding them through the formal syllabus of instruction. Moral paternalism is justified by the fact that college students are people "who have ceased to be children but are not yet men and women."[21] Second, institutions of higher learning, like the common school, must be nonpartisan and tolerant of different (Protestant) religious traditions.

> The command to love God with all our powers necessarily involves the absolute freedom of those powers. . . . Christ came to make men free in thought as well as in spirit. . . . We are bound to judge men by the integrity of their lives, rather than by the accuracy of their logic, and an unintentional error of the intellect is never to be compared with a conscious dereliction of the heart. That would be as erroneous as to compare a mistake in metaphysics with the crime of blasphemy.[22]

Mann's promotion of nonsectarianism in higher education is built on a humane recognition of human weakness in explaining the nature of moral insight (a recognition, we might note, that is in some tension with the above-mentioned claim about the clear demonstrability of moral precepts), rather than any relativism about moral belief itself. Third, Mann holds that the supremacy of the moral element in higher education demands that this education be coeducational because women require this instruction just as much as (if not more than) men, but also because a full moral education is best achieved through the proper, orderly, and well-governed integration of the sexes. These three demands all received extensive attention while Mann served the Antioch community.

Before turning to a discussion of each of these elements of Mann's work at Antioch, it is important to acknowledge the puzzle of Mann's willingness to lead the Antioch community in the first place. Mann's top priority after serving in Congress appears to have been to remain in politics and run for the governorship of Massachusetts. When it became clear, due to his conflict with Daniel Webster and the remaining core of the Whig Party in Massachusetts, that he would be unable to attain that office, Mann turned to the offer from the Antioch organizers. Over the course of the next few years, he was recruited for the presidencies of the new state universities in Iowa and Wisconsin (as well as the presidency of the private Northwest Christian College—later Butler University—in Indianapolis). Given Mann's democratic commitment to public education, it is surprising and a little mysterious that he preferred to lead a small private college rather than one of these new state universities. Cremin wonders "at Mann's failure to include public higher education within his common school system."[23] Messerli claims that Antioch became for Mann "the symbol of all he had ever worked for,"[24] but this just restates the question: why would working for a private college seem closer to Mann's lifelong project than expanding higher education through a public, more democratically accessible, institution? He had, after all, complained in the past that "the uniform policy of governments has been to create a few men of great learning rather than to diffuse knowledge among the many."[25] One might expect that the desire to "diffuse knowledge among the many," rather than create a "few men of great learning," would have made the new state universities exciting educational projects for Mann.

Addressing this puzzle leads us to recognize the one significant distinction Mann drew between higher and primary education: his understanding of the relevant student constituency. Mann's work as secretary had always stressed the rough equality of children's intellectual capacity and the need to bring all future citizens to a similar level of intellectual and moral development. Higher education, in contrast, is reserved for a few distinctive young men and women. In the baccalaureate address to the graduating class in 1858, Mann explains that the "higher forms of education are for the exemplary and the faithful, to robe them and crown them with glory and joy."[26] Higher education, in short, is restricted to a moral elite, the most distinctive and praiseworthy young people (as opposed to "a few men of great learning"). It is not restricted by religious denomination, because no religious denomination has a monopoly on virtue.[27] Higher education is reserved for an aristocracy of the virtuous, and its purpose is to provide society with superior citizens who will assume positions of leadership for reform in the future. Mann's conception of higher education, therefore, stresses the meritocratic selection and training of morally outstanding (and intellectually capable) young people, rather than the democratic accessibility of advanced learning. The inclusiveness and utilitarianism of state universities apparently failed to interest him. The commitment to nonsectarianism and coeducation made the Antioch experiment attractive to Mann, and he clearly thought this new college was poised to provide him with the opportunity to train a moral elite.[28]

Mann's commitment to coeducation reflects an extension of his views about the moral sphere and duties naturally suited to women. As secretary, Mann pushed vigorously for the training and employment of women as teachers of the youngest children. Although he sometimes promoted this program with a crass appeal to the lesser expense associated with hiring women teachers, his more considered judgment, which emerged over time, was that the gap between women's and men's pay was morally unjustifiable.[29] The real reason to employ women was not their low wages but their natural ability as teachers of the young.[30] Although Mann believed in a sexual division of labor, this did not break down neatly between public and private life but rather between different (although occasionally overlapping) sets of gender-specific public and private duties.

In one of his popular lectures, *A Few Thoughts on the Powers and Duties of Women*, published the year he went to Antioch, Mann criticizes those who overly romanticize women. Poets who present an ethereal portrait of womanhood, for example, have missed the true point about woman's virtue and thereby encourage too restrictive an understanding of the nature and purposes of women. In contrast, it would be a great improvement if the authors of such portraits "would take off their [women's] wings, and set them to doing something useful."[31] Indeed, women have been both oppressed and "debased by adulation."[32] Mann claims a higher regard for women and would not "insult her by adulation."[33] He hopes to lead women instead to their natural duties.[34] The difficulty in coming to terms with the proper role of women is to accept the division of labor between the sexes and to understand how gender differences naturally lead to different capacities, talents, and thereby obligations.

The natural differences Mann has in mind are not surprising or particularly original. Men are intellectual; women are "sympathetic" and emotional. Men are more combative; women are more pacific and capable of loving outreach to others. When we remember that, for Mann, emotional and moral life occupies a higher plane than intellectual life, we understand why, in his view, even though man and woman are each superior in their respective spheres, the sphere that women occupy is the higher of the two. "Female nature is male nature, once more refined."[35] This higher nature is what makes women the natural educators of children and men the natural governors of adults: "this great work, like others, is naturally divided between the sexes,—the nobler government of children belonging to women, the less noble government of adults to men."[36] Coming from other thinkers, such comments might be suspected of harboring a great deal of patronizing pandering; for Mann, however, the sentiment accords with his consistent view of education as the greatest tool available for producing the deepest, most meaningful social reform. As he says in his "Investiture of Office" comments upon assuming the presidency at Antioch, "the work of education" is "always paramount to all others."[37] Women's role as natural educators is in accord with and reflects the superiority of their natural attributes. Mary Mann notes that her husband "had never been pleased with any desire on woman's part to shine in public; but it was his opinion that the divinely appointed mission of woman is to teach, and it was his wish to introduce her into every department of instruction as soon as it could be done with good effect."[38] Woman's suitability for teaching could extend, in Mann's view, to higher education; he hired his own niece to teach at Antioch.

There are other spheres besides the domestic and the educational that fit women's nature, however, and Mann's view is that it is unjust to exclude them from these opportunities. Work relating to the fine arts, the ministry, and medicine should be open to women, since these fields draw on women's natural aesthetic, moral, and nurturing senses, respectively. More combative and public occupations, however, such as law, government, and the military, are appropriately masculine by nature. Such activities and careers would pervert, distort, and disastrously corrupt women's best qualities, and women may rightly be prevented from entering these professions.

Because women naturally occupy the higher ground in the hierarchy of human capacities, Mann fears they are also capable of greater corruption. The education of women is therefore required on the basis of simple prudence; too much of the moral life is at stake to leave women's education to chance. But Mann believes that the education of women is also a matter of right, built on the fundamental Protestant insight of personal responsibility. "The great idea of Protestantism,—that of making each individual soul responsible for itself, and, there, in the last resort, sovereign arbiter over its own conclusions and conduct,—has done more than anything else for the elevation of women."[39] Mann's contention that women are less intellectual than men in no way disqualifies women from higher education, given the supremacy of the moral element in all education. In his view, women obviously have sufficient intellectual capacity to understand the types of science and natural law required to perform their rightful duties and pursue professional careers. The argument for higher coeducation is that a properly designed college can prepare women to perform their highest duties, and it can do so in a context in which they learn to be chaste even while working with and around men.

> It is more than desirable that a certain degree of social intercourse should subsist between those who have ceased to be children but are not yet men and women. Without such intercourse the manners grow rude and awkward, the sentiments grow coarse and impure. How painfully this is illustrated in the life of sailors, soldiers, and pioneers. In education, the problem is to facilitate this appropriate degree of intercourse while avoiding all dangerous or indecorous familiarity.[40]

Mann also suggests that it is economically inefficient and wasteful to provide sexually segregated colleges,[41] and we can expect better marriages from couples who have had the opportunity to know members of the opposite sex in closer (but rigorously regulated) social and educational contexts than are frequently available to young adults.[42] Ultimately, however, the case for coeducation rests on the claim that both men and women will be best prepared to assume their proper roles and perform their assigned duties in such an environment. In large part because women's duties often require them to work side by side with men in some sectors of the public world, "one of the Demands of the Age is that both sexes shall be educated together."[43]

In addition to coeducation, the nonsectarian nature of Antioch was all-important to Mann. When he was preparing to assume the presidency, he wrote to a correspondent, "As far as possible, I would prepare every human being for that most important of all duties, the determining of his religious belief for himself."[44] He strongly denied anyone's right to question him on issues of Christian doctrine, claiming that these are matters of personal conscience rather than institutional discipline.[45] He also refused to allow religious revival meetings on campus, arguing that they could not be of interest to such thoughtful students as his own; the enthusiasms they generated could only grow from a vicious community and could never reflect the response of an engaged, serious, and virtuous student body.[46] Clear religious thinking, however, in no way guarantees doctrinal agreement. We know that the world is full of disagreement about religious truth, and this alone "should teach us diffidence and modesty, and not presumption or dogmatism."[47] Indeed, Mann argues that no two people, given their different life experiences, can have precisely the same conception of God. In addition, given God's enormity and our own human limitations, no individual's conception can be anything other than fractionally accurate, nor can any individual's conception claim to be more accurate than any other's. Superior intellect and education, in short, are no guarantee of superior religious truth or insight.[48]

Despite our limitations, Mann believes that all genuine religious experience provides certain similar lessons. Every great religious tradition, he claims, teaches the omnipotence and justice of God.[49] Most important, "there is one point of absolute uniformity among all His true worshippers! In ideas they conflict, but in love they all harmonize. Love is the same in all worlds and in all natures."[50] The unity of all religious people is a unity not of doctrine but of "spirit."[51] Love is the constant: "The bond of love engirdles the universe; it is the oneness of Creator and created."[52]

There are three points to make about Mann's understanding and justification of nonsectarian higher education. First, he is still trying, as he did when he served as secretary, to find a defensible distinction between particularistic doctrines and more universally shared beliefs. We may not be able to agree on the specifics of doctrine, he thinks, but we should be able to agree on the spirit that underlies all different doctrinal understandings. Second, this claim is as unpersuasive in his Antioch sermons as it was in his political speeches as secretary of the Board of Education of Massachusetts. It is simply not true that the different intellectual architecture promoted by different religious groups reflects a similar underlying spirit. For example, Mann's own Unitarianism conceives of sin quite differently than conventional Calvinism does. The underlying structure of the moral universe for Mann is (potentially) much more harmonious than it was for his Puritan forebears, and although both he and they could speak to a similar degree about God's love, only the latter could speak as well and as clearly about human perversity of will, God's wrath, and divine vengeance. The cosmology between even these two Protestant perspectives is noticeably different, Mann's protestations to the contrary notwithstanding. His own distinctions between the doctrine and spirit of religion could not help but look like an overtly doctrinal claim to his opponents.

For our purposes, however, the third and most critical issue concerning Mann's commitment to nonsectarian higher education relates to higher education's more general commitment to moral development. Mann may have deluded himself about how strictly nonpartisan he was, about the degree to which he avoided dogma in his own views, but his Antioch sermons convey a kind of epistemological and theological modesty about the limits on human beings' knowledge of ultimate moral and religious truth: "no mortal man ever had or can have an adequate idea of the one living and true God."[53] In a lecture delivered during his Antioch years, Mann charged, "when any being less than omniscient binds himself to verbal article or dogma, he thereby turns language, which should be his instrument, into an iron incasement for imprisoning his soul."[54] The key, as we know from the earlier discussion of Mann's commitment to natural religion, is for religion to take its cue from science. The beauty and appeal of science, he believes, are precisely in its transcendence of dogma, its appeal to commonly held truths, evidence, and demonstration. Science, in short, "is not sectarian."[55] Because no natural reality can contradict any other, the "greatest Demand of the Age is that religion and science should be reconciled, harmonized, and led to work lovingly together."[56] Science has proved that only nonsectarian discussion can lead to an increased (and mutual) understanding of the truth. If religion is to maintain its commitment to the truth, it must learn to incorporate the sensibility of scientific thinking as well as the conclusions of scientific analysis. And the "only religion . . . with which science will freely and rejoicingly consent to live and work, is an unsectarian religion."[57] No religion committed to dogmatic certainty is justifiable in a world increasingly understood by science.[58] For Mann, no general moral perspective out of step with a scientific epistemological modesty is defensible or compelling.

Mann's actual treatment of his undergraduates, however, sent a noticeably different message. His goal, as Mary Mann put it, was to develop the moral superiority above the literary reputation of the college.[59] Assuming the "character of parent" to his students,[60] Mann developed a code of conduct that disapproved of dancing, card games, practical jokes, and most other forms of youthful humor, as well as marriage among his students,[61] not to mention the more obvious vices of tobacco and alcohol. Mann not only set these rules; in his paternal role he would plead, even cry,[62] to persuade students to pursue a righteous path of behavior. Rather than promoting a morally relaxed, open, and tolerant community, as we might expect in light of some of his comments about moral modesty, Mann's code of conduct for students was severe and enforced with liberal helpings of both guilt and sanctions. In one of his sermons he argued that sin is "the weakness and disease of the moral faculties."[63] He was convinced, apparently, that if he reinforced the proper forms of chaste, upright, morally admirable behavior, the moral faculties of his students would gain health and strength, and the desire to stray would disappear and be replaced by a fully voluntary embrace of a moral lifestyle. "The glorious truth," he proclaimed in Antioch's first graduation address in 1857, "is that habit has as much power to elevate as to debase us."[64] Mann was nothing if not enthusiastic in the enforcement of proper moral habits among his student body. Robert Straker's claim that "Mann did not trust himself, or anyone else, to indoctrinate others" seems at best a half-truth.[65]

Mann used those first baccalaureate exercises to fully develop his understanding of the moral project of higher education. The cultivation of moral sensibility begins "in a subjugation of the bodily appetites and desires."[66] Therefore, for example, he condemns "all brawling jollities or sports unworthy [of] the nobler faculties of man" and advances "an earnest plea in behalf of elegant and refined mirthfulness."[67] Such mirthfulness, however, "should always be associated with the higher faculties," since it is always "debasing" when "allied with the lower or animal propensities of men."[68] There is a sense of urgency in Mann's tone, reflecting his view that "college is a place where character is developed with fearful rapidity."[69] Mann led his life at Antioch at a high moral pitch, and he obviously expected those around him to do so as well. The time is short and the stakes are high, since the development of even the most modest and seemingly innocuous vice in college can lead to profound moral perversion later in private life and public career. "A college should be a nursery for the principles of sobriety and for all noble aspirations."[70] Mann's analysis here is almost hysterical, imagining immoral college graduates acting as judges overturning temperance laws, lawyers defending criminals even when they are aware of their criminality, and other such outrages.[71] Just as it is the "sacred function of the common school" to "extirpate and abolish" the "vicious sentiments and noxious habits into whose midst so many children are born, and which, therefore, they imbibe as inevitably as they do their mother's milk,"[72] the college is charged with ensuring that students do not take the germs of any moral viciousness into their postgraduate careers. Any immoral individual is undeserving of the "prerogatives of a college education and the honors of a college diploma."[73] The highest responsibility for a college, therefore, is to make sure that all its graduates are of the very highest character. "I proclaim it to be an offense against pubic morality for any college to graduate a vicious young man."[74]

Mann's conclusion to this speech suggests that he sees no contradiction between his demand for moral uniformity and his condemnation of doctrinal dogma. On the contrary, the assumption appears to be that moral consensus is the natural outcome of tolerant, nondogmatic inquiry. "Let colleges . . . bend their energies to secure, not uniformity of a supposed good creed, but universality of known good morals. Conscience has a higher function than intellect; the love of truth is better than the love of logic."[75] This is a startling comment on a number of levels: its significant distinction between conscience and intellect, its promotion of the nonrational over the rational as the primary program for an institution of higher learning, and its assumption that a tenable distinction can be made between dogma and moral conscience and principles. I return to all these points later. Mann wanted to promote a profoundly Puritanical moral code while rejecting the Calvinist commitments underlying the original development of the code itself. Liberal theology and modern "scientific" moral theory, he hoped, could generate the old-fashioned moral virtues.

Mann's moral commitments as a university president have caused a great many people to admire and revere him. The final sentence of his final public speech, delivered at the third Antioch graduation in 1859 a couple of months prior to his death, has now become famous: "*Be ashamed to die until you have won some victory for humanity*."[76] These inspiring lines were delivered by a sincere, beloved, and exhausted man; they no doubt moved his audience and have certainly moved later generations. But Mann's project of moral education has a darker side as well. Most significantly, his moral righteousness led him to demand that students report all breaches of conduct by their peers.[77] Encountering resistance to the idea of student informants, Mann delivered a sermon, later published as "Testimony against Evil—A Duty." The argument here, and also in "Report of the 'Code of Honor,' Falsely So Called," authored for a convention of university presidents and delegates in 1856, supports Mary Mann's claim that, to her husband, "Principles were more to him than even friends."[78] In the sermon, Mann claims, "Honest men are interested in having the whole world honest, in suppressing all fraud, violence, and wrong."[79] No distinctions in judgment are allowed among "fraud, violence, and wrong" of differing degrees. In fact, there is a theory of escalating wrong that suggests that by overlooking minor vices, we are only ensuring the increasing severity of future vicious, even criminal, behavior. The greatest good may actually be to nip this process in the bud by doing everything we can to prevent even minor infractions of good behavior.[80] Our obligation to love one another requires us to rescue those who are sinning by reporting them to the appropriate authorities. Far from "tattling," this is actually an act of charity and commitment to the wrongdoer. "No, my young friends, it is wholly a false code of honor which prevents any one, student or citizen, from preventing wrong-doing."[81] We should all view good laws as our "friends and protectors,"[82] not as threats to our (or others') liberty. Failure to report a breach of these laws allows not only the obvious harm to the community that such acts may overtly produce; it also positively harms the guilty party by allowing his or her moral corruption to be reinforced and nurtured:[83] "He who saves one's character is a greater benefactor than he who saves his life."[84] Any student who fails to inform on another is guilty of a self-inflicted wound as well; that student becomes a kind of liar and, to that degree, is as vicious as the original offender. The influence of such lying can only be harmful. "A lying state of mind in youth has its natural culmination in the falsehoods and perjuries of manhood."[85] Mann makes it a positive moral good and obligation for students to inform on friends and colleagues even for the smallest infractions of the college's code of conduct. Mann's friend Samuel Gridley Howe was right to fear that Mann "was seeking the liberal goals of co-education and nonsectarianism by increasingly illiberal means."[86]

When one surveys Mann's moral project, both for Antioch and for American society in general, a number of points need to be appreciated. First, regarding the relationship between bodily health and moral character, there is no reason to think that Mann's own life experience in any way reinforced his moral conclusions. Mann's claim, in his final baccalaureate address, that "good digestion is part and parcel of a good man,"[87] is particularly poignant, given his own lifelong struggle with poor digestion. Whatever guilt or self-loathing Mann's views of the relationship between bad health and moral degeneracy may or may not reflect, it is undeniably true that the people he admired most were often the victims of diseases that he identified as retribution for violations of natural moral law. The most powerful case here is Mann's first wife, Charlotte, who succumbed to tuberculosis after less than two years of marriage. Mann was devastated by her death for many years, and he never thought of his wife as anything other than a chaste and morally pure woman. There is, in short, very little in his life that suggests a correlation between moral virtue and good health. To the contrary, much of his experience—from his own chronic ill health to the suffering of those within his personal circle of loved ones—suggests at best the horribly random and inequitably distributed nature of physical suffering. One can only surmise that the theoretical correlation (granted legitimacy by Combe's theory) between health and virtue that Mann insisted on was, for him, both a moral necessity and a deep longing, a projection of his understanding of how a benevolent God must have made the universe. This particular dogma reflects the intensity of Mann's idealism, the degree to which moral commitment could and did sometimes overcome his own lived experience.

Second, Mann believed that the problem facing society generally, and therefore education in particular, was how to wield the powers generated by the growth of science, technology, and industrialization. "In Bacon's time, the grand inquiry was how to obtain power; in our time, the grand inquiry is how to use the power we have obtained."[88] Mann simply did not believe that we still needed to generate huge amounts of new knowledge about the physical laws of nature. On the contrary, he believed that Bacon's revolution had been successful and that we now needed to generate an equally sufficient revolution in moral knowledge to help us make sense of and control our intellectual and scientific powers. Our problems, in short, concerned moral rather than physical nature, and our entire educational apparatus, from the common school to higher education, must be oriented toward addressing these problems.

This leads to a third and related point: Mann thought that although this new moral knowledge had not been widely distributed, it was available and waiting to be taught to the world. When Mann speaks of moral truth and law, he seems to believe that all reflective people of goodwill are naturally disposed to discovering the same elements of the moral life. Such moral knowledge does not appear to be particularly hard to understand. It is the insufficient reinforcement of appropriate habits that encourages the inferior elements of our character to dominate the most admirable and allows counterproductive behavior to overwhelm demonstrably better ways of living. Anyone in our own time who has listened to conversations about "social justice" on contemporary university campuses will understand and appreciate the degree to which Mann's frustration was not a result of moral doubt; it grew from what he believed to be the archaic customs, false beliefs, and poor socialization that prevented people from seeing what was obviously and clearly the best set of moral principles and practices. Likewise, our contemporaries argue the veracity of social justice, as if the content of such justice were intellectually obvious and obscured from sight only by ignorance or moral laziness, at best, and viciousness, at worst.

This leads to a final point: Mann's distinction between this accessible set of moral laws and what he criticizes as dogma and sectarian belief is neither theoretically nor practically convincing. It is not theoretically convincing because he fails to demonstrate how his own moral commitments avoid dogmatic assumptions (for example, that the universe must have been made by a benevolent God) in a way that is different from the assumptions informing other perspectives. It is not practically convincing because of the strongly coercive and impositional character of Mann's moral program at Antioch. Mann began his career at Antioch with the question, "what do youth need in order to become ministers of good in the world?" The answers to that question pulled him in opposing directions—sometimes toward tolerance and openness, sometimes toward the close regulation of moral life that such morally fraught goals seemed to demand. At the end of the day, the intensity of moral commitment overwhelmed him, leading him away from more liberal sensibilities. Mann's vestigial Puritan moral authoritarianism ultimately got the best of him.

To gain some critical perspective on Mann's approach to higher education, it is helpful to compare his views and projects with the views expressed by John Stuart Mill, Mann's British contemporary. Serving as rector of the University of Saint Andrews from 1865 to 1868, Mill delivered his "Inaugural Address" fourteen years after Mann delivered his "Dedicatory and

Inaugural Address" at Antioch. The contrast between the comments of America's (arguably) greatest living educator and Great Britain's (arguably) greatest living intellectual is instructive and in some ways remarkable.

Like Mann, Mill argues that the role of higher education is not vocational in any narrow sense. Although there should be schools for professional training, the role of undergraduate liberal education is to produce not "ministers of good in the world" but "capable and cultivated human beings."[89] Mill's vision is perhaps less ambitious than Mann's, but it is significantly normative: "What professional men should carry away with them from an University, is not professional knowledge, but that which should direct the use of their professional knowledge, and bring the light of general culture to illuminate the technicalities of a special pursuit."[90] The "general culture" to be conveyed to the undergraduate, the "crown and consummation of a liberal education," is the integrative knowledge that brings all specific fields together into a kind of unity.[91] Ideally, universities provide this liberal knowledge, situated beyond the remedial schooling of secondary education but not yet focused on training for professional and specialized careers.

The curriculum Mann implemented at Antioch did not differ dramatically from that defended and explained by Mill. Messerli suggests that Mann hoped the Antioch curriculum would be as "broad and liberal" as that found in any college or university in the country.[92] Antioch students would study ancient languages, Latin and Greek, as well as a wide array of arts and sciences, including mathematics, history, English, philosophy, and natural science; in addition, they would enjoy an elective system offering courses in art and teaching preparation. Modern languages could be substituted for the advanced study of Greek. English instruction would emphasize composition and public speaking over the study and appreciation of literature.[93] Mill defended a curriculum more evenly balanced between literature and science than Mann's,[94] but he stressed a similar attention to ancient languages and moral philosophy. His address also included a much greater appeal to instruction in the fine arts than one can find in Mann.

It is the rationale for this curriculum and the discussion of the ends of education, however, that most clearly distinguish Mill from Mann. There are three key points to note here. First, Mill's curricular views convey a much greater interest in the development of what might be called the creative and moral imaginations of students than we find in Mann's program of study. There are two important illustrations of this. In the first instance, Mill explains why students should study the ancient languages. He argues that the Greeks and Romans wrote with real leisure and therefore aimed for a kind of literary perfection that is no longer even imaginable in our busy modern world.[95] This means that, in Mill's view, Greek and Roman writings are the main sources for a true literary education. An even more important reason for studying the ancients, however, is their profound foreignness, their vast separation from us across time and experience. Their lives were so different from ours, and their ways of thinking reflect these huge differences. When we gain access to their lives and thoughts by learning their languages, we gain access to truly distinct cultures that differ greatly from our own. If we are to be independent thinkers, we must have the comparative knowledge of radically different ways of looking at the world, of organizing society, and of achieving human meaning. Only through such study will we gain the kind of critical distance from our own experience to be able to subject it to a serious evaluation. Mill argues that the modern university need not teach contemporary European languages, since European communities are both accessible to the contemporary student and not terribly different from the British community overall. Only the ancients provide a radical contrast to our own experience and therefore educate us to a higher level of critical independence than we can expect to develop by studying contemporary European societies. Mill's argument for learning the ancient languages is similar to that offered by many educators in our own time for promoting international study, especially now that international travel is so widely available, allowing students to venture beyond the cultural boundaries of western Europe. Knowledge of real cultural difference, in short, is required for the development of a genuinely independent perspective.[96]

In the second instance, Mill makes a case for the centrality of the fine arts in a liberal education. His most important argument is that exposure to and the cultivated appreciation of beauty can take us beyond ourselves, teach us to care about the bigger, more important things in life. The "mere contemplation of beauty of a high order produces in no small degree this elevating effect on character." It can raise us "at least temporarily . . . above the littleness of humanity" and bring us to the "nobler pleasures which all might share." There is, Mill claims, "a natural affinity between goodness and the cultivation of the Beautiful."[97] In fact, Mill defines art as "the endeavour after perfection in execution."[98] The fine arts (Mill has the visual arts in mind here) take us outside ourselves and bring us face-to-face with the greatest human aspirations. They cultivate in the student an appreciation of and a longing for the highest goods available to human beings.[99]

The main lesson in Mill's discussion of the importance of ancient languages and fine arts in a liberal education is this: for him, a key element of the educational experience is the development of a kind of imaginative intelligence, the ability to think outside oneself and take the view of another. For Mill, this ability is critical to the educational process and is equal in status to the development of scientific knowledge and understanding. In fact, the relationship of this kind of learning to the learning of science provides an instructive contrast. The truths of science are singular and unique. The more developed and successful the science, the more certainty there is in a particular and exclusive answer to a relevant question. The scientist may need imagination to develop creative tests and experiments, but the interpretation of scientific results requires the application of rigorous logical methods and standards. Mill believes, however, that in many other spheres of life—particularly those pertaining to normative and aesthetic matters, where judgment and wisdom rather than scientific truth are required—what we need is not a rigorous science but rather a creative imagination, stimulated by true comparative information and aesthetically moving objects.

This appeal to comparative and aesthetic judgment stands in stark contrast to Mann's desire for the creation of a moral science. As we saw in chapter 2, to Mann, the art of literature appeals to self-indulgent emotion and nothing more. In a lecture presented to inspire young men, Mann's view is recognizable to us: "Men love fiction because they love wonder and excitement; but nothing is more true than that truth is more wonderful than fiction."[100] He holds out hope, however, that a new kind of literature, presumably didactic and based on the moral laws of nature, can be developed in the future. "But there is no reason why literature should not hereafter be founded on science, have constant reference to its truths, and thus become its most delightful illustrator."[101] In saying this, Mann demonstrates his inability to understand Mill's position, which is built on the presumption that education must prepare us to live in a world not fully explicable in scientific terms, not fully susceptible to scientific knowledge and analysis, a world in which imperfect judgment and uncertainty are to be managed wisely but never overcome. Even imagining such a world, for Mann, is morally unacceptable; to admit it is to admit moral defeat. His hope is for a moral education that will make moral judgment obsolete. In an education dedicated to a science of morality, we need not be "decentered," in Elaine

Scarry's words,[102] since moral science will demonstrate the perfect unity of our own needs and interests with the true needs and interests of all those around us. Mill hopes we learn to think outside of ourselves, that we are drawn, from time to time, to challenge our own particular impulses, thoughts, prejudices, and interests. Mann hopes these impulses, thoughts, prejudices, and interests can be so transformed by moral knowledge that a project like Mill's, with all its attendant uncertainty, will never be necessary at all.

This leads us to appreciate a second great difference between Mill's and Mann's hopes for higher education. Mill's educational project, like Mann's, is a normative one, aiming to develop within students a moral compass that they can apply to their lives after they leave the university. The two men view the nature of this moral compass quite differently, however. Mill's refusal to conflate the arts and humanities with science is a sign of his acceptance of a more modest moral purpose than that driving Mann. Compare Mann's enthusiasm for the scientific moral philosophy derived from Combe's phrenology with Mill's interest in debates about the possibility of free will. "But it is a part of liberal education to know that such controversies exist, and, in a general way, what has been said on both sides of them. It is instructive to know the failures of the human intellect as well as its successes."[103] Mill, like Mann, understands that the highest goal of liberal education is to prepare students for "the exercise of thought on the great interests of mankind as moral and social beings—ethics and politics, in the largest sense."[104] This does not mean, however, teaching students the ethical and political truths generated by science; rather, it means helping them develop the background knowledge and judicious sensibilities that allow them to become their own teachers. "Education is not entitled, on this subject, to recommend any set of opinions as resting on the authority of established science. But it can supply the student with materials for his own mind, and helps to use them."[105] The goal is for students to become measured, thoughtful, informed, and judicious citizens. The university has no authority or responsibility to move beyond this to "educate morally or religiously."[106] Mill understands that universities set a moral tone through the high sense of duty and purpose properly communicated by the behavior of its faculty and officers. His wish, however, is for education in moral philosophy to become "more expository, less polemical, and above all less dogmatic" than is commonly the case.[107] Students should be made familiar with the different ethical schools and major contrasts in thinking about important subjects. In the end, however, "it is not the teacher's business to impose his own judgment, but to inform and discipline that of his pupil."[108] Although Mann, too, stresses the development of individual judgment, the overall emphasis of his moral education is significantly more didactic than Mill's.

It is important to stress that this does not mean that Mill lacks high normative aspirations for liberal education. The final passage of his address is actually quite stunning for the moral vision it presents:

> I do not attempt to instigate you by the prospect of direct rewards, either earthly or heavenly; the less we think about being rewarded in either way, the better for us. But there is one reward which will not fail you, and which may be called disinterested, because it is not a consequence, but is inherent in the very fact of deserving it; the deeper and more varied interest you will feel in life: which will give it tenfold its value, and a value which will last to the end. All merely personal objects grow less valuable as we advance in life: this not only endures but increases.[109]

Like Mann, Mill is inspired by a vision of disinterested service. He also believes that a good liberal education can stimulate individuals to pursue this goal. His pedagogy for promoting this moral commitment, however, is less didactic than Mann's and more hopeful that curricula stressing a free and open exchange of ideas and the imaginative exposure to contrasting worlds and views will help produce it.

Finally, this leads us to the differing civic visions informing Mill's and Mann's understanding of higher education. Underlying Mann's promotion of a new moral science is the hope for a consensual moral world. It is not only that properly educated individuals become disinterested; it is that they long for a disinterestedness that is committed to a unitary vision of the good. The moral problem for Mann is less to discover right and wrong than it is to produce individuals willing to accept and embrace what is clearly, in the eyes of uncorrupted individuals, the true and the good. The moral problem for Mill, in contrast, is to educate individuals with the virtues required in a world where the true and the good are terribly uncertain. These virtues, ranging from significant knowledge of the realities of the world to the judicious ability to weigh evidence and imagine answers that transcend our own desires and interests, are required by individuals confronting a confusing world that contains an infinity of conflicting interests, opinions, and possibilities. The purpose of higher education is less to produce individuals committed to what is right than to encourage individuals to be responsible as they participate in a world where what is right is deeply uncertain and contested even among individuals of goodwill. Put crudely, Mann is more concerned about creating "right thinking" individuals, and Mill will settle for "conscientiously thinking" graduates. Mann's graduates will constitute a cadre of the righteous. Mill's, in contrast, will be responsible citizens and nothing more.[110]

This contrast between Mill and Mann is helpful because it clarifies the degree to which Mann's understanding of higher education moves away from toleration, openness, and diversity of opinion and toward a kind of intellectual uniformity. The contrast is not between a moral and a nonmoral vision of higher education; rather, it is between competing normative visions. We can see a kind of secularized Puritanism in Mann's project, an extension of the desire to create moral consensus evident in his rationale for the common school. Mill, in contrast, stresses the development of skills and knowledge required in a world beyond consensus, where people need to negotiate their significantly different values and understandings of the good. Although the constituency from which students are drawn has narrowed significantly at the college level, Mann's program of higher education recognizes no fundamental change in moral emphasis between primary and higher education; both aim to bring the student into conformity with the norms of moral community. The curriculum for young adults needs to be much more sophisticated than that for children, of course, but the moral project is fundamentally similar insofar as a singular civic virtue trumps all purely intellectual educational goods. Mill's program is designed to encourage the development of individuals capable of dealing with the ambiguities of a society without clear or universally accepted moral norms, and it relies on the intellectual goods promoted by the full array of arts and sciences to achieve this goal. Mann's project tries to cope with the conflicts generated by democratic society by educating in such a way as to make these conflicts dissolve, at least among the moral elite (who will, presumably, lead the rest of society toward this moral consensus). In contrast, Mill's hope for liberal education is that it will produce conscientious and independent individuals capable of negotiating and managing the conflicts themselves.

There is a noticeable element of extremity in Mann's experiences at Antioch. He wept in 1853 when he left Massachusetts, and Straker reports that by the spring of 1859 he "could neither eat nor sleep, and he wished only to be relieved of the intolerable burden of Antioch."[111] He offered his resignation, but the trustees refused it, and he died of typhus during the summer. Over the course of his presidency he struggled mightily with Antioch's bankruptcy, religious dissension among the faculty (a faculty he had hoped would transcend doctrinal differences and conflict), significant personal health and financial problems, and the terrible unhappiness Mary experienced as a result of the move to Ohio.[112] Hinsdale refers to the Antioch years as "the most painful period in Mr. Mann's public life" and claims that this chapter in Mann's biography is "indeed a pathetic one, almost a tragedy."[113] Mann certainly suffered the burdens associated with a remarkably difficult situation during Antioch's founding, and he sacrificed dearly to bring this young institution through numerous crises. In a sense, we need to view Mann's thoughts, reflections, and arguments from this period of his life with a certain amount of charity and sympathy. If Mann sounds shrill at times, such as when he demands a level of moral commitment and purity from his young undergraduates that cannot reasonably be expected, we should keep in mind the trying circumstances Mann was managing. There is a hysterical quality to his Antioch speeches and policies, but there is a heroic quality as well.

With this caveat in mind, there are a number of important conclusions we can draw from our investigation of Mann's experience with and contribution to higher education. First, Mann's concern for higher education, like his concern for the common school, is fundamentally civic in nature; the dangers and potentials of democracy should be the driving concern in our educational efforts. Second, this similarity of purpose leads him to approach the basic educational project of higher education in the same way he approached the teaching of children: moral education trumps purely intellectual instruction, and the civic virtues trump purely intellectual virtues. The third conclusion grows from the second. We see in Mann's Antioch writings, particularly those concerning religious nonsectarianism, an appeal to the virtues of toleration, epistemic modesty, and moral humility. We also clearly see, in the practice of enforcing the primary moral and political values, how easy it is for this toleration, modesty, and humility to be overwhelmed by civic and moral commitment. For Mann, virtue is to be cultivated above understanding, and the demand for moral harmony overrides the appeal to toleration. Finally, the moral vision informing Mann's civic goals is inspired by science, with its promise of nondoctrinaire consensus. All these elements drove Mann in a direction quite different from that sketched by Mill in his "Inaugural Address," and all are strongly representative of developments we continue to wrestle with in American higher education today.

Chapter 5

Democracy and Education

We have seen that Horace Mann's democratic anxiety shaped both his common school and higher education careers. Whether serving the children of Massachusetts or the young adults at Antioch, he designed his educational mission around what I called in chapter 1 the democratic paradox, what he believed was the (dramatic) need to prepare democratic citizens for responsible citizenship. Mann's democratic commitments produced much to be admired: In his work with primary education, Mann insisted on equal access to quality education for all children, regardless of their varied backgrounds and family conditions; he also insisted that all children be treated humanely and appropriately for their age and maturity. In his work with college students, he demanded that education be both rigorous and informed by a deep moral seriousness and integrity. In both educational contexts, however, his promotion of civic purposes over all other ends strained the intellectual integrity of his projects. His protestations to the contrary notwithstanding, he politicized and moralized his educational projects to the point where they were in real danger of becoming dogmatic and ideological. What began in both aspects of his educational career as a commitment to nonpartisan and nondogmatic principles was transformed, at the end of the day, into clearly partisan and potentially dogmatic educational programs.

When we look ahead from Mann's time to our own, it is not surprising to see that Mann was not alone in wrestling with these problems; they can be thought of as endemic or fundamental to democratic politics. What *is* of interest is the degree to which Mann's approach to these problems provides something of a template or a pattern for important episodes in American educational philosophy and politics. Horace Mann's legacy frames the work of the twentieth century's greatest educational theorist, John Dewey, as well as some of the key philosophical debates about education in contemporary America. We need not make any deep causal claims about Mann's influence on later thinkers to be impressed by the degree to which his thinking can help us understand the strengths and weaknesses of debates beyond his lifetime, including those informing our own.

Perhaps the most striking element in John Dewey's educational thought is the degree to which he clearly, even bluntly and irreverently, breaks with what he takes to be older scholarly perspectives. In *School and Society* he suggests that the "merely intellectual life" of conventional scholarship is a vestige from predemocratic, class-dominated society.[1] He approves of the degree to which words such as *academic* and *scholastic* are becoming terms of reproach rather than praise, and he suggests that this represents the degree to which knowledge is no longer being controlled and monopolized by narrow class interests and has begun to flourish for democratic use and benefit. "Learning has been put into circulation. . . . The merely intellectual life, the life of scholarship and of learning, thus gets a very altered value."[2] In later essays Dewey writes that enthusiasm for classical learning is "socially reactionary"[3] and that literary training, "whatever it may have accomplished elsewhere, produces only a feebly pretentious snobbishness of culture."[4] The individualism and elitism of traditional scholarship are the inheritance of aristocratic and priestly cultures committed to using knowledge for their own narrow and tightly proscribed purposes and reinforcing their claims to social and political superiority. Appeals to traditional scholarship today are either cynically reactionary or the result of confusion and alienation from contemporary democratic culture.[5] Education aimed at traditional scholarly accomplishment produces only "sharps" (not a term of praise) and "egoistic specialists."[6] Just as Mann views literature as decadent, Dewey thinks of the conventional humanities as vain and reactionary.

In addition, it is evident that democratic culture is neither capable of nor particularly interested in understanding the traditions of learning, thinking, and scholarship developed in predemocratic societies. "The simple facts of the case are that in the great majority of human beings the distinctively intellectual interest is not dominant."[7] Such intellectual experiences are not in the cards for the demos because of a lack of either inclination or ability. Education growing out of these intellectual traditions is too "exclusive" and uninteresting to be the foundation for democratic education.[8] Conventional intellectual life is unfit for democratic society because it is too demanding and deeply uninteresting for the many.

Dewey holds to a kind of Darwinian functionalism in arguing that we must look more closely at what children *want* to learn and how they want to learn it in developing our educational programs; after all, it is only natural for them to want what they in fact need to develop into sound, healthy, happy adults: "Strange it would be, indeed, if intelligent and serious attention to what the child *now* needs and is capable of in the way of a rich, valuable, and expanded life should somehow conflict with the needs and possibilities of later, adult life."[9] We must trust and cultivate the impulses of the young as they grow in response to the society around them. Looking to earlier educational traditions to guide this process is egregiously and counterproductively beside the point.

What democratic society requires, then, is not the development and transmission of conventional scholarship through the efforts of its educational institutions but rather a commitment to the development of a "common spirit" and "common aims" among its maturing citizens. A society is a community built around these commonalities, and it is education's task to produce and reinforce this shared life. "A society is a number of people held together because they are working along common lines, in a common spirit, and with reference to common aims. The common needs and aims demand a growing interchange of thought and growing unity of sympathetic feeling."[10] In *Democracy and Education*, Dewey calls this educational process the creation of "social dispositions."[11] In contrast to a "bookish . . . pseudo-intellectual spirit," the goal of the schools is to produce a genuine social consciousness and disposition among the young.[12] Dewey is actually concerned that conventional education often aims at a kind of liberal autonomy or individualism that serves to undermine the more important social goals of schooling.[13] Developing a strong sense of independence "often makes an individual so insensitive in his relations to others as to develop an illusion of being really able to stand and act alone—an unnamed form of insanity which is responsible for a large part of the remediable suffering in the world."[14] The individual development of each student misses the broader educational task: to socialize each student into an understanding of his or her relationship to the broader democratic society.[15]

The instrumental purpose of this education is to increase the overall control a democratic society has over its environment. All true education leads to increased social control. In fact, Dewey defines education as "the reconstruction or reorganization of experience which adds to the meaning of experience, and which increases ability to direct the course of subsequent experience."[16] Any understanding of education that looks to the inner life of the student is a retrograde dead end: "the idea of perfecting an 'inner' personality is a sure sign of social divisions. What is called inner is simply that which does not connect with others—which is not capable of free and full communication."[17] Education must be oriented outward, away from private life and concerns, and toward social experience. The strong implication is that social experience alone is real, and the rest is just mystification and alienation (or even, as suggested above, a kind of "insanity"). The mind must be "socialized." This process "is actively concerned in making experiences more communicable; in breaking down the barriers of social stratification which make individuals impervious to the interests of others."[18]

The knowledge conveyed by education must be tied actively to doing if it is to have any relevance or even reality. Knowledge or information "severed from thoughtful action is dead, a mind-crushing load."[19] The model for true knowledge is science, which Dewey says is a name for "knowledge in its most characteristic form" and is "both logically and educationally . . . the perfecting of knowing, its last stage."[20] If the goal of education is the "forming of a socialized disposition,"[21] science represents the activity most closely approximating such a disposition. This is because the community of scientists shares a commitment to both the methods and the ends of the community and can therefore work harmoniously together to address the problems the community has agreed to focus on. Knowing has no genuine substance outside of problem solving, and problems are real only to the degree that they can be formulated and addressed in a social context. Science is the "agency of progress in action" and "experience becoming rational."[22] It represents rationality because of the way it "socializes" the minds and dispositions of scientists; it represents progress because this rationality is focused entirely, in Leo Strauss's (disapproving) words, on the "relief of man's estate."[23]

The distance we travel from Horace Mann to John Dewey is obviously great. Dewey's pragmatic philosophy is a significant departure from Mann's phrenology and moral idealism, Dewey's secular humanism contrasts dramatically with Mann's Unitarianism, and Dewey's democratic socialism is a far cry from Mann's Whig principles. Despite all these obvious differences, however, we can see that Dewey shares with Mann a core educational commitment. While Mann insists that we emphasize the civic and social over the intellectual elements of schooling, Dewey's claim is even more dramatic: it is meaningless, he suggests, to speak of real education as anything other than a fundamentally civic activity. This means that, for Dewey, it is nonsense to speak of meaningful intellectual education apart from civic concerns and issues. It also means that normatively we must either focus on these civic issues or fall prey to antisocial cynicism and elitist posturing and thus potentially to reactionary and antidemocratic politics. Not only *should* we focus on the civic content of education; we *must* focus on it to have any meaningful and politically acceptable education at all. Stephen Macedo is certainly right when he comments that "Dewey seems to . . . flirt with a civic totalism that leaves too little to the extrapolitical dimensions of human experience."[24] I might quibble with Macedo only by saying that Dewey leaves not too little but rather nothing at all beyond the political for education to address. Dewey has built an even more extreme theory of and commitment to civic education than that developed by Mann. Indeed, it would be hard to imagine a more thoroughly civic understanding of the educational process than this.[25]

Despite concerns like those expressed by Macedo, Dewey's position continues to find strong advocates today. Political theorist Benjamin Barber argues that there is no compromise to be made between civic and intellectual educational missions. In a democracy "there is only one essential task for the educator: teaching liberty."[26] Claiming what he takes to be the mantle of Jefferson and Dewey, Barber insists that the civic purposes of higher education are the only significant purposes to be cultivated: "I am not arguing that the university has a civic mission, but that the university *is* a civic mission."[27] The key to developing the appropriate university is to replace conventional academic study with "education-based community service."[28] Casting aspersions on the "ivory tower" and the "complacent professionalism and research orientation of the modern university,"[29] Barber insists that the only standard by which to measure our educational institutions is that of political relevance, engagement, and commitment to students' civic development. Fashioning himself as a modern Rousseau, he suggests that we can force our students to freedom by transforming the curriculum into a service learning model.[30]

Horace Mann's legacy of civic education is built on both a profound anxiety about the current quality of democratic citizenship and an equally profound faith in the ability of educational institutions, at all levels, to remedy our failures. Lee Benson and his coauthors warn today's educators that without an "effective democratic schooling system," we can expect there to be "no democratic society."[31] They even scold Dewey for not taking his own principles seriously enough—by not designing the social experience in the laboratory school to truly reflect the social conditions in American society[32] and by abandoning the civic mission of higher education when he retreated to "the traditionally scholastic Department of Philosophy at Columbia University."[33] Dewey may have pointed the way in thinking about the civic nature of education, but it is up to us to design a "New Democratic Cosmopolitan Civic University."[34] Referring to their professional home at the University of Pennsylvania, they write: "we believe that, as is true of all American universities, Penn's highest, most basic, and most enduring responsibility is to help America realize in concrete practice the egalitarian promise of the Declaration of Independence."[35] Once again, the view is that the political purposes of education are not only significant but all-encompassing (or at least close to it).

As noted in chapter 1, even among less alarmed philosophers and political theorists, there has been a great deal of interest in civic education in the past generation. Among these thinkers the theme is the same: although they may not be as expressly overwhelmed by the current state of civic virtue as those authors mentioned above, and although they are therefore less apt to collapse all of education into civic education, both the alarm and the educational optimism are present to a significant degree. Eamonn Callan begins his important book, *Creating Citizens*, with a thought experiment designed to illustrate the potential "brave new world" of polarization and illiberal tendencies growing from the dynamics of liberal society.[36] The first assumption is that unless we consciously promote the "common dispositions that liberal dialogue presupposes,"[37] there is no reason to think that a liberal political order will be stable and secure: "creating virtuous citizens is as necessary an undertaking in a liberal democracy as it is under any other constitution."[38] The second assumption is that the political education on which the health of our political order depends is tied to the formal schooling of children. For example, Callan clearly believes that "schooling is . . . likely to be the most promising institutional vehicle" for teaching (future) citizens to understand and be sensitive to ethical diversity. It is "simply wrong," he believes, "to say that the relevant understanding of ethical diversity is picked up in the public world of contemporary pluralistic societies."[39] The political life of adults, in Callan's view, comes too late and teaches lessons contrary to the moral requirements of thoughtful citizenship. Macedo observes that "public schools have undertaken this project [of forming citizens] more directly and persistently than any other public institution,"[40] and he strongly approves of public schools' intervention "between children and their parents and communities of birth to shape the deepest beliefs and commitments of 'private' communities and future generations."[41] William Galston agrees that it "is both necessary and possible to carry out civic education in the liberal state."[42] Although there are many (widely discussed) differences in the views of these (and other) contemporary liberal and democratic theorists, they all share the belief that the civic purposes of schooling are significant and at least potentially effective.[43]

It is not only liberal political theorists, of course, who emphasize the role of educational institutions in producing capable and virtuous democratic citizens. Justice Sandra Day O'Connor criticized the "No Child Left Behind" program for crowding out civic education from the public school curriculum. "This leaves a huge gap, and we can't forget that the primary purpose of the public schools in America has always been to help produce citizens who have the knowledge and the skills and the values to sustain our republic as a nation, our democratic form of government."[44] O'Connor's fellow justice David Souter, soon after stepping down from the Supreme Court, announced that he, too, would be working to improve civic education in the public schools of his home state of New Hampshire. Citing studies that illustrate the American citizenry's deep ignorance about government and politics, Souter suggested that our democratic government "can be lost, it is being lost, and it is lost, if it is not understood."[45] The burden of our civic culture traditionally falls, as these retired justices observe, on our educational system. Generation after generation has looked to our educational institutions, as Mann did, to solve the problems of our political culture. Our history as a democratic experiment and an immigrant nation has generated a deep democratic insecurity and uncertainty about our own civic sufficiency for contending with the demands of democratic government.[46] These uncertainties haunt both our popular and philosophical discussions of education. As Diane Ravitch and Joseph Viteritti write, "Ever since the late nineteenth century, Americans have relied upon government schools as a principal purveyor of deeply cherished democratic values."[47] Mann's democratic anxiety has been our own for much of our history.[48]

This civic burden borne by American education is all the more striking in light of the paltry empirical evidence for the effectiveness of formal civic education. We know, as Richard Niemi and Jane Junn report, that "formal education is the strongest, most consistent correlate . . . of political knowledge,"[49] but we know very little about where this political knowledge comes from. Niemi and Junn admit that many researchers find no correlation between this political knowledge and civics classes, although in their view, the overall evidence is mixed. They conclude that there are measurable gains in political knowledge when students study civics in their senior year of high school;[50] students are more likely to learn and retain political knowledge the closer they are to entering the adult world.[51] This, of course, is a profoundly modest finding; after all, the purpose of the entire system of public education, from kindergarten through high school, has been defined by overwhelmingly civic concerns.

Even these modest successes, however, fail to address the critical issue of the degree to which schooling can encourage the development of democratic norms, values, and commitments. Concerning normative knowledge and these moral dispositions, the empirical evidence is even less impressive than that for basic political knowledge. We know that students' verbal aptitude is positively correlated with political engagement and that math aptitude is negatively correlated.[52] (It is depressing to note that for college students, an engineering major is associated with not only declining writing ability but also declining cultural awareness, political participation, and commitment to racial understanding.[53]) In the college curriculum, only exposure to the social sciences seems positively correlated with political engagement.[54] And teacher training has no positive effect on the civic engagement of teachers themselves, who, as a group, are not "among the civic-minded."[55] Norman Nie and his colleagues conclude their major study, *Education and Democratic Citizenship in America*, by suggesting that the political values of a "democratically enlightened citizenry," such as tolerance, political engagement, knowledge of political principles, and commitment to democratic norms, increase with years of education, at least to the degree that these years are correlated with the growth of basic verbal competency.[56] Given our dramatic hope that schools will produce a knowledgeable and democratically committed citizenry, these findings of the empirical success of our educational institutions seem meager at best. There is certainly little evidence that the overall stability of our political order is generated primarily from the educational system, that this system is the main source of political learning and socialization, or that this system is particularly effective at promoting this learning and socialization. As James Murphy points out, "If schooling itself were effective in fostering civic virtue, then we should expect Americans today to exhibit a much higher degree of civic virtue than Americans of the mid-twentieth century."[57] The opposite seems to be the case, however. Murphy adds, ironically, that "those of us who object to the whole endeavor of using public schools as instruments of partisan civic indoctrination may take some comfort in its near total failure."[58]

Serious ethical concerns have been raised about our preoccupation with civic education as well. Harry Brighouse argues that the contemporary political theory of civic education has promoted a kind of disrespect for the autonomy of individual students. Consider, he suggests, the claim that schooling should be used to shape "the characters of future citizens so as to stabilize and legitimize" the democratic order.

> To see education in that way is to treat children, and the adults they will become, not as potentially self-determining citizens but as sub-

> jects of a predetermined order. This violates both the liberal ideals that persons should be self-governing and that social institutions are legitimized only by the freely offered and critical consent of reasonable persons; and the individualist ideal that each person counts in his or her own right, and should not be treated merely as a means to some collective end.[59]

Our obligation to teach children, Brighouse argues, grows from our moral obligation to them as individuals, not from the needs of our political order:[60] "the central point of educating someone is for her own benefit."[61] To educate for the good of the political community is to attempt to engineer, and thereby perversely to delegitimate, the consent of citizens. As Brian Barry puts it, "Liberal democracy, unlike other forms of government, depends for its legitimacy on consent. But the quality of that consent is compromised if it is simply manufactured by the state through the school system."[62]

A generation earlier, and in rather different terms, Hannah Arendt criticized the progressive tradition of American public education for confusing its true obligations to children. The purpose of schooling, Arendt argues, is to "teach children what the world is like and not to instruct them in the art of living."[63] The duty of adults is to present the reality of the world to children as accurately and thoroughly as possible, to make them familiar with and aware of the accumulated and evolving human knowledge. Children should be left free, when they enter adulthood and citizenship, to make of this world as they wish, without being instructed on the proper way of living in it. In short, for the sake of adult freedom, children's education should be conservative and nonpolitical. Although Arendt emphasizes the language of political freedom rather than liberal theory's "autonomy" and "consent," her point grows from a concern similar to Brighouse's and Barry's.

In addition to inappropriately attempting to prejudice or predetermine the choices of citizens through the political instruction of children, civic education may subvert more conventional academic goals. Murphy stresses that the academic commitment to truth is all too easily and too often subordinated to political purposes:

> What happens to academic education in the context of schools committed to civic education? Whether we look to the history of civic education or to the ideas of civic educators, the answer is quite certain: the academic pursuit of knowledge will be corrupted through

> a subordination of truth-seeking to some civic agenda. The history of civic education in the United States is a cautionary tale, indeed.[64]

Although the political agenda of schooling has changed from Mann's time to our own, from the promotion of liberal Protestantism to contemporary multiculturalism, "nothing has changed in the American passion for subordinating truth-seeking to moral and civic uplift."[65] As Barry argues, the pragmatic argument against civic education is that it "politicizes education in an unwholesome and potentially even destructive way."[66] Promoting civic virtue all too easily threatens and trumps the pursuit of truth and rational inquiry.

Much of the debate between advocates and critics of civic education grows from their differing senses of the threats to democratic culture and their optimism about schools' ability to address these threats. As we have seen, Murphy is unimpressed by the evidence for civic education's success in the schools. He is equally unimpressed by claims that civic education is necessary for the creation of committed citizens. "No advocate of patriotic education in schools has ever furnished any evidence suggesting that American students do not love their country."[67] He holds that providing a quality academic education is all that is required to prepare children for responsible adulthood. We should have confidence in the moral power of knowledge, including straightforward political and civic knowledge, and resist the temptation to drag didactic lessons about political and moral life into the curriculum. "Instead of constantly subordinating knowledge to moral uplift, we ought to have more confidence in the sheer moral value of knowledge."[68] For Barry, the gain to democratic government must likewise be a by-product of academic education rather than the directly and purposefully manufactured outcome of a normative civic education. The "possibility of democratic government depends upon shared criteria of rational discourse," and these are promoted through academic integrity rather than an overt project in civic education.[69] In contrast, the advocates of civic education share with Horace Mann a conviction that without such a civic orientation in education, democratic political culture is in significant danger of disintegrating. In Macedo's words, "There is no reason to think that the dispositions that characterize good liberal citizens come about naturally: good citizens are not simply born that way, they must be educated by schools and a variety of other social and political institutions."[70] Much of the difference between advocates and critics of civic education thus reflects their varying assessments of the empirical dangers facing democratic culture and the possibility of successfully addressing these threats through civic education. There are real normative differences between the two positions, of course, but these differences themselves assume diverse empirical assessments of the needs and possibilities of civic education.

Arguments against civic education tend to draw one of two normative conclusions. Addressing higher education, Stanley Fish has clearly articulated the view that universities are in the "pursuit-of-truth business" and should be completely detached from all political purposes and goals.[71] When professors attempt to teach political values, they assume a responsibility for which they have no professional expertise or legitimate authority. "Once we cross the line that separates academic work from these other kinds, we are guilty both of practicing without a license and of defaulting on our professional responsibilities."[72] The value of scholarship is intrinsic to the activity itself and can only be corrupted by appeal to external moral or political norms. What is the value of a liberal college education? Fish asks. "Beats me!" he provocatively answers. "As far as I can tell those habits of thought and the liberal arts education that provides them don't enable you to do anything, and, even worse, neither do they prevent you from doing anything."[73] The point here is that scholarship and education at the university level can only be justified in terms completely divorced from any political consequences (and, indeed, from any direct vocational utility as well). Addressing the justification of primary schooling, Brighouse also forswears any advantage his argument might receive by appealing to positive civic outcomes. "The common good may well be served by providing a good education for children, but it would be incumbent on us to provide a good education to them even if that did not serve the common good. Providing education is properly seen as a matter of justice, not of democracy or of the common good."[74] Academic values alone (for Fish) or the benefit to individuals alone (for Brighouse) must define the purposes of education. Justifying the educational project by appealing to broader social or political outcomes threatens to undermine the integrity of the project as a whole.

Other critics oppose the overt pursuit of civic education but nonetheless expect that properly focused and disciplined nonpoliticized education will have politically fortuitous outcomes. The argument implied in Murphy's and Barry's comments is that civic goods will result from educational programs that emphasize academic achievement alone. For Murphy, civic trust will be strengthened when we stop using the schools to promote what he views as inevitably parochial political perspectives.[75] For Barry, emphasizing academic goods will promote a respect for reason required by democracy. John Henry Newman famously promoted university education on nonutilitarian grounds, arguing that "that alone is liberal knowledge, which stands on its own pretensions, which is independent of sequel, expects no complement, refuses to be *informed* (as it is called) by any end, or absorbed into any art, in order duly to present itself to our contemplation."[76] University education must be based on the conviction that "knowledge is capable of being its own end."[77] Despite this philosophical, rather than practical, understanding of knowledge and educational commitment, Newman is absolutely persuaded that liberally educated individuals will become "gentlemen" and thereby "good members of society."[78]

> But a University training is the great ordinary means to a great but ordinary end; it aims at raising the intellectual tone of society, at cultivating the public mind, at purifying the national taste, at supplying true principles to popular enthusiasm and fixed aims to popular aspirations, at giving enlargement and sobriety to the ideas of the age, at facilitating the exercise of political power, and refining the intercourse of private life.[79]

In contrast to Fish, Newman is convinced that liberally educated individuals will be prepared to live satisfying and useful private and public lives. Like Barry and Murphy, he claims that positive civic outcomes will accrue from appropriately nonpolitical educational institutions and practices.[80]

The critique of civic education, of course, is focused on the normative elements of such training; nobody is claiming that knowledge of political institutions, events, laws, rights, history, and conflicts should not be presented to students as part of a complete and essential education. The question under dispute concerns the degree to which educational institutions rightly promote particular political norms, perspectives, and values. If we put aside for a moment questions about higher education, it is hard to imagine how civic education can be avoided, at some basic level, in the common or public schools. Aside from any overt civic curriculum, these schools are public agencies and must reflect basic public norms regarding equality of access and treatment, toleration of and respect for a wide variety of backgrounds and belief systems, and so forth. These are deep liberal democratic norms, and it is difficult to see how they could, or why they should, be avoided in the design, structure, and day-to-day affairs of public schools, both in their treatment of students and their families and in the behavior expected of students. Presumably it is a positive good for a liberal democratic society to both embody and promote these norms through its routine practices. At least in this limited sense, there is no good reason to reject the view that public schools rightly promote democratic norms and enforce a kind of democratic behavior by including a diverse population of students and treating this population with an appropriately democratic equality.[81]

The strength of the critique of civic education, therefore, lies not in an extreme claim about the inappropriateness of all forms of civic education; normative civic education is not to be avoided in any publicly mandated educational system. Rather, the most powerful critical points are found in two key claims: that all attempts to incorporate overt political norms into the substance or topics of the curriculum will fail to transcend partisanship,[82] and that thinking of schooling as being driven primarily by the concerns of civic education treats students as means to political ends rather than as individuals whose interests need to be served by teachers and educational institutions. In the first case we distort and corrupt the academic mission of schooling (what Arendt describes as simply teaching students the truth about the world) with partisan political agendas; in the second case we fail to take seriously the normative demands of the educational process in our treatment of individual students. Even in light of this critique, however, we may still retain a concern about and hope for civic education; as I argue below, there is reason to think that good civic outcomes may well be a secondary benefit of a justly distributed and democratically shaped public education focused primarily on the academic education of children.

If we shift our attention to higher education, the critique of civic education is even more powerful, since higher education is not mandated for all young adults, and students are obviously more autonomous at this age than they are as young children. The degree to which Deweyan educational theory has encouraged an emphasis on experiential and service learning in higher education (in both public and private institutions) is the degree to which civic educational theories growing out of pedagogies designed for young children have become the model for the education of young adults—a fact that should give us pause. The (presumably) meritocratic nature of higher education means that admission standards, equality of treatment, and the like require different metrics than those found in public schooling. The age, freedom, and responsibility of college students make the ideological shaping of the curriculum all the more disrespectful of the students' moral and political autonomy. Although the empirical evidence suggests that the political views of professors have no measurable impact on the political opinions of their students,[83] the attempt to teach university students appropriate political values threatens the disciplinary integrity of their studies and subverts their teachers' obligation to treat them as autonomous individuals rather than as means to political ends. This is not to suggest that there is no civic education appropriate to higher education; certain basic norms of civility should be enforced in the classroom as well as in cocurricular, extracurricular, and residential settings, including toleration, equality of treatment, respect for dissent, and the like. But these elements should certainly not be viewed as the central defining norms or ends of the academic enterprise. Fish may exaggerate the degree to which civic norms can or should be expelled from the academy, but the general thrust of his position is a powerful criticism of any politicization of higher education.

All this suggests that we are not as far from both the virtues and the vices of Horace Mann's lessons as we might believe. As we have seen, Mann's attempt to promote civic education grew in two general directions. In one, the education was didactic—at both the common school and the college level—and the aim was to produce civic consensus on elemental democratic and moral values. In the other, the aim was to produce a kind of civic friendship through the mixing of students from different social classes, religious backgrounds, and general life experiences. The first approach was built around a curriculum and pedagogy. The second was built around the general institutional design, structure, and implementation of the common school. The first led to the failed attempt to present a version of liberal Protestantism and phrenological moral theory as a shared moral worldview for a democratic society. The second opened up the possibility of democratic meritocracy and a common experience for children from diverse backgrounds. All too often, as the story told in previous chapters suggests, Mann's moralism overshadowed his emphasis on democratic institutional design. But both strains of civic education were strongly developed in his thought and work, and we can learn from the difficulties raised by his characteristic synthesis of the two, as we can from the problems of our own educational thought and practice.

We have seen that the model driving the didactic strain of Mann's civic education was one that emphasized the critical need for consensus in our shared democratic lives. Without such consensus, Mann's fear was that our civic society was in profound danger of tearing apart, that our democracy would explode into a hellish struggle between an infinity of petty despots. This fear led him to build a moral theory modeled on scientific agreement and certainty. We have also seen that his great descendant, John Dewey, made a similar move in the development of his own educational theory. We can observe the full implications of this approach when we look at Dewey's famous 1937 exchange with Robert Hutchins, president of the University of Chicago.

This exchange was instigated by Dewey's review of Hutchins's *The Higher Learning in America*. Hutchins was attacking what he took to be the vocationalism and anti-intellectualism of much of contemporary higher education. He offered, as an antidote to these tendencies, a classical liberal education in the "great books." For Hutchins, the purpose of education "is to draw out the elements of our common human nature."[84] These elements, he believed, are the same in all times and places and are best expressed and discussed in the classic works of philosophical literature.[85] The truths Hutchins aimed to discover through this education in the classics were decidedly nonutilitarian, focused on what he viewed as the timeless concerns of humanity rather than the particular vocational, social, and political problems facing American society and individual American citizens at any particular moment. "If education is rightly understood, it will be understood as the cultivation of the intellect. The cultivation of the intellect is the same good for all men in all societies. It is, moreover, the good for which all other goods are only means."[86] The curricular program Hutchins proposed was a course of general studies in great books (of the West), writing, speaking, and mathematics.[87]

This was more than Dewey could take. He sarcastically comments, "As far as I can see, President Hutchins has completely evaded the problem of who is to determine the definite truths that constitute the hierarchy."[88] Dewey's pragmatism allows him to think of truth claims only in relation to some variant of practical utility, making the more idealistic, abstract ideas championed by Hutchins look arbitrary and unsubstantiated. In the end, Dewey's complaint about Hutchins comes down to two claims. First, Hutchins's appeal to philosophical first principles commits him to political authoritarianism.[89] Second, Dewey simply dismisses the philosophical traditions appealed to by Hutchins as irrelevant to the contemporary world: "We live in a different social medium. It is astounding that anyone should suppose that a return to the conceptions and methods of these writers would do for the present what they did for the Greek and Medieval eras."[90] Neither of these criticisms of Hutchins is surprising, given what we already know about Dewey; ideas separated from practical and social problem solving, he suspects, are elitist affectations at best, insidious mystifications or rationalizations at worst, and conventional intellectual perspectives are tied to predemocratic traditions and therefore have antidemocratic implications.

Hutchins defends himself from both Dewey's paths of attack. He dismisses as rhetorical excess Dewey's suggestion that he is necessarily, if perhaps unknowingly, tying himself to undemocratic or antidemocratic politics: "A graduate of my hypothetical university writing for his fellow-alumni would know that such observations were rhetoric and that they would be received as such. As a matter of fact, fascism is a consequence of the absence of philosophy."[91] Hutchins is right to suggest that this is not a strong element of Dewey's position, since it is simply false to suggest that a given metaphysical perspective (or even the rejection of metaphysics altogether on pragmatic grounds) inevitably commits one to a particular political perspective. He is also right to suggest that fascism has strong anti-intellectual and antirationalist elements (although this did not prevent some philosophers and philosophically educated individuals from being drawn to various forms of fascism). He would have been wrong to think, however, that Dewey would admit either of these points. Perhaps the weakest element of Dewey's political commentary is his dogged insistence that a philosophical perspective is tied to a singular and necessary political perspective.[92] The claim is not persuasive and sounds for all the world like little more than combative political rhetoric, but Dewey appears, for better or worse, to have believed it.[93]

The second point concerns Dewey's historicism. This element of Dewey's thought is, of course, fundamental to his perspective and is tied to his conviction that thought grows from and reflects the pragmatic problems faced by a given society.[94] Hutchins rightly points out, however, that this historicism allows Dewey to explain the origins and functional purposes of ideas without actually answering their arguments. The protagonist in C. S. Lewis's *The Screwtape Letters* observes that the "Historical Point of View, put briefly, means that when a learned man is presented with any statement in an ancient author, the one question he never asks is whether it is true."[95] Hutchins makes the same point indirectly, suggesting, "One effect of the education I propose might be that a philosopher who had received it would be willing to consider arguments. He would not assume that his appeal must be to the prejudices of his audience."[96] What looks to Dewey like a devastating historical critique looks to Hutchins like an abdication of philosophical responsibility.

Dewey's final rejoinder fails to address Hutchins's charges; he more or less observes with incredulity that Hutchins is an Aristotelian, believes in "ultimate first truths," and would replace, if he could, the dominant scientific perspective of the modern world with a more traditional Western commitment to metaphysics.[97] All this is true enough, but Dewey thinks it seals the argument against Hutchins when in fact it merely restates the differences between Hutchins and himself. Regardless of whatever power there might be in Dewey's skepticism about the historic tradition of Western philosophy, Hutchins is absolutely correct to point out that Dewey's attack on his educational program is fundamentally dogmatic and ad hominem.

This famous exchange between Dewey and Hutchins (which, frankly, was not Dewey's finest moment) is instructive on a number of levels. Not the least of these is the present-day conventional wisdom that the exchange was a devastating defeat for Hutchins (discussed later). For now, however, it helps to clarify what is at stake in Dewey's educational perspective. In *The University of Utopia*, written well after the dustup with Dewey over *The Higher Learning in America*, Hutchins again presents an argument for a conventional liberal education in the classic texts and ideas of Western civilization. Reflecting on Dewey's educational program, Hutchins writes the following: "Looking at an industrial society, he [Dewey] concluded that the young should understand it and that they should do so through considering the various economic activities of life in their moral, political, social, and scientific context. He also thought that this would be very interesting to them. His psychology appears to be false and his program impractical. At least it has never been tried."[98] As we have seen, Hutchins is probably accurate (if unflattering) in his assessment of what Dewey thinks should be the focus in educational processes, regardless of the accuracy of his critique of the practicality and psychological appeal of this form of education. Hutchins's claim, however, is that Dewey's approach to education, which privileges the scientific perspective, dangerously and dogmatically narrows the appropriate focus of education. The liberal education Hutchins champions, in contrast, is much broader and committed to a diversity of perspectives that the pragmatic infatuation with science and scientific processes blinds us to. "The reverence that science has inspired has led scholars in other disciplines, seeking equally notable results and equally high prestige, to apply the method of science to subject matters to which it is not appropriate. Only trivial results can be accomplished by these means. Science has trivialized other fields of learning."[99] One result is that we turn our back on a universe of wisdom, beauty, and ideas. "What we are looking for is wisdom, and it does not seem sensible to say that the insights and understanding offered us by the greatest creations of the human mind cannot help us in our search. . . . It would be a bold man who would say that Newton had taught the West more than Shakespeare."[100]

The key point here is that, from Hutchins's point of view, Dewey and his followers have actually narrowed education inappropriately by trying to make it "relevant" and by thinking of science as the "perfecting of knowing, its last stage." For Hutchins, the end of education is not so much the cultivation of a shared "social disposition" as it is a "conversation aimed at truth,"[101] a conversation whose "object is not agreement but communication."[102] From this perspective, the civic purpose (indeed, the fundamentally civic definition) of education as formulated by Dewey and his disciples is narrowly dogmatic and intolerant. The dream of democratic consensus has blinded Dewey to the breadth of (legitimate) democratic, philosophical, and general intellectual disagreement. This, in turn, has blinded him to the more genuinely democratic purposes of education: to provide students with the intellectual tools and experiences for imagining alternative views, articulating their own views, and tolerating those with whom they disagree. Dewey's assumption is that without a shared "social disposition" among the citizenry, democracy is in imminent danger of flying apart. Hutchins's assumption is both more modest and more ambitious than Dewey's: whereas Dewey sees the need for a kind of ideological uniformity, Hutchins sees the ability to communicate intelligently, effectively, and civilly as the fundamental set of civic skills required by democratic citizens; whereas Dewey thinks the conventional liberal education proposed by Hutchins is beyond the intellectual reach and interest of the majority of democratic citizens, Hutchins is optimistic that, properly understood, it is within the grasp and imagination of democratic citizens in general. The intellectual precedes the civic for Hutchins, whereas the intellectual has been collapsed into the civic for Dewey.

Hutchins's reputation has not worn well among American educators. The most obvious reason has to do with contemporary objections to his exclusive emphasis on a narrowly defined Western canon.[103] At least as important, however, but often less self-evident to critics, is the ease with which we can settle into something that closely resembles Dewey's understanding of the need for and nature of democratic education. An anthology of essays about the relationship of higher education and democracy published in the late 1990s contains two striking illustrations of this. Thomas Ehrlich, former president of Indiana University and a distinguished higher education administrator, revisits the Dewey-Hutchins debate and finds himself out of sympathy with Hutchins's perspective. The first problem, he suggests, is that Hutchins's conception of education is simply too narrowly intellectual to be helpful as a guide to higher education. "The goal of education is not intellectual inquiry for its own sake, as Hutchins proclaimed, but the betterment of democratic practice across the whole of American society."[104] Indeed, one of Dewey's "radical insights" was that "a life that is only of the mind is inadequate to the challenges of U.S. democracy. Our society requires civic engagement to realize the potential of its citizens and its communities."[105] Education cannot aim only at intellectual cultivation for the simple reason that intellectual cultivation does not speak to the problems education is designed to address. The needs of democracy, rather than the promotion of truth, define the purpose of education. Dewey understood this, while Hutchins remained wed to a hopelessly narrow, academic understanding of education's end.

Hutchins's overly intellectualized understanding of education is not only inadequate to meet the needs of society; it is also counterproductive because of what is viewed as its undemocratic elitism. Ehrlich objects to Hutchins's restricted understanding of who should attend college, and he is delighted that Dewey's more populist conception of university education has become the norm in American society: "Dewey has clearly won against those who wished, with Hutchins, to reserve higher education for an elite."[106] Rather than allowing higher education to be "shaped primarily by a small group of universities dedicated to training an elite cadre of intellectual leaders," he hopes we will move toward an undergraduate education "increasingly formed by the needs of its consumers and by institutions that view their primary mission as responding to those needs."[107] In part, the charge of elitism is merely the charge of restricted access to the benefits of higher education. As long as the ultimate purposes of education relate to the needs of consumers and citizens, Hutchins's conception of education is too narrow to speak to the democratic many.

Ehrlich comments that Hutchins's "elitism was expressed in terms of who should be the teachers and should control the teachings."[108] This does not seem to be the real problem, however, since presumably Ehrlich, too, believes in the need for an expert faculty to teach undergraduates; as long as we are committed to teaching as a profession built on specialized knowledge and skills, teachers "should control the teachings."[109] The problem for Ehrlich appears to be, rather, that the "teachings" are politically unsatisfactory. Dewey may have been on the winning side in the battle over democratic access to higher education, but Hutchins is on the winning side in the battle over the content and pedagogy in much of higher education. Ehrlich hopes that the cultivation of community service learning, problem-based learning, collaborative learning methods, and new interactive technologies will help move higher education away from conventional classrooms, disciplinary-based instruction, and individual learning.[110] These developments will encourage the promotion of increasingly Deweyan subject matter and learning methods. Hutchins's view is not elitist just because it appeals to the abilities and interests of fewer people; it is elitist because it reinforces a conception of education that is hopelessly individualistic, private, and disengaged from the concerns of broader society and the social skills workers and citizens need to perform their professional and political duties. Hutchins's education simply does not focus its essential energies on the needs of a democratic society.

Ehrlich's preference for Dewey over Hutchins is built on a noticeable ambivalence about the nature of intellectual life. Recall his observation of Dewey's insight that "a life . . . only of the mind is inadequate to the challenges of U.S. democracy." Just prior to this comment, he claims that Dewey's first great radical thought was that "most citizens, not just an elite, can have a life of the mind."[111] Although it is not surprising that a former president of a major state university would comment positively about the intellectual capacities of the vast majority of democratic citizens, we can see that he is less than confident about what this means. Like Dewey, he collapses the "life of the mind" into civic life to make it democratically accessible. The academy is to be democratized, but this democratization requires that it be transformed into a civic rather than an intellectual institution. Meeting the needs of democracy rather than serving knowledge and truth provides the goals, meaning, and content of intellectual life.

Ehrlich's parting shot at Hutchins is the observation that we need a "healthy skepticism about the abilities of anyone to know all the answers—whatever the questions."[112] Ehrlich, much as Dewey had many years before, misses Hutchins's essential point, which is about providing students with the tools required for informed conversation about difficult moral and political issues (rather than providing them with ready-made answers to these problems). And like Dewey, Ehrlich finds himself defending an understanding of the life of the mind that significantly underemphasizes intellectual life itself. To make education democratically available, the assumption seems to be that we must radically minimize the importance of conventional intellectual and scholarly life and maximize in its place civic adjustment, civic commitment, and civic activities. We may well be justified in thinking that Hutchins was too optimistic about the degree to which a conventional liberal education can be made democratically meaningful for the many. But arguing that Hutchins had an elitist or undemocratic educational vision misses his point. On the contrary, his conception of education was built on a faith in our ability to extend the educational goods that had always been reserved for a few to the benefit and enjoyment of the many. He did not feel the need to redefine the nature of intellectual life simply because it would now be available to more than an aristocratic elite. In this sense it is Hutchins, not Ehrlich, who maintains the democratic courage of his intellectual convictions.[113]

Alexander Astin's essay, published in the same volume as Ehrlich's, provides an even clearer illustration of the significant anti-intellectual possibilities of the Deweyan perspective. Astin, a highly regarded scholar of higher education, writes with contempt of those who, like Hutchins, hold an "extreme view" that "the university should remain walled off from the external world of practical affairs so that the students can study and learn and faculty can pursue truth undisturbed by worldly distractions."[114] Luckily, Astin observes, democratic society is simply too powerful to allow such intellectual nonsense to prosper in the United States. "Like it or not, U.S. higher education is a *creature* of society, is sanctioned and supported by that society, and has in turn pledged itself to serve that society in its mission statements, catalogues, and other public pronouncements."[115] Whatever fantasies may be entertained in some sectors of the professoriat about the independent intellectual and scholarly life, it is clear that the very foundations of our colleges and universities have been shaped and controlled by the direct civic needs of democratic society.

Two assumptions inform Astin's analysis, and they are both very familiar by now. First, American democracy is in terrible shape: "Most of our citizenry, and that includes most of our college-educated citizenry, seem neither to understand what democracy is all about nor to accept individual responsibility to make it work."[116] Astin appears to be confident that "what democracy is all about" and the nature of our "individual responsibility to make it work" are uncontroversial matters and that all we need is a commitment to promote them (as opposed to a serious and dispassionate investigation of them). This leads to his second assumption: colleges and universities are currently failing to live up to their own professed obligations to promote civic virtue. The strength of his position is his observation that most institutions of higher learning list civic commitments as central to their mission, but they fail to take this mission seriously in practice.

> While many of my faculty colleagues may argue that the failure or success of our system of representative democracy is not higher education's responsibility or concern, they forget that promoting "good citizenship" and "developing future leaders" are two of the most commonly stated values in the mission statements of colleges and universities. Like it or not, we are publicly on record as committing ourselves and our institutions to promoting leadership and citizenship.[117]

Astin's assumption that these public pronouncements are morally compelling (rather than either misguided or merely rhetorical) allows him to take the short step to asserting that civic values should be the measure of academic life. "If we really want to make good on our professed commitment to democracy and citizenship, we need to examine all aspects of our liberal educational programs with the following questions in mind: Does this course, or this requirement, or this teaching technique, or this educational policy contribute to the student's ability to become an informed, engaged, and responsible member of society?"[118] What is needed, in short, is a "real citizenship curriculum."[119]

Astin is clearly frustrated with much in the contemporary academy. For example, universities continue to focus on hiring academic superstars. He assumes that the only plausible explanation for such hiring practices is the opportunistic cultivation of professional reputation; he cannot imagine, apparently, that these behaviors might grow from a commitment to intellectual and scholarly excellence.[120] The failure to live up to service and civic obligations seems to Astin to grow from either the hypocrisy or the incompetence of the faculty. Appeals to traditional scholarship are mere covers for self-promotion, individualism, competitive ideology, and other anticivic values.[121] This concern about faculty is nicely captured by his discussion of service learning. Like Ehrlich, Astin thinks service learning offers an appropriate break with academic business as usual, but he admits that faculty cannot fully develop such a program without the aid of service learning professionals. Although it is not clear exactly what role these nonfaculty professionals will play in the development of an appropriate university curriculum (at least some of their work will be logistical, but Astin also mentions an undefined role in helping faculty create "service learning components"), it appears that scholarly training is insufficient to prepare faculty members to pursue their appropriate role as teachers of undergraduates.[122] Astin's proposed curricular shift is indicative of the degree to which we have traveled from an intellectual to a civic conception of university life. Universities, in this view, are less institutions of higher learning than institutions for the cultivation and promotion of civic virtue.

Among contemporary political theorists concerned with civic education, the Mann-Dewey appeal to the normative model of the scientific community is no longer in fashion. However, the emphasis continues to be on the teaching of shared political values that will produce a moral consensus sufficient for the reproduction of liberal democratic society. Amy Gutmann believes it is not enough, for example, that students learn a kind of outward political toleration toward others; they must be encouraged to develop "mutual respect" for one another, despite their differences.[123] Macedo argues, "Successful constitutional institutions must . . . mold *people* in a manner that helps ensure that liberal freedom is what they want,"[124] and this holds true for public schools as well as for other institutions of civic education in our society. As he says at the beginning of *Diversity and Distrust*, "Profound forms of sameness and convergence should not only be prayed for but planned for without embarrassment."[125] Although Callan understands the degree to which we rightly resist any "stifling homogeneity in soulcraft," it is equally important, he believes, to understand the degree to which the democratic integrity of our public life will be "defeated by the failure to sustain the common dispositions that liberal dialogue presupposes."[126] Political education at its best, he argues, will be "much more corrosive of some powerful and long-entrenched sources of diversity, than many would like."[127] For these philosophically sophisticated advocates of normative civic education, the task is no longer (as it was for both Mann and Dewey) to model the political and normative community on the metaphor of scientific community and certainty. The underlying task of creating and enforcing a baseline moral consensus, however, remains the same. For all, the academic disciplines and virtues need to be supplemented with political lessons to ensure the creation of appropriately virtuous democratic citizens. For all, like Dewey, the problem is to generate a "common aim" and a "common spirit" among all citizens.[128]

Looking back at the debate between Dewey and Hutchins, we can see the articulation of an alternative to the scientific and consensus model of civic education. Both Dewey and Hutchins hope to appeal to the imagination of students, and both hope to channel this appeal in an educational project that will develop civic virtues. But they have a number of basic disagreements about how to achieve these goods. First, it is obvious that they are working from profoundly different psychologies. For Dewey, anything removed from immediate material relevancy and self-interest can hardly be expected to have a significant hold on the imaginations of the vast majority of people. Any appeal to "great ideas" or "classic literature" amounts to no more than a phony "cult of culture." For Hutchins, in contrast, the "problems of men" in general (and not merely the problems of "intellectuals") include an intellectual (one might say "philosophical") component that encompasses but is broader than the immediately practical. Only a conventional liberal education, including exposure to the humanities as conventionally conceived, can begin to address these broader human concerns. Hutchins's optimism about the ability of great literature and "high culture" to speak in serious ways to a broad democratic constituency is critical for understanding the two thinkers' different conceptions of the civic virtues. For Dewey, these virtues are dependent on the successful cultivation of a shared worldview, of a kind of intellectual consensus that constrains and bounds all political disagreement. This consensus is not merely procedural or substantively trivial but includes the full array of perspectives we might think of as constituting "secular humanism."[129] For Hutchins, the goal is not consensus so much as understanding. The reason to expose students to classic literature is not to teach them the correct way of thinking or to demonstrate, as Dewey hoped to in *Democracy and Education*, that scientific thought is the only true model for thought properly understood. Rather, it is to teach about the various ways of understanding the truth, to expose students to the range of perspectives on important problems that have been articulated over the course of history, and to engage them in a broad and serious conversation about these matters.[130]

Recall the contrast drawn in chapter 4 between Mann's understanding of the moral purposes of higher education and those articulated by Mill in his "Inaugural Address" at the University of Saint Andrews. As noted there, Mill has a much more developed understanding of the importance of cultivating students' moral imaginations than we find in Mann's didactic approach to education. For Mill, the moral purpose of education is not to teach students the moral law, as it is for Mann. Rather, it is to encourage an ability to think outside of themselves, to learn to understand and to sympathize, at least to some degree, with the contrasting views of others. In normative and aesthetic contexts, what we need is judgment, and this requires a kind of creative imagination. These needs cannot be filled by scientific knowledge or by the kind of certainty found in comparable forms of understanding. Thus, although Mill's educational project is as fraught with moral purpose as Mann's is, the purpose is significantly more modest. His goal is not to generate a moral consensus. Rather, it is to encourage the development of morally independent and reasonable individuals capable of understanding (and both agreeing and disagreeing with) others.

A comparable understanding of moral and civic education can be found in the American tradition too, although it tends to be a minority theme, overshadowed by the tradition represented by Mann, carried by Dewey into the twentieth century, and surviving in our own time in the work of our most vocal advocates of civic education. For Hutchins, for example, civic education is oriented toward understanding rather than consensus, and civic skills are conceived as side effects of a proper liberal education rather than the direct target of that education. Although one should not cultivate a program of explicitly civic education, one can expect positive civic consequences to result from quality intellectual and academic education (especially one that does not shortchange the humanities and the arts). The moral complexity and ambiguity of great literature, for example, which so annoyed and frightened Mann, provide precisely the soil in which the most important moral and civic education is cultivated.

Part of the reason we can expect positive civic results from quality intellectual education is simply that civic understanding grows with education about the world in general and with the ability to access, understand, and effectively evaluate many kinds of information. Hence, overall civic engagement increases with educational attainments. But there is an explicitly moral element to the claim developed from this perspective. Consider, in this vein, novelist David Foster Wallace's comments in a commencement address at Kenyon College in 2005. Probing the conventional argument that a liberal arts education is ultimately aimed to teach us to think, Wallace suggests that for this idea to be anything other than a hackneyed cliché, it must be about not the "capacity to think, but rather . . . the choice of what to think about."[131] Once we consider the problem from this perspective, we see that for Wallace, as it is for Mill, the end of such an education is to move beyond the narrowness of our own interests and experiences: "it's a matter of my choosing to do the work of somehow altering or getting free of my natural, hardwired default setting, which is to be deeply and literally self-centered, and to see and interpret everything through this lens of self."[132] The full power of a liberal education is the power to choose to move beyond this confining experience of the self, beyond what Wallace views as the tyranny of this narrow self, and to imagine the needs, experiences, and realities of others. "And I submit that this is what the real, no-shit value of your liberal arts education is supposed to be about: How to keep from going through your comfortable, prosperous, respectable adult life dead, unconscious, a slave to your head and to your natural default setting of being uniquely, completely, imperially alone, day in and day out."[133] Wallace's concern is less civic than moral: "The really important kind of freedom involves attention, and awareness, and discipline, and effort, and being able truly to care about other people and to sacrifice for them, over and over, in myriad petty little unsexy ways, every day."[134] But his argument has a civic quality similar to that found in Mill and Hutchins: the purpose of liberal education is to allow us a kind of liberation from the constraints of our own perspective, to enable us to imagine, understand, and sympathize with the perspectives of others. Although Callan argues for a more aggressive civic education for primary and secondary school children than is implied in these comments, his approach is deeply aligned with the cultivation of this kind of creative imagination, especially one that is encouraged through exposure to excellent literature. "To give the respect due to ethical viewpoints in deep conflict with our own, we must learn to enter them imaginatively and to understand that much of the pluralism that permeates our social world is a consequence not of evil or folly but of the inherent limits of human reason."[135] Again, from this perspective, Mann's distrust of Hawthorne's stories is clearly indicative of the mistake he would make in developing his view of civic education.

As mentioned earlier, the goals of this kind of education are more modest than those proposed by Mann and his contemporary descendants. The purpose is not to create a consensus sufficient to defuse the deep disagreements found in democratic society.[136] On the contrary, the purpose is to provide both the analytical skills and the moral capacity and inclination for coping with democratic disagreement. Kwame Anthony Appiah has commented that the educative purpose of conversation is not to generate agreement: "Conversation doesn't have to lead to consensus about anything, especially not values; it's enough that it helps people get used to one another."[137] Educating children and young adults to have the moral imagination sufficient to participate in democratic conversation may seem less inspiring than teaching Mann's body of moral commitments, Dewey's shared spirit, or Gutmann's mutual respect, but it actually displays a greater respect for democratic politics than does a more aggressive approach to civic education. It is the fear of democratic politics, of democratic citizens themselves, that leads some, in Mann's footsteps, to advocate a civic education that is thorough enough to simply remove the most contentious elements from the democratic debate. The tradition promoted by Mill and others hopes to civilize democratic disagreement; the tradition growing from

Mann hopes, ultimately, to eliminate it. The former tradition emphasizes the educative effects of democratic politics on adult citizens. The latter is built on a deep distrust of adult citizens' ability to develop civic virtue simply through the practice and experience of democratic politics and therefore aspires to something approaching a whole and complete civic education during childhood. Murphy argues that the thrust of conventional political theory emphasizes civic education that grows from civic participation by adults and not the political socialization (or, worse, indoctrination) of children.[138] Although he exaggerates the degree to which conventional political theory refrains from focusing on childhood education,[139] his overall point has power. The American educational impulse has grown out of a great fear that democratic practice will subvert rather than support the cultivation of civic virtues. All too often, the presumption has been that democratic practice is not sustainable; only the cultivation of a deep consensus among a democracy's children can ensure a democratic practice mild enough and sufficiently civilized to sustain itself.

The alternative to a preoccupation with the cultivation of civic virtue and consensus is the tradition that views civic virtues as an expected outgrowth of intellectual virtues. English classes appear to be at least as significantly correlated with tolerance and other civic virtues as civics classes,[140] and increasing language competency is the best means of developing effective and appropriate habits of democratic citizenship. Offering children a sufficient academic education is more likely than any heavy-handed civic education to actually contribute to the goals of civic education. This indirect approach to civic education not only promises the most satisfactory results; it can also be cultivated with the least danger of politicizing the curriculum. Civic education is not to be avoided, but it can take a much more gentle, modest, and less ideological form than that which is often advocated. To be gained are not particular civic beliefs but the more general disposition and inclination toward effective democratic participation and engagement.

How, then, should we understand and address the necessary, appropriate, even inevitable civic elements of any mass educational system in a liberal democracy? I have suggested that the best approach to democratic civic education is to provide the most complete and thorough intellectual education possible to all children. There is good reason to believe that this academic preparation will provide not only helpful knowledge but also intellectual virtues associated with rationality as well as with imagination and sympathy for the diversity of human experience, accomplishment, potential, and limitation. To overtly stress civic virtues, beyond those necessary for basic civility, mutual accommodation, the recognition of equal standing, and the corollary requirement for equal treatment, necessarily threatens the intellectual content of the academic education provided.[141] As we have seen, there is empirical evidence that intellectual development, especially in language and literacy sophistication, is correlated with civic virtues. There are two essential conclusions to keep in mind about this observation. First, academic education cannot shortchange the conventional humanities in favor of a narrow vocationalism or civic utility. Some of the greatest social goods to be reaped from both common schooling and higher education flow naturally from a healthy liberal education built on the humanities. It is here that the creative imagination of (future) democratic citizens is most likely to be cultivated.[142] Second, as Brighouse and Arendt point out in their different ways, it is our obligation to provide this rich liberal education to all children, even if we are not certain of the positive civic rewards. Democratic equality in education is a requirement of civic standing, regardless of the degree to which such treatment may or may not promote civic education.

As we appropriately shift our focus from civic to intellectual education, we can begin to appreciate that the primary normative problem facing our schools is not the paucity, ineffectiveness, or perversity of civic education currently being provided; instead, our attention is drawn to questions of justice and the quality of the intellectual education provided to American children. The differences in educational quality experienced by the least and most advantaged children in American society are profound, disturbing, and destructive. Almost two decades ago, Jonathan Kozol reported on these "savage inequalities" and their devastating effects.[143] More recently, Kozol has argued, "In a nation in which fairness was respected, children of the poorest and least educated mothers would receive the most extensive and most costly preschool preparation, not the least and cheapest, because children in these families need it so much more than those whose educated parents can deliver the same benefits of early learning to them in their homes."[144] Although there is still much work to be done in examining the demands of educational justice,[145] Kozol is certainly right to draw our attention to these problems as the most immediate, difficult, and significant normative matters facing our educational institutions. He is also right to chronicle how educational injustice erodes civic solidarity, trust, and community. Perhaps the most basic civic education of all must grow from the experience of educational equality.

The challenge offered to us by Horace Mann is the challenge of addressing the democratic paradox of civic education in a way that is respectful of our democratic values overall. There are clearly two tendencies in Mann's work. The first and most influential of these leads to an overly aggressive, pedantic, and didactic understanding of civic education. But Mann also points toward another understanding of civic education that is structural and institutional and reflects the civic values that must inform all public agencies in a democratic society. The stress here is on common access, shared experience, equality of treatment, toleration, and mutual accommodation. These basic civic commitments, properly reflected in the public schools as well as in our colleges and universities, provide a civic educational context for the intellectual education required by free individuals. These commitments, combined with the intellectual virtues associated with rationality, broadmindedness, inquisitiveness, sympathetic evaluation, and self-doubt, represent a meaningful foundation for shared democratic public life, even if they fall well short of the ideological consensus so often promoted by advocates of civic education.

A particular challenge today for those of us who have inherited Mann's democratic project is the fact that we can no longer take for granted something that Mann simply assumed: that people from all walks of life will live in close proximity to one another. This allowed Mann to hope that the common school would embody two appropriate and complementary democratic goods (and lessons) at once: providing the opportunity for civic friendship across boundaries of difference, and instituting equality of treatment for all children. Because our residential patterns have become so dramatically segregated by race and social class, we can no longer assume that both these goods can be achieved simultaneously in the community-based common school. Today we need to sort through the competing goods of common experience and equal treatment. For example, given contemporary housing patterns, in order to achieve a shared school experience that transcends racial and class differences, we would need to engage in wholesale social engineering by busing, with all the attendant problems and political disruptions associated with such policies in the past. Likewise, to achieve equality of treatment, we clearly need to move away from funding based on property taxes, given the dramatic disparity in property values in differing (often neighboring) communities.[146] We must also find ways to attract the most skilled, committed, and successful teachers to our most needy schools.[147] Much of our work, as Horace Mann's children, must be to weigh these competing values of shared experience and equality of treatment. It is important to note that many in the African American community are much more concerned about the control over, safety of, and academic achievement within underresourced schools than they are about promoting racial integration within them.[148] Given the inequalities and injustices of the broader social order, perhaps we must first work to overcome the relevant inequalities among our schools before we can hope to fully or satisfactorily address the issues of shared experience across race and class.[149] Perhaps the most basic level of shared experience for American children should be equality in their educational opportunities. Turning our attention and democratic energy from concerns about civic education to a commitment to educational justice would probably, in the long run, be best for both issues.

We are committed to the education of all our children, and this requires that we function within, reflect, and enforce the constraints and commitments of democratic society as we provide this education. It is possible to recognize the rightful, if subordinate, role of civic education while turning down the moral heat on our demands for the cultivation and reach of this education. To this degree, we need to emphasize the structural and institutional rather than the didactic elements of Mann's legacy in shaping the common school, and perhaps remember Elizabeth Peabody's desire for a more morally relaxed, intellectually focused educational program than the one ultimately advocated by Mann. Although present-day champions of a vigorous civic education would not demand, with Mann, that we create "godlike men," there remains a strong sense of the need to shape a moral consensus that simply dissolves many of the deep-seated moral differences and disagreements in American society. Our schools, colleges, and universities, however, are as unlikely to create such a consensus as they are to produce the godlike people Mann so longed for, and any attempt to produce such consensus threatens to undermine the core intellectual mission of our educational institutions. We should place greater trust in the value and moral impact of quality intellectual education. Instead of aiming for consensus, we should promote the more modest intellectual and democratic virtues that help students understand, tolerate, and civilly negotiate difference and disagreement. The democratic paradox cannot be entirely avoided, but it can and should be mitigated and managed in a manner most respectful of the intellectual integrity of the educational process and the individual autonomy of citizens. Mann did not always succeed in living up to this goal, but he provides us with the tools, and sometimes even the example, for thinking about these matters today.

NOTES

Chapter 1. Horace Mann's Legacy

1. Horace Mann, *Tenth Annual Report* (facsimile edition of original report for 1846, published by the Horace Mann League and the Hugh Birch–Horace Mann Fund of the National Education Association, 1952), 144.

2. Horace Mann, *Lectures on Education* (Boston: Lemuel N. Ide, 1850), 93.

3. Alexander Hamilton, James Madison, and John Jay, *The Federalist Papers* (New York: New American Library, 1961), 322.

4. The phrase is from James Russell Lowell (1888), quoted in Michael Kammen, *A Machine That Would Go of Itself* (New York: Alfred A. Knopf, 1987), 18.

5. Madison famously reminds us, in *Federalist* 10, that we must constitutionally control the effects of faction, since "Enlightened statesmen will not always be at the helm" (*Federalist Papers*, 80). When discussing the Senate, however, in *Federalist* 63, he defends the upper chamber in these terms: "I shall not scruple to add that such an institution may be sometimes necessary as a defense to the people against their own temporary errors and delusions. As the cool and deliberate sense of the community ought, in all governments, and actually will, in all free governments, ultimately prevail over the views of its rulers; so there are particular moments in public affairs when the people, stimulated by some irregular passion, or some illicit advantage, or misled by the artful misrepresentations of interested men, may call for measures which they themselves will afterwards be the most ready to lament and condemn. In these critical moments, how salutary will be the interference of some temperate and respectable body of citizens, in order to check the misguided career and to suspend the blow mediated by the people against themselves, until reason, justice, and truth can again regain their authority over the public mind?" (*Federalist Papers*, 384).

6. It is often pointed out that his authorship of the Declaration of Independence and Virginia's Statute of Religious Freedom and his work in founding the University of Virginia are the three accomplishments Jefferson made certain were mentioned on his tombstone.

7. "The science of politics . . . like most other sciences, has received great improvement." *Federalist Papers* (no. 9), 72.

8. The hard-boiled evaluation of the "American Democrat" offered by James Fenimore Cooper, in the same year that Horace Mann assumed his position as sec-

retary, suggests that "the peculiar danger of a democracy, arises from the arts of demagogues." James Fenimore Cooper, *The American Democrat* (New York: Penguin, 1989), 141.

9. A contemporary economist has complained that citizens' common attempt to attend to the public good is the very reason that American politics is in such disarray: "Precisely because people put personal interests aside when they enter the political arena, intellectual errors readily blossom into foolish policies." Bryan Caplan, *The Myth of the Rational Voter* (Princeton, NJ: Princeton University Press, 2007), 153.

10. Jean-Jacques Rousseau, *Basic Political Writings* (Indianapolis and Cambridge: Hackett, 1987), 55.

11. Ibid.

12. Henry David Thoreau, *Collected Essays and Poems* (New York: Library of America, 2001), 203–204.

13. "O for a man who is a *man*, and, as my neighbor says, has a bone in his back which you cannot pass your hand through!" Ibid., 209.

14. Plato writes of the moral chaos within the democratic man: "Then he . . . lives along day by day, gratifying the desire that occurs to him, at one time drinking and listening to the flute, at another downing water and reducing; now practicing gymnastic, and again idling and neglecting everything; and sometimes spending his time as though he were occupied with philosophy. Often he engages in politics and, jumping up, says and does whatever chances to come to him; and if he ever admires any soldiers, he turns in that direction; and if it's money-makers, in that one. And there is neither order nor necessity in his life, but calling this life sweet, free, and blessed he follows it throughout." Plato, *The Republic* (New York: Basic Books, 1991), 239–240. Although contemporary social scientists also criticize the moral views or qualities of democratic citizens, the more common complaint is their simple political ignorance. Data illustrating how much American citizens do not know about politics are ubiquitous. One particularly troubling finding is that although Americans today receive much more schooling than they did a generation ago, their political knowledge has remained more or less constant—college graduates today know no more about politics than high school graduates did fifty years ago. See Stephen Macedo, ed., *Democracy at Risk* (Washington, DC: Brookings, 2005), 1. For a classic study of the topic, see Michael Delli Carpini and Scott Keeter, *What Americans Know About Politics and Why It Matters* (New Haven, CT: Yale University Press, 1997).

15. See *On the Social Contract*, Book II, chapter 7, and Book IV, chapter 8, in Rousseau, *Basic Political Writings*.

16. Paul Woodruff, *First Democracy* (New York: Oxford University Press, 2005), 162.

17. Horace Mann, *Ninth Annual Report* (facsimile edition of original report for 1845, published by the Horace Mann League and the Hugh Birch–Horace Mann Fund of the National Education Association, 1951), 68.

18. Ibid., 66.

19. Mary Peabody Mann, *Life of Horace Mann* (Washington, DC: National Education Association of the United States, 1937), 102.

20. Perry Miller, *The Responsibility of Mind in a Civilization of Machines: Essays by Perry Miller* (Amherst: University of Massachusetts Press, 1979), 78.

21. John Dewey, "Education, the Foundation for Social Organization," in *Later Works*, vol. 11 (Carbondale: Southern Illinois University Press, 2008), 226.

22. "Washington and Lincoln represent the highest types of heroism, patriotism, and wisdom in the great crisis of republic-building; Horace Mann, the quiet inner building, the soul development of the nation." Quoted in E. I. F. Williams, *Horace Mann: Educational Statesman* (New York: Macmillan, 1937), 353. Williams echoes Parker's view, writing that Mann "deserves to be ranked with Washington and Lincoln in his influence upon the development of a democratic America." Ibid., x.

23. Joy Elmer Morgan claims that "Horace Mann and his followers were destined to lay the foundations for cultural democracy." Joy Elmer Morgan, *Horace Mann: His Ideas and Ideals* (Washington, DC: National Home Library Foundation, 1936), 7.

24. For example, Samuel Bowles and Herbert Gintis argue that Mann is significant because his educational work helped foil the development of class-consciousness among American workers: "Mann's reforms had the intent (and most likely the effect as well) of forestalling the development of class consciousness among the working people of the state and preserving the legal and economic foundations of the society in which he had been raised. The reformed school system of Massachusetts was Mann's crowning achievement. It was truly an innovative solution to the problem of conservative adaption to change. It was soon to be duplicated around the country." Samuel Bowles and Herbert Gintis, *Schooling in Capitalist America* (New York: Basic Books, 1976), 173.

25. Jonathan Messerli, *Horace Mann* (New York: Alfred A. Knopf, 1972). For the best of the remaining studies of Mann, see Raymond B. Culver, *Horace Mann and Religion in the Massachusetts Public Schools* (New Haven, CT: Yale University Press, 1929); B. A. Hinsdale, *Horace Mann and the Common School Revival in the United States* (New York: Charles Scribner's Sons, 1900); Neil Gerard McCluskey, *Public Schools and Moral Education* (New York: Columbia University Press, 1958); Louise Hall Tharp, *Until Victory: Horace Mann and Mary Peabody* (Boston: Little, Brown, 1953); Williams, *Horace Mann*.

26. Hinsdale, *Horace Mann and the Common School Revival*, 266.

27. Messerli, *Horace Mann*, 336.

28. Although, as David Tyack and Elisabeth Hansot point out, "No one better expressed the range of arguments for public education or better symbolized the idealism of the social movement for the common school than did Horace Mann." David Tyack and Elisabeth Hansot, *Managers of Virtue: Public School Leadership in America, 1820–1980* (New York: Basic Books, 1982), 56. For a discussion of some of Mann's

educational forebears, see Hinsdale, *Horace Mann and the Common School Revival*. For a study of the politics of public involvement in education in the nineteenth century, see Julie M. Walsh, *The Intellectual Origins of Mass Parties and Mass Schools in the Jacksonian Period: Creating a Conformed Citizenry* (New York: Garland, 1998). For a more general history of American public education in the nineteenth century and before, see Carl F. Kaestle, *Pillars of the Republic* (New York: Hill and Wang, 1983).

29. Mann, *Lectures on Education*, 229.

30. George Combe, *The Constitution of Man* (Boston: Marsh, Capen, and Lyon; New York: Daniel Appleton, 1836).

31. See Mary Mann's comment in her *Life of Horace Mann*, 47. Later in the same volume (132), she reports that Mann wrote of Combe: "The world knows him not. In the next century, I have no doubt, he will be looked back upon as the greatest man of the present." In Mary's favor, it is true that Mann was willing to criticize Combe when he found his work failed to live up to its usual standards (see 139–140).

32. Robert Straker claims that Mann "specifically denied any interest in cranial topography." Robert L. Straker, *The Unseen Harvest: Horace Mann and Antioch College* (Yellow Springs, OH: Antioch Press, 1955), 15.

33. For example, see Mann's phrenological analysis of Henry Clay's head in Mary Mann's *Life of Horace Mann*, 282. Messerli reports that while attending an elegant social event in England, Mann complained that "he did not see a single head which gave phrenological evidence of 'strength and benevolence.'" Soon thereafter, viewing the great portraits at Versailles, he claimed that, "phrenologically, Louis XVI had the 'head of an idiot,' while that of Napoleon was 'magnificent.'" He also worried about the phrenological implications of the shape of his son's, Horace Junior's, head. Messerli, *Horace Mann*, 389, 398, 426–427.

34. "Purity is more precious than life," he writes, after criticizing literary wit and conventions that seem to him to praise crime or immorality; he is shocked to his core by what he takes to be the pornography of Byron's poetry—"what licentious passions!" Horace Mann, *Life and Works*, vol. 5 (Boston: Lee and Shepard, 1891), 140, 148.

35. Mann resisted allowing the stories of Nathaniel Hawthorne (his brother-in-law) to be used as texts in the common schools, as they were insufficiently didactic and morally unambiguous. Megan Marshall reports that "Mann had . . . expressed . . . his dislike of Hawthorne's tales, his preference for something 'nearer home to duty and business,' and his outright incomprehension of the darker stories, such as 'The Wedding Knell': 'wherefore is it and to what does it tend?' As far as literature itself was concerned, Mann considered the whole enterprise a slight one, writing once to his friend Samuel Gridley Howe, 'I should rather have built up the Blind Asylum than to have written *Hamlet*.'" Megan Marshall, *The Peabody Sisters* (Boston and New York: Houghton Mifflin, 2005), 402.

36. As just one example, he characterized the opponents of the Board of Education as "bigots and vandals" and "wicked." Mann, *Life of Horace Mann*, 125.

37. Messerli, *Horace Mann*, 337.

38. Messerli (ibid., 303) reports that Mann distrusted New England town meetings. Mann's hatred of political parties is expressed in many of his writings throughout his career. This comment, from a letter to Combe, is typical: "What an enemy to the human race is a party-man! To get ashore himself is his only object: he cares not who else sinks." Mann, *Life of Horace Mann*, 123.

39. Horace Mann, *Twelfth Annual Report* (facsimile edition of original report for 1848, published by the Horace Mann League and the Hugh Birch–Horace Mann Fund of the National Education Association, 1952), 19.

40. For example, in his excellent study of Mann's disputes with religious conservatives over the role of Congregationalist orthodoxy in the common schools, Raymond Culver is restrained but clear in this observation about Mann's prickly inability to tolerate criticism: "His was an extremely sensitive nature, and quite lacking in that saving sense of humor that would have spared another man frequent annoyances." Culver, *Horace Mann and Religion*, 230.

41. See, for example, Amy Gutmann, *Democratic Education* (Princeton, NJ: Princeton University Press, 1987); Eamonn Callan, *Creating Citizens* (Oxford and New York: Oxford University Press, 1997); Harry Brighouse, *School Choice and Social Justice* (Oxford and New York: Oxford University Press, 2000); Stephen Macedo, *Diversity and Distrust* (Cambridge, MA: Harvard University Press, 2000); Brian Barry, *Culture and Equality* (Cambridge, MA: Harvard University Press, 2001); Rob Reich, *Bridging Liberalism and Multiculturalism in American Education* (Chicago: University of Chicago Press, 2002). I return to this and related literature in chapter 5.

42. It seems to me that Lawrence Cremin is exactly right on this issue: Mann's "quest was for a *public philosophy*, a sense of community which might be shared by Americans of every variety and persuasion." Lawrence A. Cremin, ed., *The Republic and the School: Horace Mann on the Education of Free Men* (New York: Teachers College, Columbia University, 1957), 8.

43. For my reading of Dewey's preoccupation with modern science and the impact this has on his educational theory, see my *Citizenship and Democratic Doubt: The Legacy of Progressive Thought* (Lawrence: University Press of Kansas, 2004), chapter 2.

44. Miller, *Responsibility of Mind*, 82.

45. "It [anti-intellectualism] first got its strong grip on our ways of thinking because it was fostered by an evangelical religion that also purveyed many humane and democratic sentiments. It made its way into our politics because it became associated with our passion for equality. It has become formidable in our education partly because our educational beliefs are evangelically egalitarian." Richard Hofstadter, *Anti-Intellectualism in American Life* (New York: Alfred A. Knopf, 1963), 22–23.

Chapter 2. The Need for Common Schooling

1. Ralph Waldo Emerson, *Essays and Lectures* (New York: Library of America, 1983), 53.

2. Messerli, *Horace Mann*, 265.

3. Mann, *Lectures*, 142.

4. It is important to note, in all that follows about Mann's democratic theory, that his definition of a *republic* is "government of the people by the people." That is, he uses the terms *republic* and *democracy* interchangeably. See Mann, *Twelfth Annual Report*, 83.

5. "In the end nothing illustrates better the transforming power of the American Revolution than the way its intellectual and political leaders, that remarkable group of men, contributed to their own demise." Gordon Wood, *Revolutionary Characters* (New York: Penguin, 2006), 274.

6. Other themes and claims in "The American Scholar" would resonate in Mann's work over the next few years as well. Consider just three: Emerson's claim that "character is higher than intellect"; that "he then learns, that in going down into the secrets of his own mind, he has descended into the secrets of all minds"; and that "I embrace the common, I explore and sit at the feel of the familiar, the low." Each of these has clear parallels in the theory Mann develops, as will become clear in what follows. Emerson, *Essays and Lectures*, 62, 64, 68–69.

7. Mann, *Lectures*, 123.

8. Ibid., 148.

9. Horace Mann, *Eighth Annual Report* (facsimile edition of original report for 1844, published by the Horace Mann League and the Hugh Birch–Horace Mann Fund of the National Education Association, 1950), 135.

10. Mann, *Twelfth Annual Report*, 80–83.

11. Mann, *Lectures*, 153.

12. Ibid., 242. In the *Ninth Annual Report* (71), Mann is deeply critical of West Point, suggesting that it represents a primitive martial inheritance we would do well to transcend. Messerli tells the story of Mann's inspection of West Point as a U.S. representative in 1850, and his comments to the graduating class to the effect that military education needed to change its focus from warfare to working for peace. Messerli, *Horace Mann*, 501–502. Mann became noticeably pacific and antimilitarist in midlife, although he had been quite militaristic and particularly enthusiastic about the development of American naval power when he was a young man. See ibid., 43; Hinsdale, *Horace Mann and the Common School Revival*, 81–82.

13. Mann, *Life of Horace Mann*, 302.

14. Mann, *Twelfth Annual Report*, 57.

15. Horace Mann, *A Few Thoughts for a Young Man* (Boston: Ticknor, Reed, and Fields, 1850), 61. Merle Curti reports that "Mann's outspoken criticism of indus-

trial and commercial capitalism provoked bitter denunciations." Merle Curti, *The Social Ideas of American Educators* (Totowa, NJ: Littlefield, Adams, 1959), 117.

16. See Mann, *Lectures*, 249, where he rants about the favorable reception given to two female European dancers whom he considered to be obscene. "It is said that Celeste received *fifty thousand dollars*, in this country, in one year, for the combined exhibition of skill and person; and that devotee to Venus, Fanny Ellsler, was paid the enormous sum of *sixty thousand dollars*, in three months, for the same meritorious consideration, or *value received*. . . . And I blush while I reflect, that amongst all the daughters of New England who witnessed the unreserved displays of these Cyprian women, there was not one to be found, in whose veins flowed the chaste blood of the Puritan mothers, prompting her to approach these female *sans culottes*, backwards, and perform for them the same friendly service, which, on a like necessity, the sons of Noah performed for him."

17. See chapter 1, note 35.

18. Mann's criticism of literature was long-standing. As a college student in the fall of 1817, he had written two essays attacking fiction. The first of these, "Against Novels," argues that "perhaps few kinds of amusement are more predjudicial [*sic*] to the attainment of solid science, or productive of more injury to the mind, than . . . that of fictitious history embraced in novels and romances." In the second, "Against Fiction," Mann continues the assault: "When . . . months and years have been wasted on gaining a knowledge of the whole range of novels and romances which infest the world, we shall find, that the mind has received no improvement, principles no correction, nor ideas enlargement. All the benefit derived was a transitory satisfaction, and of this naught remains but the recollection." These essays can be found in the Horace Mann Papers I–V, Reel 2 of 40, at the Massachusetts Historical Society. It is somewhat melancholy to note that Mary Peabody Mann, always loyal to and supportive of her husband, had been a "voracious reader, chiefly of fiction," as a young woman. See Marshall, *Peabody Sisters*, 147.

19. Horace Mann, *Third Annual Report* (facsimile edition of original report for 1839, published by the Horace Mann League and the Hugh Birch–Horace Mann Fund of the National Education Association, 1948), 69–70.

20. Ibid., 69.

21. Ibid., 68.

22. Ibid., 64.

23. Mann, *Lectures*, 297.

24. Ibid., 296.

25. Ibid.

26. Mann, *Third Annual Report*, 71.

27. In a wonderful essay, historian Jill Lepore points out that the eighteenth and early nineteenth centuries saw many attacks—almost always by men—on fictional literature, an art form appreciated and consumed primarily by women. Jill Lepore,

"Just the Facts, Ma'am: Fake Memoirs, Factual Fictions, and the History of History," *New Yorker*, 24 March 2008, 79–83. Noah Webster, for example, wrote in 1790, "At best, novels may be considered as the toys of youth, the rattle boxes of sixteen." Noah Webster, "On the Education of Youth in America," in *Essays on Education in the Early Republic*, ed. Frederick Rudolph (Cambridge, MA: Harvard University Press, 1965), 71.

28. Again, see chapter 1, note 35.

29. One author, asked by Mann to rewrite his own book to make it more didactic, was astounded by Mann's presumptuousness and referred to him as a "school-master gone crazy." Messerli, *Horace Mann*, 346.

30. Mann, *Lectures*, 297.

31. Marshall, *Peabody Sisters*, 241. For Combe's offer at the University of Michigan, see Hinsdale, *Horace Mann and the Common School Revival*, 99. Hinsdale (97) argues that "the breakdown of phrenology as a science should not blind us to the fact that its cultivators started with a sound postulate, and that their general method was right. Their postulate was the doctrine of localization; their method, observation and experiment. They were the experimental psychologists of their time." Neil McCluskey is one commentator who is less willing to be charitable about Mann's interest in phrenology. See McCluskey, *Public Schools and Moral Education*, 24, 27.

32. "*Morality becomes a science*." Combe, *Constitution of Man*, 223.

33. See ibid., 52–56, for the full list and explanation of these mental faculties.

34. Ibid., 21–23.

35. Ibid., 247.

36. Ibid., 37.

37. Ibid., 61.

38. Ibid., 110–111.

39. "Neither disease nor death, in early and middle life, can take place under the ordinary administration of Providence, except when the laws have been infringed." Ibid., 214.

40. Ibid., 3.

41. See ibid., 164, 186.

42. Ibid., 202.

43. See ibid., 273.

44. See Messerli, *Horace Mann*, 351.

45. Combe, *Constitution of Man*, 191.

46. Ibid., 390.

47. Ibid., 241.

48. "A perception of the importance of the natural laws will lead to their observance, and this will be attended with an improved development of brain, thereby increasing the desire and capacity for obedience." Ibid., 391. "By teaching mankind the philosophy of their own nature and of the world in which they live . . . they may be induced to modify the latter, and to intrench the moral powers; and then the tri-

umph of virtue and religion will be complete." Ibid., 393. It is interesting to note that Emerson had no such optimism about phrenology's compatibility with free will. "Very odious, I confess, are the lessons of Fate. Who likes to have a dapper phrenologist pronouncing on his fortunes?" Emerson, "Fate," in *Essays and Lectures*, 960.

49. Combe, *Constitution of Man*, 58.

50. Mann refers to Locke's *Thoughts on Education* as "that admirable treatise" and then continues: "but while his system of metaphysics, which is the poorest of all his works, has been made a text-book both in the universities of England and America, this excellent treatise, which is by far better than any thing which had ever then been written, has been almost wholly neglected and forgotten." Mann, *Lectures*, 229.

51. As discussed in chapter 3, a number of Mann's critics were very sensitive to this issue.

52. Combe, *Constitution of Man*, 25.

53. Combe writes, "There is reason to believe, that, in the state of nature, death is attended with very little suffering to the lower creatures." He suggests that when we humans get our lives in line with natural law, the same will be true for us. Ibid., 209, 211, 217.

54. "Physical has far outstripped moral science; and it appears to me, that, unless mankind shall have their eyes opened to the real constitution of the world, and be at length induced to regulate their conduct in harmony with the laws of the Creator, their future physical discoveries will tend only to deepen their wretchedness." Ibid., 278.

55. Ibid., 113.

56. Williams, *Horace Mann*, 232.

57. Mann, *Ninth Annual Report*, 69.

58. Mann, *Lectures*, 127.

59. Mann, *Twelfth Annual Report*, 90.

60. Mann, *Lectures*, 140.

61. Ibid., 124.

62. Ibid., 125.

63. Mann, *Ninth Annual Report*, 69.

64. Mann, *Lectures*, 238–239.

65. Mann, *Ninth Annual Report*, 28.

66. Hamilton, Madison, and Jay, *Federalist Papers*, 322.

67. Mann, *Lectures*, 216.

68. Ibid., 169.

69. Ibid., 124.

70. "But his faith in endless progress grew stronger with every experience, till his very aspect was irradiated by it." Mann, *Life of Horace Mann*, vii.

71. For example, we find Mann writing of "the sublime law of human progress" in the *Common School Journal*. Horace Mann, *Life and Works*, vol. 2 (Boston: Lee and Shepard, 1891), 7.

72. Combe, *Constitution of Man*, 4.

73. Messserli writes: "Progress and human perfectibility were undeniably part of a providential plan. He [Mann] simply arrogated to himself the task of accelerating the agenda of the Almighty." Messerli, *Horace Mann*, 403.

74. Mann, *Lectures*, 125.

75. Ibid., 169.

76. Ibid., 171.

77. Mann, *Twelfth Annual Report*, 78.

78. Mann, *Life and Works*, 5:314.

79. Mann, *Lectures*, 159.

80. Ibid., 161.

81. Mann, *Twelfth Annual Report*, 42.

82. Mann, *Life and Works*, 5:314.

83. Messerli, *Horace Mann*, 249.

84. Mann, *Lectures*, 172.

85. Mann, *Ninth Annual Report*, 95.

86. Mann, *Lectures*, 13.

87. Carl Kaestle and Maris Vinovskis have shown that the number of students attending private schools in Massachusetts in 1840 was only 13.8 percent of the total school population. They also demonstrated that between 1840 and 1880, the growth of the common school did less to displace students from elite private schools (enrollment declined to about 8.4 percent of the total school population by 1880) than to replace other nonelite options ("low-priced pay schools, local academies, and subscriptions schools") for students. Carl Kaestle and Maris Vinovskis, *Education and Social Change in Nineteenth-Century Massachusetts* (Cambridge: Cambridge University Press, 1980), 34.

88. See Horace Mann, *First Annual Report* (facsimile edition of original report for 1837, published by the Horace Mann League and the Hugh Birch–Horace Mann Fund of the National Education Association, 1947), 48; Horace Mann, *Fourth Annual Report* (facsimile edition of original report for 1840, published by the Horace Mann League and the Hugh Birch–Horace Mann Fund of the National Education Association, 1949), 34, 41.

89. Mann, *First Annual Report*, 56–57.

90. Horace Mann, *Seventh Annual Report* (facsimile edition of original report for 1843, published by the Horace Mann League and the Hugh Birch–Horace Mann Fund of the National Education Association, 1950), 36.

91. Mann, *Twelfth Annual Report*, 132.

92. Mann argues that the best students are drained out of the public schools by private schools, as the wealthier and most capable seek to purchase the best educational services available. "The lower classes in a school have no abstract standard of excellence, and seldom aim at higher attainments than such as they daily witness. All children, like all men, rise easily to the common level. There, the mass stop;

strong minds only ascend higher. But raise the standard, and, by a spontaneous movement, the mass will rise again and reach it. Hence the removal of the most forward scholars from a school is not a small misfortune." Mann, *First Annual Report*, 50. If private schools threaten the attainments of all students by robbing them of high standards at which to aim, they also threaten to rob public schools of the commitment of the teaching profession. See Mann, *Seventh Annual Report*, 37.

93. Mann, *Eighth Annual Report*, 109.

94. Mann, *Seventh Annual Report*, 37.

95. Mann, *Fourth Annual Report*, 41.

96. Ibid., 42.

97. See his discussion of this problem in Horace Mann, *Eleventh Annual Report* (facsimile edition of original report for 1847, published by the Horace Mann League and the Hugh Birch–Horace Mann Fund of the National Education Association, 1952), 94–99.

98. See Mann's discussion of this problem, for example, in his *Fourth Annual Report*, 87–91.

99. Mann, *Tenth Annual Report*, 111.

100. Ibid., 69.

101. Here are just a couple of examples. Mann laments those children "who suffer under the amazing parental folly of being delicately brought up." Later he writes, "But parents are deplorably ignorant. Hence they allow unhealthful indulgences. They inculcate false principles. They establish bad habits. As an inevitable consequence, sickness and suffering abound." Horace Mann, *Sixth Annual Report* (facsimile edition of original report for 1842, published by the Horace Mann League and the Hugh Birch–Horace Mann Fund of the National Education Association, 1949), 64, 77.

102. Mann, *Third Annual Report*, 42.

103. Mann, *Tenth Annual Report*, 113.

104. See Mann, *First Annual Report*, 43–44.

105. Mann, *Sixth Annual Report*, 21.

106. Mann, *Ninth Annual Report*, 65–66.

107. Mann, *Twelfth Annual Report*, 94.

108. Mann, *Lectures*, 77.

109. Mann, *Third Annual Report*, 46.

110. Mann, *Life of Horace Mann*, 142.

111. Mann, *Eighth Annual Report*, 60.

112. "The founders of the public schools were often well-educated academy or college graduates who loved to read and write and reflect upon society and its problems. But theirs was a moral mission. They did not believe that the schools should focus only on intellectual training, however important. Even Ralph Waldo Emerson, who found many of the reformers distasteful, frequently told his lyceum audiences that the aim of education was to make a life, not a living. Character was

everything in an age of fast deals, confidence men, geographical mobility, and changes that battered the body and soul." William J. Reese, *America's Public Schools* (Baltimore: Johns Hopkins University Press, 2005), 34. Maxine Greene writes, "Both Mann and Emerson . . . were working in the matrix of tradition when they placed their stress on moral or spiritual development rather than on intellectual excellence." Maxine Greene, *The Public School and the Private Vision* (New York: Random House, 1965), 29.

113. Mann, *Lectures*, 84.

114. Ibid., 89.

115. Messerli, *Horace Mann*, 214.

116. Ibid., 281–282. Messerli later (346) refers to Mann's desire to "housebreak the masses."

117. Quoted in Culver, *Horace Mann and Religion*, 22.

118. Cremin, *The Republic and the School*, 9.

Chapter 3. The Ends of Common Schooling

1. Horace Mann, *Life and Works*, vol. 4 (Boston: Lee and Shepard, 1891), 346.

2. Ibid., 353.

3. Ibid., 403.

4. Messerli, *Horace Mann*, 380.

5. Mann, *First Annual Report*, 55.

6. "If Prussia can pervert the benign influences of education to the support of arbitrary power, we surely can employ them for the support and perpetuation of republican institutions." Mann, *Seventh Annual Report*, 23.

7. "We can never fully estimate the debt of gratitude we owe to our ancestors for establishing our system of Common Schools." Ibid., 46.

8. Ibid., 68–69.

9. Ibid., 52.

10. See ibid., 87–99.

11. Ibid., 104.

12. See ibid., 90, 106.

13. See ibid., 104, 123, 125.

14. Ibid., 110.

15. "It is a moral means of great efficacy." Ibid., 126.

16. Ibid., 134–135.

17. Ibid., 86.

18. Ibid., 137.

19. Ibid., 127.

20. In the *Fourth Annual Report*, Mann wrote, "That females are incomparably better teachers for young children than males, cannot admit of a doubt" (45). Thirteen years later, in a lecture published under the title *A Few Thoughts on the Powers*

and Duties of Women (Syracuse, NY: Hall, Mills, 1852), Mann would write, "That woman should be the educator of children, I believe to be as much a requirement of nature as that she should be the mother of children" (82). In the *Seventh Annual Report*, however, he is impressed by the Prussian schoolmasters' gentle effectiveness with little children. Here he suggests that perhaps his views concerning female teachers "are calculated only for particular meridians" (140).

21. Mann, *Seventh Annual Report*, 138.

22. Ibid., 165–170.

23. Ibid., 125–126.

24. Ibid., 179, 181.

25. McCluskey, *Public Schools and Moral Education*, 78.

26. These topics are the primary focus of Horace Mann, *Second Annual Report* (facsimile edition of original report for 1838, published by the Horace Mann League and the Hugh Birch–Horace Mann Fund of the National Education Association, 1948). The discussion begins on page 37 and continues until the end of the report.

27. See ibid., 65.

28. Ibid., 44.

29. Ibid., 45.

30. Mann, *Third Annual Report*, 70–71.

31. Ibid., 88. See, too, Mann, *Sixth Annual Report*, for an extensive discussion of the teaching of human physiology. He concludes this report by claiming that "an acquaintance with the fundamental laws of health and life, may be and must be *popularized*" (159).

32. Mann, *Ninth Annual Report*, 150.

33. Mann, *Lectures*, 41.

34. At one point, Mann suggests that a teacher "wants capacity to govern" if he "has no expedients for enkindling a love of knowledge and a zeal for improvement, among his pupils, but the low and anti-social one of rivalry,—that is, a desire to surpass one's classmates or fellow-students, for the sake of winning a prize, or of standing, conspicuous, at the head of a class, at the final examination of the school." Horace Mann, *Fifth Annual Report* (facsimile edition of original report for 1841, published by the Horace Mann League and the Hugh Birch–Horace Mann Fund of the National Education Association, 1949), 56.

35. "The object of punishment is, prevention from evil; it never can be made impulsive to good. . . . In all cases, therefore, the very fact of punishment supposes that a great deal else is to be done." Mann, *Lectures*, 311.

36. See Mann, *Eighth Annual Report*, passage beginning on page 117.

37. Mann, *Sixth Annual Report*, 156.

38. "Remarks on the Seventh Annual Report of the Hon. Horace Mann, Secretary of the Massachusetts Board of Education" (Boston: Charles C. Little and James Brown, 1844). This can be found in the Horace Mann Papers and Pamphlets collection at the Massachusetts Historical Society.

39. Ibid., 10.
40. Ibid., 20.
41. Ibid., 8–9.
42. Ibid., 20.
43. Ibid., 43–44. The schoolmasters are not the only ones to conclude that Mann's tour of Prussian schools was superficial at best. Lawrence Cremin dryly observes, "If ever an inspection confirmed what the inspector was searching for, this was it." Cremin, *The Republic and the School*, 16. See, too, McCluskey, *Public Schools and Moral Education*, 78.
44. "Remarks," 54, 56.
45. Ibid., 60.
46. Ibid., 101.
47. Ibid., 83.
48. Ibid., 85.
49. Ibid., 127.
50. Ibid., 128.
51. Ibid., 136.
52. Ibid., 144.
53. Horace Mann, "Reply to the Remarks of Thirty-one Boston Schoolmasters on the Seventh Annual Report of the Secretary of the Massachusetts Board of Education" (Boston: Wm. B. Fowle and Nahum Chapen, 1844). This can be found in the Horace Mann Papers and Pamphlets collection at the Massachusetts Historical Society.
54. Ibid., 3.
55. Ibid., 167.
56. Ibid., 171.
57. Ibid., 3.
58. Mann explains that he had taught in district schools for three seasons as a young man, had tutored in a college (Brown University) for two years, and had served as a school committeeman for eight years until he moved to Boston in 1833. Ibid., 8–9.
59. Ibid., 7.
60. Mann responds: "The Masters call it severe. I acknowledge it had the sharpest of all severities,—that of truth." This comment is found in Mann's last round in this pamphlet war, his "Answer to the 'Rejoinder' of Twenty-nine Boston Schoolmasters, part of the Thirty-one who published 'Remarks' on the Seventh Annual Report of the Secretary of the Massachusetts Board of Education" (Boston: Wm. B. Fowle and Nahum Capen, 1845), 17. This material can be found in the Horace Mann Papers and Pamphlets collection at the Massachusetts Historical Society.
61. Tharp, *Until Victory*, 214.
62. Mann, "Reply," 132.
63. Ibid., 127.

64. Ibid., 133.

65. Ibid., 135.

66. Quoted in Culver, *Horace Mann and Religion*, 231.

67. Mann wrote to Combe, "I have suffered severely in the conflict, so far as my feelings are concerned; and doubtless I have suffered considerably in my reputation." Mann, *Life of Horace Mann*, 241.

68. Culver, *Horace Mann and Religion*, 197–198.

69. Mann, *Life of Horace Mann*, 16–17.

70. Ibid., 479–480.

71. Ibid., 257.

72. Mann once wrote to Combe that he "preferred the religion of Black Hawk to the religion of John Calvin." Hinsdale, *Horace Mann and the Common School Revival*, 268.

73. Ibid.

74. Culver, *Horace Mann and Religion*, 22.

75. Ibid., 221.

76. Ibid.

77. This material can be found in the Horace Mann Papers and Pamphlets collection at the Massachusetts Historical Society, published in a single pamphlet entitled "The Common School Controversy; Consisting of Three Letters of the Secretary of the Board of Education of the State of Massachusetts, in Reply to Charges Preferred against the Board, by the Editor of the Christian Witness and by Edward A. Newton, Esq. of Pittsfield, Once a Member of the Board; to Which Are Added Extracts from the Daily Press in Regard to the Controversy" (Boston: J. N. Bradley and Co., 1844).

78. Ibid., 14.

79. "Never did he question the validity of his ideology. Nor would he tolerate less than total allegiance from others. Those who did not agree with him were against him and his cause." Messerli, *Horace Mann*, 282.

80. Mann, "Common School Controversy," 16.

81. Ibid., 23.

82. Ibid.

83. Ibid.

84. Ibid., 24.

85. Horace Mann, "Letter to the Rev. Matthew Hale Smith in Answer to His 'Reply' or 'Supplement'" (Boston: William B. Fowle, 1847), 12–14. This pamphlet can be found in the Horace Mann Papers and Pamphlets collection at the Massachusetts Historical Society.

86. Matthew Hale Smith, "Horace Mann and M. Hale Smith" (Boston, 30 April 1847), 8. This pamphlet can be found in the Horace Mann Papers and Pamphlets collection at the Massachusetts Historical Society. See, too, the earlier pamphlet by Smith, "Reply to the Sequel of Hon. Horace Mann, Being a Supplement to the

Bible, the Rod, and Religion, in Common Schools," 2nd ed. (Boston: J. M. Wittemore, 1847), available in the same collection. There he writes: "He [Mann] no where forgets to magnify himself, in all things; and his boastings have passed into a proverb" (32).

87. Smith, "Reply to the Sequel," 24.

88. Ibid., 26.

89. Mann, "Common School Controversy," 24–25.

90. Ibid., 31.

91. Horace Mann, "Sequel to the So Called Correspondence between the Rev. M. H. Smith and Horace Mann, Surreptitiously Published by Mr. Smith; Containing a Letter from Mr. Mann, Suppressed by Mr. Smith, with the Reply Therein Promised" (Boston: William B. Fowle, 1847), 31. This material is available in the Horace Mann Papers and Pamphlets collection at the Massachusetts Historical Society.

92. Mann, "Common School Controversy," 30.

93. Carl Kaestle and Maris Vinovskis have demonstrated that the growth of the common school did not significantly change the percentage of children attending schools in the nineteenth century. Rather, it constituted a shift away from a mix of local private and public tuition schools and toward tax-supported "free" common schools. Such a shift clearly presented the possibility of greater public and centralized oversight of education and less parental and local control. It is also of interest that Mann had hoped to see the establishment of a "Department of Public Instruction" as an office in the federal government. See Kaestle and Vinovskis, *Education and Social Change*, 9, 35; Mann, *Life of Horace Mann*, 259.

94. Mann, *Third Annual Report*, 70–71.

95. In the *First Annual Report*, Mann writes that schools should be "nurseries of intelligence and morality" (69).

96. Ibid., 65–66.

97. Mann, *Second Annual Report*, 75.

98. For example, Mann writes in the *Twelfth Annual Report*, "It is a lesson of unspeakable importance, to learn that nourishment and not pleasure is the primary object of food" (49). He also writes in this passage that a proper understanding of health "will restrain the caprices and follies of Fashion, in regard to dress and amusement, and subordinate its ridiculous excesses to the laws of health and decency."

99. Mann, *Life and Works*, 5:27.

100. Mann, *Life of Horace Mann*, 113.

101. Mann, *Lectures*, 253.

102. Mann, *First Annual Report*, 58.

103. Mann, *Eighth Annual Report*, 121.

104. Ibid., 124.

105. Mann lists moral goods ranging from "regard and sympathy for domestic animals" to "a passion for duty and a homage for all men who do it" when considering the potential moral uplift provided by songs. Ibid., 132.

106. Ibid., 126.
107. Ibid., 129.
108. Mann, *Lectures*, 47.
109. "I know it may be said . . . that the instinct or propensity of emulation is implanted in us by nature, and therefore to be cultivated like any other natural endowment. So, also, are the instincts of anger, and pride, and avarice, and war, and of other selfish or sensual passions, implanted in us by nature. One answer applies equally to them all. From some cause, they are too strong already. They do not need inflaming, but repression." Mann, *Fifth Annual Report*, 58–59.
110. See Mann, *Ninth Annual Report*, passage beginning on page 140.
111. Mann, *Fourth Annual Report*, 59.
112. Mann, *Ninth Annual Report*, 90.
113. It is important to remember that teachers in the nineteenth century lived in much more intimate proximity to their students than they usually do today; indeed, they often lived in their students' homes.
114. Mann, *Life of Horace Mann*, 263.
115. See Mann, *Twelfth Annual Report*, 26.
116. See Mann, *Fourth Annual Report*, 59.
117. Mann gives a stunning example of the moral message (or, in this case, a monstrously immoral message) that can be sent simply in the way a mathematics problem is formulated. This problem was taken from a contemporary arithmetic text: "A sea captain, on a voyage, had a crew of 30 men, half of whom were blacks. Being becalmed, on the passage, for a long time, their provisions began to fail, and the captain became satisfied that, unless the number of men was greatly diminished, all would perish of hunger before they reached any friendly port. He, therefore, proposed to the sailors that they should stand in a row on deck, and that every ninth man should be thrown overboard, until one half of the crew were thus destroyed. To this they all agreed. How should they stand *to save the whites?*" *Ninth Annual Report*, 127–128n.
118. Mann, *First Annual Report*, 64.
119. Mann, *Third Annual Report*, 59. Mann shared this view with John Locke. See Nathan Tarcov, *Locke's Education for Liberty* (Chicago: University of Chicago Press, 1984), 164–165.
120. "Seldom does woman emerge from her obscurity,—indeed, hardly should we know that she existed,—but for her appearance to grace the triumphs of the conqueror." Mann, *Third Annual Report*, 58–59.
121. Ibid., 59.
122. Ibid., 90.
123. Ibid., 91.
124. Mann, *Second Annual Report*, 73.
125. Mann, *Ninth Annual Report*, 156.
126. Mann, *First Annual Report*, 65.

127. Ibid., 64.
128. Mann, *Ninth Annual Report*, 64.
129. Ibid., 94.
130. Mann, *Lectures*, 118.
131. Mann, *Ninth Annual Report*, 64.
132. Mann, *Twelfth Annual Report*, 103.
133. Ibid., 98.
134. "The believer is bound to live by his belief under all circumstances, in the face of all perils, and at the cost of any sacrifice. But his standard of truth is the standard for himself alone; *never for his neighbor*." Ibid., 108.
135. Ibid., 111.
136. Ibid., 118.
137. Ibid., 121.
138. Ibid., 131.
139. Ibid., 124.
140. Ibid., 138.
141. McCluskey writes, "the charge that Mann himself was sectarian will not easily down." McCluskey, *Public Schools and Moral Education*, 88.
142. See Mann, *Life and Works*, 5:31.
143. Ibid., 32.
144. Ibid., 37.
145. Ibid., 59.
146. Ibid., 63.
147. Culver, for example, writes that despite the intensity of the attack on Mann, orthodox opposition to him "does not appear to have been widespread." Culver, *Horace Mann and Religion*, 198.
148. The most thoughtful critic of Mann along these lines is Neil McCluskey, a Jesuit priest. McCluskey contends, "The assumption of general Protestant or Christian unity that Mann followed was of questionable validity even during his years as secretary." McCluskey, *Public Schools and Moral Education*, 97.
149. Mann, *Eleventh Annual Report*, 49–58, 55.
150. Ibid., 86. Mann is not entirely clear on how these views fully respect or reflect the doctrine of original sin. He also argues (87) that those who believe in original sin, as well as those who believe in the environmental determinism of character, can still agree on the benefits of common schools. In short, he is not as forthright or consistent on this issue as he might be.
151. Ibid., 63.
152. Mann, *Tenth Annual Report*, 112.
153. Mann, *Twelfth Annual Report*, 89.
154. Mann, *Lectures*, 56.
155. Mann, *Eighth Annual Report*, 107.
156. Mann, *Lectures*, 52.

157. Ibid., 53.
158. Ibid.
159. Mann, *Life of Horace Mann*, 285.
160. Mann, *Twelfth Annual Report*, 138.
161. Mann, *Fifth Annual Report*, 65.
162. Mann, *Twelfth Annual Report*, 89.
163. See ibid., 86.
164. Ibid., 89. Mann apparently lacks self-awareness of the degree to which he himself is guilty of being an "intolerant zealot" in his political life.
165. See ibid., 118.
166. Mann, *Lectures*, 261.
167. Ibid., 207.
168. Mann, *First Annual Report*, 56.
169. "We want men who feel a sentiment, a *consciousness*, of brotherhood for the whole human race." Mann, *Lectures*, 105.
170. Mann, *Ninth Annual Report*, 64.
171. In the *Fifth Annual Report*, 66–69, Mann discusses the problem caused by two Shaker communities that withdrew their schools from broader community oversight (they refused to allow the district committees to visit, and so forth). He notes that this is not as bad as it could be, since there are no local minorities being oppressed in the Shaker-controlled schools. However, he also notes that the logic of the situation is one that will lead to disintegration of the common school into multiple sectarian schools, which was already happening in New York between Catholics and Protestants. Although he admits respect for the Shakers, he greatly fears the precedent they created.
172. Mann, *Eighth Annual Report*, 51.
173. Mann, *Twelfth Annual Report*, 55.
174. Ibid., 59. It is interesting to note that this report appeared in the same year, 1848, as the *Communist Manifesto*, with its demand for public education for all children. See Karl Marx and Friedrich Engels, *Selected Works*, vol. 1 (Moscow: Progressive Publishers, 1977), 127.
175. Mann, *Twelfth Annual Report*, 59.
176. Ibid., 60.
177. Mann, *Fifth Annual Report*, 102. Mann's point here is comparable to Lincoln's defense of free labor: "The man who labored for another last year, this year labors for himself, and next year he will hire others to labor for him." Abraham Lincoln, "Speech at Kalamazoo, Michigan," in *Speeches and Writings, 1832–1858* (New York: Library of America, 1989), 380.
178. Mann, *Tenth Annual Report*, 114.
179. Mann, *Seventh Annual Report*, 22.
180. Mann, *Fourth Annual Report*, 32.
181. Ibid., 36–37.

182. Ibid., 42.
183. Ibid.
184. Mann, *Fifth Annual Report*, 78.
185. Ibid., 82. Perhaps Mann was thinking of Aristotle's comment about education in the final book of *Politics*: "It is completely inappropriate for magnanimous and free people to be always asking what use something is." Aristotle, *Politics* (Indianapolis and Cambridge: Hackett, 1998), 230.
186. Mann, *Fifth Annual Report*, 81.
187. See, too, Mann, *Eleventh Annual Report*, 114.
188. Mann, *Fifth Annual Report*, 82.
189. Ibid., 101.
190. Maris A. Vinovskis, *Education, Society, and Economic Opportunity* (New Haven, CT: Yale University Press, 1995), 79.
191. "Thanks to the work of Mann and his supporters the economic productivity of elementary education was recognized and praised by the time of the Civil War." Ibid.
192. Mann, *Fifth Annual Report*, 81.
193. Ibid., 81–82.
194. Ibid., 120.
195. Ibid., 108.
196. Orestes Brownson, "The Second Annual Report of the Board of Education, Together with the Second Annual Report of the Secretary of the Board," *Boston Quarterly Review* 2 (October 1839): 393–434.
197. Ibid., 403.
198. Ibid., 404.
199. Ibid., 405.
200. Ibid., 408–409.
201. Ibid., 405.
202. Ibid., 412.
203. Ibid., 416.
204. Ibid.
205. Morgan, *Horace Mann*, 17.
206. For a defense of Brownson's appeal to localism and parental control of education, see Christopher Lasch, *The True and Only Heaven* (New York: W. W. Norton, 1991), 187–189.
207. Brownson, "Second Annual Report," 418–419.
208. When the governor and the legislature moved against the board in 1840, Mann referred to his legislative opponents as "political madmen" and "partisan men," and he accused the Democratic governor of committing "that high treason to the truth which consists in perverting great principles to selfish ends." Messerli, *Horace Mann*, 329–330.
209. "Horace Mann and the Whigs never fully appreciated the depth of the fears of

the Democrats that the creation of a state agency to do good might eventually result in a serious danger to freedom within the Republic." Kaestle and Vinovskis, *Education and Social Change*, 231.

210. "When will society, like a mother, take care of *all* her children?" Mann, *Life of Horace Mann*, 73. Perhaps "maternalistic" would be more accurate.

211. Robert Westbrook argues that Mann (like other common school reformers) was merely a "conservative Whig" who aimed to use the common schools to control the common people. This perspective, however, not only underestimates Mann's democratic egalitarianism; it also profoundly underestimates both the fears and ambitions driving his work and writings. Mann's focus is not on protecting the privileged from the working class; it is on saving the entire democratic citizenry from itself. See Robert Westbrook, *Democratic Hope* (Ithaca, NY: Cornell University Press, 2005), 222–223.

212. Vinovskis shrewdly observes, "Instead of seeing mass education as the result of mid-nineteenth-century industrial development, it is more accurate to view it as a continuation of the colonial Puritan activities to ensure that everyone was able to read the Bible." Vinovskis, *Education, Society, and Economic Opportunity*, 77.

213. Nathaniel Hawthorne, "A Bell's Biography," in *Tales and Sketches* (New York: Library of America, 1982), 480.

Chapter 4. Higher Education

1. Joy Elmer Morgan, *Horace Mann at Antioch* (Washington, DC: Horace Mann Centennial Fund, National Education Association, 1938), 198.
2. Ibid., 191.
3. Ibid., 198.
4. Ibid., 200.
5. Ibid., 203.
6. Ibid., 209.
7. Ibid., 205.
8. Ibid., 211.
9. Ibid., 235.
10. Ibid., 222.
11. Ibid.
12. Ibid., 225.
13. Ibid., 230.
14. Ibid., 247.
15. Ibid., 241.
16. Ibid., 251–252.
17. Ibid., 250.
18. Ibid., 248.
19. Ibid., 250.

20. Ibid., 245.
21. Ibid., 258.
22. Ibid., 240.
23. Cremin, *The Republic and the School*, 25.
24. Messerli, *Horace Mann*, 576.
25. Mann, *Lectures*, 285.
26. Morgan, *Horace Mann at Antioch*, 498.
27. "So the youth of our country ought to receive the prerogatives of a higher education, not at all as they belong to this or that religious sect or denomination, but wholly and exclusively as they give promise of becoming honorable and virtuous citizens." Ibid., 499.
28. Mann's experience in Congress solidified not only his hatred of slavery but also his hatred of compromise with injustice. This, in turn, reinforced and strengthened his view that much of our political leadership (not just that from the South) was terribly corrupt. He saw Webster's support of the Compromise of 1850, for example, as nothing less than a treasonous act of political opportunism and self-promotion. His Washington experience, in short, encouraged Mann's belief that our democracy was deteriorating ("truth compels me to acknowledge that, during the last three quarters of a century, our course, in this country, has been downward") and that we required a renewed moral elite to lead and reshape our democracy: "In selecting men to be our political leaders, we have sometimes committed the gravest moral error. We have assumed the falsity of a distinction between a man's public and his private life. We have supposed that the same individual might be a bad man and a good citizen; might be a patriot and an inebriate, a faithful officer and a debauchee, at the same time; might serve his country during 'office hours,' and the powers of darkness the rest of the twenty-four. But I say, as of old, no man can serve God and mammon." Horace Mann, *Slavery: Letters and Speeches* (Boston: B. B. Mussey, 1851), 473, 517. For comments about Webster, see "Speech, Delivered at Lancaster, MA, May 19, 1851" (473–522), "Speech, Delivered in Boston, April 8, 1851" (523–535), and "Speech, Delivered at Worcester, Sept. 16, 1851" (536–564).
29. Mann, *A Few Thoughts on the Powers and Duties of Women*, 75.
30. Recall that Mann was impressed by the ability of Prussian men to effectively teach young children. In the long run, he appears to have viewed the Prussian example more as an exception to the rule rather than a challenge to the rule itself.
31. Mann, *A Few Thoughts on the Powers and Duties of Women*, 14.
32. Ibid.
33. Ibid., 15.
34. Ibid.
35. Ibid., 24.
36. Ibid., 101.
37. Mann, *Life and Works*, 5:314. In *A Few Thoughts on the Powers and Duties of Women*, Mann comments, "Politics, at its best, is but a crude instrument of reform"

(99). As we have seen, this perspective informs Mann's entire career as an educator. When he accepted the nomination to replace John Quincy Adams in Congress, however, he temporarily entertained higher hopes for politics: "The enactment of laws which shall cover waste territory, to be applied to the myriads of human beings who are hereafter to occupy that territory, is a work which seems to precede and outrank even education itself." Mann, *Slavery*, 9.

38. Mann, *Life of Horace Mann*, 424.

39. Mann, *A Few Thoughts on the Powers and Duties of Women*, 50.

40. Morgan, *Horace Mann at Antioch*, 258.

41. Ibid., 257.

42. Ibid., 259.

43. Ibid., 274.

44. Mann, *Life of Horace Mann*, 366.

45. See ibid., 533–539.

46. "It is said we have no revivals here. The reason of this is the serious and thoughtful character of our students on religious subjects. Take a set of drinking, gambling, swearing, blaspheming, and godless students, come upon them suddenly, make them see their sinful condition, and they will be frightened into as vehement a demonstration of their alarms as they had before given of their profligacies and revellings. But this effect can never be produced upon a company of thoughtful, serious young people, whose minds have been systematically turned in the direction of their religious condition, and to whom the ideas of their duty and their destiny are familiar, and who have led an exemplary life. This is precisely the case with our students. They do not receive religious excitements like savages, but like men of intelligence and morals, and generally pure and correct purposes. This is the true explanation of the complaint made against us." Ibid., 539.

47. Morgan, *Horace Mann at Antioch*, 414.

48. Ibid., 402–405.

49. Ibid., 422, 423.

50. Ibid., 414.

51. Ibid., 408.

52. Ibid.

53. Ibid., 413.

54. Ibid., 316.

55. Ibid., 313.

56. Ibid., 297.

57. Ibid., 314.

58. In addition, no contemporary religion is justified in believing in miracles. Science has taught us there is no chance in the universe, Mann argues, so any supernatural religion can be experienced only by ignorant people. Horace Mann, *Twelve Sermons* (Boston: Ticknor and Fields, 1961), 69–70.

59. Mann, *Life of Horace Mann*, 504.

60. Ibid., 420.

61. “It is known that no precocious attachment that may spring up [between a male and female student] can be consummated until after the college life is completed without forfeiting all connection with the college itself.” Morgan, *Horace Mann at Antioch*, 260.

62. In an 1858 letter to Combe, Mann wrote, “When I have an interview with a reckless or perverse student, and pass into his consciousness, and try to make him see mine, I always shed tears, I cannot help it; and there is a force in honest tears not to be found in logic.” Messerli, *Horace Mann*, 569.

63. Mann, *Twelve Sermons*, 93.

64. Morgan, *Horace Mann at Antioch*, 332.

65. Straker, *Unseen Harvest*, 15.

66. Morgan, *Horace Mann at Antioch*, 334.

67. Ibid., 336.

68. Ibid., 337.

69. Ibid., 326.

70. Ibid., 343.

71. See ibid., 346–349. Mann’s understanding of legal ethics does not include what we think of today as a commitment to a strictly adversarial legal process in which even the guilty are rightly defended with the greatest vigor allowed by law.

72. Ibid., 340.

73. Ibid., 325.

74. Ibid., 341.

75. Ibid., 358.

76. Ibid., 389.

77. Mann reacted with deep anger and moral indignation when a student newspaper poked fun at him and reported that Antioch students had visited a local brothel. Four students were expelled over this incident, and Mann was incensed that students refused to inform on their peers. See Tharp, *Until Victory*, 300–301.

78. Mann, *Life of Horace Mann*, vi.

79. Mann, *Twelve Sermons*, 120.

80. Ibid., 122.

81. Ibid., 124.

82. Morgan, *Horace Mann at Antioch*, 523.

83. Ibid., 525.

84. Ibid., 526.

85. Ibid., 524.

86. Messerli, *Horace Mann*, 570. Mann also appears to have forgotten his own criticism of Dorothy Dix’s extreme moralism when she worked with the Lexington Normal School in Massachusetts. Ibid., 582.

87. Morgan, *Horace Mann at Antioch*, 378.

88. Ibid., 291.

89. John Stuart Mill, "Inaugural Address Delivered to the University of St. Andrews, 1867," in *The Collected Works of John Stuart Mill*, vol. 21, *Essays on Equality, Law, and Education*, ed. John M. Robson (Toronto: University of Toronto Press; London: Routledge and Kegan Paul, 1984), 218.

90. Ibid.

91. Ibid., 219.

92. Messerli, *Horace Mann*, 557.

93. Ibid., 543.

94. "Can anything deserve the name of a good education which does not include literature and science too?" Mill, "Inaugural Address," 221. Mann was criticized by Cornelius Conway Felton, a professor and future president of Harvard, for undervaluing classical studies and overvaluing natural science in the Antioch curriculum. Straker, *Unseen Harvest*, 16.

95. Mill, "Inaugural Address," 227–230.

96. Ibid., 226.

97. Ibid., 255.

98. Ibid., 256.

99. Elaine Scarry, like Mill, argues, "At the moment we see something beautiful, we undergo a radical decentering." In fact, she takes the argument a step further and argues that beauty "incites deliberation" and "is a starting place for education." Elaine Scarry, *On Beauty and Being Just* (Princeton, NJ: Princeton University Press, 1999), 111, 28, 31.

100. Mann, *A Few Thoughts for a Young Man*, 50.

101. Ibid.

102. See note 99 above.

103. Mill, "Inaugural Address," 243.

104. Ibid., 243–244.

105. Ibid., 244.

106. Ibid., 247.

107. Ibid., 248.

108. Ibid., 249.

109. Ibid., 257.

110. The normative modesty of this position is much more complex and plausible than Daniel Cottom gives Mill credit for when he asks, "is there anyone who can still take this image of the 'better man' as anything but the product of a dangerously narrow and parochial vision?" Cottom makes a more compelling point when he observes that Mill's ideal must be "massively counterintuitive" to "anyone who has ever spent any considerable period of time in the company of academics." Daniel Cottom, *Why Education Is Useless* (Philadelphia: University of Pennsylvania Press, 2003), 35.

111. Robert L. Straker, *Horace Mann and Others* (Yellow Springs, OH: Antioch Press, 1963), 41.

112. Mann had to lecture for income, since Antioch was chronically unable to pay him his salary. Messerli reports that in 1856 Mann suffered some sort of breakdown, including a partial paralysis of speech, the uttering of nonsense words, and the inability to control himself. Tharp reports that Mary begged Mann to leave Antioch. See Messerli, *Horace Mann*, 577; Tharp, *Until Victory*, 287.

113. Hinsdale, *Horace Mann and the Common School Revival*, 242. Hinsdale concludes that Mann "died a martyr to Antioch College." Ibid., 264.

Chapter 5. Democracy and Education

1. John Dewey, *The School and Society*, in *Middle Works*, vol. 1 (Carbondale: Southern Illinois University Press, 1976), 17.

2. Ibid.

3. "For wherever you find a social reactionary there you find an enthusiast for either classical learning on the one hand or technical or specialized training on the other—usually both." John Dewey, "The Modern Trend toward Vocational Education in Its Effect upon the Professional and Non-Professional Studies of the University," in *Middle Works*, vol. 10 (Carbondale: Southern Illinois University Press, 1985), 157.

4. John Dewey, "Our Educational Ideal in Wartime," in *Middle Works*, 10:181.

5. "So-called cultural education has always been reserved for a small limited class as a luxury. Even at that it has been very largely an education for vocations, especially for those vocations which happened to be esteemed as indicating social superiority or which were useful to the ruling powers of the given period." John Dewey, "Learning to Earn: The Place of Vocational Education in a Comprehensive Scheme of Public Education," in *Middle Works*, 10:144.

6. John Dewey, *Democracy and Education*, in *Middle Works*, vol. 9 (Carbondale: Southern Illinois University Press, 1985), 12.

7. Dewey, *School and Society*, 18.

8. Ibid., 19.

9. Ibid., 37.

10. Ibid., 10.

11. Dewey, *Democracy and Education*, 12.

12. Ibid., 44.

13. Alan Ryan dryly observes: "The freedom at which liberal education aims is the freedom that comes from understanding our own intellectual resources and being fully in possession of them. This is an ideal that animated Aristotle as well as Arnold and John Stuart Mill; James displayed it in person. It was not something that Dewey had much feeling for." Alan Ryan, "No Consensus in Sight," in Bruce A. Kimball, *The Condition of American Liberal Education*, ed. Robert Orrill (New York: College Entrance Examination Board, 1995), 246.

14. Dewey, *Democracy and Education*, 49.

15. Dewey's perspective provides a significant contrast to Jonathan Kozol's irritation with the contemporary pedagogical emphasis on encouraging group solidarity, cooperation, and identity: "Many of the brightest, most creative, independent-minded, and ambitious kids I know are not 'team players' and don't *want* to be and, indeed, would lose the very essence of what makes them full, complex, and interesting people if they were." Jonathan Kozol, *The Shame of the Nation* (New York: Three Rivers Press, 2005), 106.

16. Dewey, *Democracy and Education*, 82.

17. Ibid., 129.

18. Ibid., 127.

19. Ibid., 159.

20. Ibid., 196, 227.

21. Ibid., 204.

22. Ibid., 231, 233.

23. Leo Strauss, "Liberal Education and Mass Democracy," in *Higher Education and Modern Democracy: The Crisis of the Few and Many*, ed. Martin Meyerson and Robert A. Goldwin (Chicago: Rand McNally, 1967), 89.

24. Macedo, *Diversity and Distrust*, 139.

25. In preparation for the upcoming centennial of Mann's assumption of the secretaryship, Dewey published a brief article in 1936 entitled "Horace Mann Today." He explained that although American society had changed so much since Mann's time that we needed new conceptions of democracy and education to fit the twentieth-century world, Mann's spirit continued to be exactly right because he understood the fundamentally and completely civic nature of education. "But our chief problem is to find out what is the business of the school in relation to the democratic way of life and by what means that business shall be executed. The issue of the relation of education to our national life and institutions still remains." Dewey, *Later Works*, 11:389. Robert Westbrook is concerned that Dewey "had relatively little to say about the particulars of civic education." This could be true only to the degree that his educational philosophy was simply too vague or poorly defined for implementation, since the project itself had no obvious aims beyond the civic. Westbrook, *Democratic Hope*, 231.

26. Benjamin Barber, *An Aristocracy of Everyone* (New York: Ballantine Books, 1992), 15.

27. Ibid., 222. R. Freeman Butts expands the point to include primary and public schooling as well: "We need to put citizenship values at the heart of American education." R. Freeman Butts, *The Civic Mission in Educational Reform* (Stanford, CA: Hoover Institution Press, 1989), 225.

28. Barber, *Aristocracy of Everyone*, 229.

29. Ibid., 247, 248.

30. Ibid., 251.

31. Lee Benson, Ira Harkavy, and John Puckett, *Dewey's Dream: Universities and Democracies in an Age of Educational Reform* (Philadelphia: Temple University Press, 2007), 21.

32. Ibid., 29.

33. Ibid., 45.

34. Ibid., 82.

35. Ibid., 86–87.

36. Callan, *Creating Citizens*, 1–3.

37. Ibid., 7.

38. Ibid., 3.

39. Ibid., 133–134.

40. Macedo, *Diversity and Distrust*, ix.

41. Ibid., 39.

42. William Galston, *Liberal Purposes* (New York: Cambridge University Press, 1991), 242.

43. Will Kymlicka writes, "I believe the schools have an unavoidable role [in civic education], in part because no other social institution can take their place." Rob Reich agrees: "The fact of pluralism . . . makes the common school necessary in that the schoolhouse is perhaps the best vehicle available to the state to unite a diverse citizenry under common ideals and to help forge a common national identity." E. D. Hirsch is even more enthusiastic about what he takes to be the historic successes in the civic education provided by public schools: "The strong patriotic sense of most Americans is not an accident but the fortunate residue of a time when the writers of American schoolbooks deliberately instilled common ideals and shared knowledge." Will Kymlicka, *Politics in the Vernacular* (Oxford and New York: Oxford University Press, 2001), 300; Rob Reich, "How and Why to Support Common Schooling and Educational Choice at the Same Time," *Journal of the Philosophy of Education* 41 (2007): 711; E. D. Hirsch, *The Making of Americans: Democracy and Our Schools* (New Haven, CT: Yale University Press, 2009), 66.

44. http://www.nytimes.com/2008/06/09/arts/09sand.html?scp=4&sq=Justice%20Sandra%20Day%20O%27Connor%202008&st=cse.

45. http://legaltimes.typepad.com/blt/2009/05/souter-republic-is-lost-unless-civic-education-improves-.html.

46. According to British philosopher Brian Barry, the benefits of education for individuals in a democratic society are so obvious that we need only appeal to the government's paternalistic obligation to provide this good for all citizens to justify public education. Why, he asks, do Americans require such a crass and convoluted instrumental justification for the universal education of children, when it is clear that such an explanation is entirely unnecessary? Barry suggests that it is our antipathy to governmental paternalism that leads us to justify universal education on the grounds of civic education—only if the stability of the political community is at stake do we agree to give the government such power and authority. My suspicion is that

the explanations offered above, however, are sufficient to explain the democratic anxiety from which our preoccupation with civic education has grown. See Barry, *Culture and Equality*, 222.

47. Diane Ravitch and Joseph P. Viteritti, eds., "Introduction," in *Making Good Citizens* (New Haven, CT: Yale University Press, 2001), 5.

48. Even conservatives and religious traditionalists who object to what they see as the overwhelmingly liberal educational establishment and hope to dismantle the public or common school through voucher systems and other comparable policy initiatives are sometimes willing to appeal to civic education's benefits growing from a diverse array of school options (and not simply build their case on the questionable ground of absolute parental authority over the content of children's education). Michael McConnell, for example, writes: "It thus appears that the apparent conflict between liberal pluralism and democratic education may be illusory. A pluralist approach to educational institutions, like the pluralist approach to religion adopted 200 years ago, may better achieve the purposes of democratic education as well as better comporting with the disestablishmentarian principles of the regime." McConnell points to empirical evidence that parochial schools are more effective than public schools at "inculcating the virtues and values essential for democratic citizenship." He also notes that there is no evidence to support the claim that racially integrated schools necessarily lead to increased racial tolerance: "Sadly, the experience of integrated education has more often *increased* than *decreased* the levels of racial prejudice." Michael W. McConnell, "Educational Disestablishment: Why Democratic Values are Ill-Served by Democratic Control of Schooling," in *Nomos XLIII: Moral and Political Education*, ed. Stephen Macedo and Yael Tamir (New York: NYU Press, 2002), 133, 127, 131.

49. Richard Niemi and Jane Junn, *Civic Education: What Makes Students Learn?* (New Haven, CT: Yale University Press, 1998), 13.

50. "The most important message to come out of our study of the political knowledge of high school seniors is that the school civics curriculum does indeed enhance what and how much they know about America government and politics." Ibid., 147.

51. Ibid., 88.

52. Norman Nie and D. Sunshine Hillygus, "Education and Democratic Citizenship," in Ravitch and Viteritti, *Making Good Citizens*, 41.

53. Derek Bok, *Our Underachieving Colleges* (Princeton, NJ: Princeton University Press, 2006), 141.

54. Nie and Hillygus, "Education and Democratic Citizenship," 47.

55. Ibid., 46.

56. Norman H. Nie, Jane Junn, Kenneth Stehlik-Barry, *Education and Democratic Citizenship in America* (Chicago: University of Chicago Press, 1996), 194.

57. James Bernard Murphy, "Against Civic Schooling," *Social Philosophy and Policy* 21 (2004): 239.

58. Ibid., 244. It is striking to note the degree to which advocates of civic educa-

tion either ignore or sidestep this issue of the empirical effectiveness of their education programs. See, for example, Macedo, *Diversity and Distrust*, 201, 324n28.

59. Brighouse, *School Choice and Social Justice*, 61.

60. "While education is a public good, it is its status as a private good to which all have a right that obliges us to provide it." Ibid., 45.

61. Harry Brighouse, *On Education* (London and New York: Routledge, 2006), 37. In light of this point, Messerli's comment that "the education of a single child held no interest for" Horace Mann is both compelling and disturbing. Mann was so concerned for the stability and virtue of the political community that he viewed individuals as a means to this end rather than as all educators should view them—as ends in themselves. See Messerli, *Horace Mann*, 342.

62. Barry, *Culture and Equality*, 231.

63. Hannah Arendt, "The Crisis in Education," in *Between Past and Future* (New York: Penguin, 1968), 195.

64. Murphy, "Against Civic Schooling," 248. Robin Barrow shares Murphy's concern about the corruption of the intellectual mission of the schools: "My concern is that both in theory and practice the educational mission of the school is being eroded or ignored as a result of a disproportionate emphasis on socialisation. The pursuit of social harmony and a commitment to social engineering in the schools are taking precedence over a concern to educate each individual as fully and effectively as possible." Robin Barrow, "Common Schooling and the Need for Distinction," *Journal of the Philosophy of Education* 41 (2007): 565.

65. Murphy, "Against Civic Schooling," 250.

66. Barry, *Culture and Equality*, 231.

67. Murphy, "Against Civic Schooling," 253. Civic education, of course, is not always or necessarily conceived of as patriotic education; in many formulations, it may emphasize civic virtues such as toleration, political engagement, and so forth.

68. Ibid., 261.

69. Barry, *Culture and Equality*, 247.

70. Macedo, *Diversity and Distrust*, 16.

71. "If you're not in the pursuit-of-truth business, you should not be in the university." Stanley Fish, *Save the World on Your Own Time* (New York: Oxford University Press, 2008), 20.

72. Ibid., 67.

73. Ibid., 53.

74. Brighouse, *School Choice and Social Justice*, 65.

75. "We ought to be confident that we are contributing significantly to civic virtue merely by attempting to impart to our students genuine knowledge and, in particular, civic knowledge." Murphy, "Against Civic Schooling," 262.

76. John Henry Newman, *The Idea of the University* (New Haven, CT: Yale University Press, 1996), 81.

77. Ibid., 78.

78. Ibid., 125.

79. Ibid., 125–126.

80. As mentioned in chapter 4 (see note 110), Daniel Cottom has vigorously objected to this claim that education, and in particular liberal education in the humanities, has a potentially positive moral and civic influence on students. Providing an accounting of the moral and civic crimes committed by well- and liberally educated individuals, he writes, "Who can dare to assert that education is useful, much less that it improves us, in this historical context?" In fact, he claims, "one has to become a barbarian to argue that literature makes us better people." After this flamboyant charge, however, Cottom concludes that professors are not doing their jobs if "we are not doing our best to create dissatisfaction among" students. He means by this that good teachers make their students critically aware of the hypocrisy, injustice, and general disingenuous nastiness in the world, which is another way of saying, of course, that they will become better citizens (in, presumably, the true sense of the word). See Cottom, *Why Education Is Useless*, 25, 27, 206.

81. It is not my intention to provide an account of what such democratic equality means and requires in the context of primary, secondary, and higher education.

82. "Unfortunately, civic education aimed at civic virtue turns out to be no more truly ecumenical than was nondenominational Protestantism." Murphy, "Against Civic Schooling," 228.

83. See a summary of recent findings on this issue in the *New York Times* at http://www.nytimes.com/2008/11/03/books/03infl.html?scp=6&sq=professors%20political%20opinions%202008&st=cse.

84. Robert Maynard Hutchins, *The Higher Learning in America* (New Haven, CT, and London: Yale University Press, 1936), 66.

85. "A classic is a book that is contemporary in every age. That is why it is a classic." Ibid., 78.

86. Ibid., 67.

87. Ibid., 85.

88. John Dewey, "President Hutchins' Proposals to Remake Higher Education," in *Later Works*, 11:400.

89. "Any scheme based on the existence of ultimate first principles, with their dependent hierarchy of subsidiary principles, does not escape authoritarianism by calling the principles 'truths.' I would not intimate that the author has any sympathy with fascism. But basically his idea as to the proper course to be taken is akin to the distrust of freedom and the consequent appeal to *some* fixed authority that is now overrunning the world. There is implicit in every assertion of fixed and eternal first truths the necessity for some *human* authority to decide, in this world of conflicts, just what these truths are and how they shall be taught. This problem is conveniently ignored. Doubtless much may be said for selecting Aristotle and St. Thomas as competent promulgators of first truths. But it took the authority of a powerful ecclesiastic organization to secure their wide recognition. Others may prefer Hegel, or

Karl Marx, or even Mussolini as the seers of first truths; and there are those who prefer Nazism." Ibid.

90. Ibid., 401.

91. Robert M. Hutchins, "Grammar, Rhetoric, and Mr. Dewey," in Dewey, *Later Works*, 11:596.

92. In 1915 Dewey published *German Philosophy and Politics*, in which he argues that "absolutism" in German philosophy has both reflected and exacerbated German political authoritarianism and imperialist aggression. He reissued the book in 1942 in response to World War II and the Nazi regime. He continued to be persuaded, obviously, of the intimate and necessary correlation between political commitments and philosophical style. See John Dewey, *German Philosophy and Politics*, in *Middle Works*, vol. 8 (Carbondale: Southern Illinois University Press, 1985), 135–204. See also the thoughtful and critical comments about Dewey's thesis in this work by Sidney Hook in the volume's introduction, xxvii–xxxi.

93. As Donald Levine points out, "Hutchins *never* endorsed the view of truth as a fixed body of doctrine that was secured by an elite and imposed dogmatically upon hapless students." Donald N. Levine, *Powers of the Mind: The Reinvention of Liberal Learning in America* (Chicago: University of Chicago Press, 2006), 77.

94. "Common frankness requires that it be stated that this account of the origin of philosophies claiming to deal with absolute Being in a systematic way has been given with malice prepense. It seems to me that this genetic method of approach is a more effective way of undermining this type of philosophic theorizing than any attempt at logical refutation could be. . . . Considered in this way, the history of philosophy will take on a new significance. What is lost from the standpoint of would-be science is regained from the standpoint of humanity. Instead of disputes of rivals about the nature of reality, we have the scene of human clash of social purpose and aspirations. Instead of impossible attempts to transcend experience, we have the significant record of the efforts of men to formulate the things of experience to which they are most deeply and passionately attached." John Dewey, *Reconstruction in Philosophy*, in *Middle Works*, vol. 12 (Carbondale: Southern Illinois University Press, 1988), 93–94.

95. C. S. Lewis, *The Screwtape Letters* (New York: New American Library, 1988), 113.

96. Hutchins, "Grammar, Rhetoric, and Mr. Dewey," 597.

97. John Dewey, "The Higher Learning in America," in *Later Works*, 11:402–407.

98. Robert M. Hutchins, *The University of Utopia* (Chicago: University of Chicago Press, 1953), 28–29.

99. Ibid., 15–16.

100. Ibid., 16.

101. Ibid., 56.

102. Ibid., 67.

103. For a contemporary defense of the educational focus on the Western canon

of "great books," see Anthony Kronman, *Education's End: Why Our Colleges and Universities Have Given Up on the Meaning of Life* (New Haven, CT: Yale University Press, 2007). Although Hutchins limited his philosophical vision to the conventional list of canonical Western texts, there is no reason to believe that the basic structure of his argument, as I have presented it here, requires such a limited understanding of the relevant philosophical and literary resources to be investigated in a satisfactory liberal education. On the contrary, the intellectual project is probably best thought of in much more expansive, cosmopolitan terms.

104. Thomas Ehrlich, "Dewey versus Hutchins: The Next Round," in *Education and Democracy: Re-imagining Liberal Learning in America*, ed. Robert Orrill (New York: College Entrance Examination Board, 1997), 227.

105. Ibid., 259.

106. Ibid., 257.

107. Ibid., 255. It is hard not to note the institutional interest higher education administrators have in expanding the consumer base for higher education.

108. Ibid., 233.

109. Ehrlich himself represents an increasingly elite cadre of higher education administrators with impressively expanding professional control over the practices and institutional commitments of our colleges and universities.

110. Ehrlich, "Dewey versus Hutchins," 237.

111. Ibid., 259.

112. Ibid., 260.

113. It is certainly true that universities, in Hutchins's view, should be much smaller and more elite than Ehrlich would prefer. Hutchins claimed that this was necessary to prevent them from getting sidetracked from their central purpose of advanced academic study. He also held, however, that our primary and secondary schools should be designed to provide a more effective general liberal education than they currently do (rather than assuming that liberal education is the responsibility of colleges and universities). The key point is that Hutchins was committed to the idea that a conventional liberal education is the "education every free citizen . . . ought to have." Robert Maynard Hutchins, *Education for Freedom* (Baton Rouge: Louisiana State University Press, 1943), 67.

114. Alexander W. Astin, "Liberal Education and Democracy: The Case for Prgamatism," in Orrill, *Education and Democracy*, 208–209.

115. Ibid., 209.

116. Ibid., 221.

117. Ibid., 213.

118. Ibid., 216.

119. Ibid.

120. Ibid., 220.

121. Ibid.

122. Ibid., 215.

123. Amy Gutmann, "Civic Education and Social Diversity," *Ethics* 105 (April 1995): 557–579.
124. Macedo, *Diversity and Distrust*, 15.
125. Ibid., 2.
126. Callan, *Creating Citizens*, 7.
127. Ibid., 13.
128. During Dewey's lifetime, the report of the Harvard Committee on General Education had argued that "democracy, however much by ensuring the right to differ it may foster difference . . . yet depends equally on the binding ties of common standards." Therefore, "a supreme need of American education is for a unifying purpose and idea." Harvard University Committee on the Objectives of a General Education in a Free Society, *General Education in a Free Society* (Cambridge, MA: Harvard University Press, 1945), 12, 43.
129. See John Dewey, *A Common Faith*, in *Later Works*, vol. 9 (Carbondale: Southern Illinois University Press, 1989), 1–58. See chapter 2 of my *Citizenship and Democratic Doubt* for a discussion of the consensus Dewey hoped to reach.
130. "What belongs in education is what helps the student to learn to think for himself, to form an independent judgment, and to take his part as a responsible adult." Robert Maynard Hutchins, *The Conflict in Education in a Democratic Society* (New York: Harper and Brothers, 1953), 13.
131. David Foster Wallace, *This Is Water* (New York: Little, Brown, 2009), 14.
132. Ibid., 44. In this passage, Wallace argues that his position is less moral ("This is not a matter of virtue") than pragmatically oriented toward the cultivation of a meaningful, rewarding life. But his overall position is clearly moral (or "virtuous") if we mean by this that he is concerned with cultivating a life worth living.
133. Ibid., 60.
134. Ibid., 120.
135. Callan, *Creating Citizens*, 43.
136. Education built on intellectual integrity is unlikely to produce a stable ideological consensus and thus will always represent something of a threat to civic educators. Historian Edmund Morgan, in an essay about the subversive impact of the new library in the early years of Yale College, observes, "If we allow young men and women to read and think, we must expect that their thoughts will not be our thoughts and that they will violate much that we hold dear." Democracy may require a thoughtful, knowledgeable, rational—in short, educated—citizenry, but one quality of such a citizenry will be precisely its unpredictability, its freedom, for better or worse, to continually invent and reinvent itself. Edmund S. Morgan, *American Heroes* (New York: W. W. Norton, 2009), 34.
137. Kwame Anthony Appiah, *Cosmopolitanism* (New York: W. W. Norton, 2006), 85.
138. Murphy, "Against Civic Schooling," 233. Murphy observes, "Admittedly, it requires truly heroic forbearance to refrain from taking advantage of the naiveté of small children who are a captive audience for all manner of idealistic moral and civic

uplift" (264). This comment seems particularly poignant in light of Mann's emphasis that children are much more susceptible to moral education than adults. Nancy Rosenblum also notes that much of the debate concerning civic education in schools can "undervalue democratic education outside of schools, in civil society generally, lifelong." Nancy Rosenblum, "Pluralism and Democratic Education: Stopping Short by Stopping with Schools," in Macedo and Tamir, *Nomos XLIII*, 163.

139. One need only look at the interior books of Plato's *Republic* or the final book of Aristotle's *Politics*, for example, to appreciate the ancient concern with the political socialization of children.

140. "English courses proved to be one of the major arenas for 'informal civics education.'" Pamela Johnston Conover and Donald D. Searing, "A Political Socialization Perspective," in *Rediscovering the Democratic Purposes of Education*, ed. Lorraine M. McDonnell, P. Michael Timpane, and Roger Benjamin (Lawrence: University Press of Kansas, 2000), 111.

141. As Perry Miller writes, "Unless [the educator] is to surrender entirely his function, and to become merely an instrument of national policy, he must keep alive a passion for knowledge that is first and foremost its own excuse for being, and take the position that under present conditions, this insistence is his major responsibility to the future of democracy." Miller, *Responsibility of Mind*, 96. The disturbing degree to which the aggressive use of our educational system to promote political programs and values has perverted the intellectual integrity of American schooling is a matter of clear historical record. For a discussion of nineteenth- and early-twentieth-century education, see Hofstadter, *Anti-Intellectualism in American Life*, pt. 5. For a discussion of these problems in our own time, see Diane Ravitch, *The Language Police: How Pressure Groups Restrict What Students Learn* (New York: Vintage Books, 2004).

142. "A school that sticks to its job of intellectual training is not thereby indifferent to the vocational needs of its students, to their physical development, or to the problem of moral conduct. Such a school merely recognizes that it must deal with these matters within the context provided by its own characteristic activity." Arthur Bestor, *Educational Wastelands: The Retreat from Learning in Our Public Schools* (Urbana and Chicago: University of Illinois Press, 1953, 1985), 15.

143. Jonathan Kozol, *Savage Inequalities* (New York: Crown, 1991). The terrible power of these inequalities is poignantly illustrated by Kozol's report of a girl in East St. Louis who asks, when reflecting on the radically different nature of the schools in her neighborhood and those in more affluent sections of the city, "Are we citizens of East St. Louis or America?" (30).

144. Kozol, *Shame of the Nation*, 54.

145. See, for example, Martha Minow, Richard A. Shweder, and Hazel Rose Markus, *Just Schools: Pursuing Equality in Societies of Difference* (New York: Russell Sage Foundation, 2008).

146. Claudia Goldin and Lawrence Katz report that the "actual inequality in per

pupil expenditure was far greater in the past than today." Be this as it may, the inequalities between affluent and poor communities remain, in many cases, dramatic. Claudia Goldin and Lawrence F. Katz, *The Race between Education and Technology* (Cambridge, MA: Harvard University Press, 2008), 339.

147. A recent Brookings Institution study suggests that if the least advantaged children had access to the most successful teachers, the achievement gap between black and white students could be erased. See Robert Gordon, Thomas J. Kane, and Douglas O. Staiger, "Identifying Effective Teachers Using Performance on the Job" (Brookings Institution, April 2006), 8.

148. See Jennifer L. Hochschild and Nathan Scovronick, "Democratic Education and the American Dream," in McDonnell, Timpane, and Benjamin, *Rediscovering the Democratic Purposes of Education*, 221.

149. E. D. Hirsch holds the view that "integration as such is far less critical to equality of educational opportunity than the quality of education actually received." Hirsch, *The Making of Americans*, 135.

WORKS CITED

Appiah, Kwame Anthony. *Cosmopolitanism*. New York: W. W. Norton, 2006.

Arendt, Hannah. *Between Past and Future*. New York: Penguin, 1968.

Aristotle. *Politics*. Indianapolis and Cambridge: Hackett, 1998.

Astin, Alexander W. "Liberal Education and Democracy: The Case for Pragmatism." In *Education and Democracy*, edited by Robert Orrill, 207–223. New York: College Entrance Examination Board, 1997.

Barber, Benjamin. *An Aristocracy of Everyone*. New York: Ballantine Books, 1992.

Barrow, Robin. "Common Schooling and the Need for Distinction." *Journal of the Philosophy of Education* 41 (2007): 559–573.

Barry, Brian. *Culture and Equality*. Cambridge, MA: Harvard University Press, 2001.

Benson, Lee, Ira Harkavy, and John Puckett. *Dewey's Dream: Universities and Democracies in an Age of Educational Reform*. Philadelphia: Temple University Press, 2007.

Bestor, Arthur. *Educational Wastelands: The Retreat from Learning in Our Public Schools*. Urbana and Chicago: University of Illinois Press, 1953, 1985.

Bok, Derek. *Our Underachieving Colleges*. Princeton, NJ: Princeton University Press, 2006.

Boston Schoolmasters. "Remarks on the Seventh Annual Report of the Hon. Horace Mann, Secretary of the Massachusetts Board of Education." Boston: Charles C. Little and James Brown, 1844.

Bowles, Samuel, and Herbert Gintis. *Schooling in Capitalist America*. New York: Basic Books, 1976.

Brighouse, Harry. *On Education*. London and New York: Routledge, 2006.

———. *School Choice and Social Justice*. Oxford and New York: Oxford University Press, 2000.

Brownson, Orestes. "The Second Annual Report of the Board of Education, Together with the Second Annual Report of the Secretary of the Board." *Boston Quarterly Review* 2 (October 1839): 393–434.

Butts, R. Freeman. *The Civic Mission in Educational Reform*. Stanford, CA: Hoover Institution Press, 1989.

Callan, Eamonn. *Creating Citizens*. Oxford and New York: Oxford University Press, 1997.

Caplan, Bryan. *The Myth of the Rational Voter*. Princeton, NJ: Princeton University Press, 2007.

Coetzee, J. M. *Waiting for the Barbarians*. New York: Penguin, 1980.

Combe, George. *The Constitution of Man*. Boston: Marsh, Capen, and Lyon; New York: Daniel Appleton, 1836.

Conover, Pamela Johnston, and Donald D. Searing. "A Political Socialization Perspective." In *Rediscovering the Democratic Purposes of Education*, edited by Lorraine M. McDonnell, P. Michael Timpane, and Roger Benjamin, 91–124. Lawrence: University Press of Kansas, 2000.

Cooper, James Fenimore. *The American Democrat*. New York: Penguin, 1989.

Cottom, Daniel. *Why Education Is Useless*. Philadelphia: University of Pennsylvania Press, 2003.

Cremin, Lawrence A., ed. *The Republic and the School: Horace Mann on the Education of Free Men*. New York: Teachers College, Columbia University, 1957.

Culver, Raymond B. *Horace Mann and Religion in the Massachusetts Public Schools*. New Haven, CT: Yale University Press, 1929.

Curti, Merle. *The Social Ideas of American Educators*. Totowa, NJ: Littlefield, Adams, 1959.

Delli Carpini, Michael, and Scott Keeter. *What Americans Know About Politics and Why It Matters*. New Haven, CT: Yale University Press, 1997.

Dewey, John. *Later Works*. 17 vols. Carbondale: Southern Illinois University Press, 1981–2008.

———. *Middle Works*. 15 vols. Carbondale: Southern Illinois University Press, 1976–1988.

Ehrlich, Thomas. "Dewey Versus Hutchins: The Next Round." In *Education and Democracy: Re-imagining Liberal Learning in America*, edited by Robert Orrill, 225–262. New York: College Entrance Examination Board, 1997.

Emerson, Ralph Waldo. *Essays and Lectures*. New York: Library of America, 1983.

Fish, Stanley. *Save the World on Your Own Time*. New York: Oxford University Press, 2008.

Galston, William. *Liberal Purposes*. New York: Cambridge University Press, 1991.

Goldin, Claudia, and Lawrence F. Katz. *The Race Between Education and Technology*. Cambridge, MA: Harvard University Press, 2008.

Gordon, Robert, Thomas J. Kane, and Douglas O. Staiger. "Identifying Effective Teachers Using Performance on the Job." Washington, DC: Brookings Institution, April 2006.

Greene, Maxine. *The Public School and the Private Vision*. New York: Random House, 1965.

Gutmann, Amy. "Civic Education and Social Diversity." *Ethics* 105 (April 1995): 557–579.

———. *Democratic Education*. Princeton, NJ: Princeton University Press, 1987.

Hamilton, Alexander, James Madison, and John Jay. *The Federalist Papers*. New York: New American Library, 1961.

Harvard University Committee on the Objectives of a General Education in a Free Society. *General Education in a Free Society*. Cambridge, MA: Harvard University Press, 1945.

Hawthorne, Nathaniel. *Tales and Sketches*. New York: Library of America, 1982.

Hinsdale, B. A. *Horace Mann and the Common School Revival in the United States*. New York: Charles Scribner's Sons, 1900.

Hirsch, E. D. *The Making of Americans: Democracy and Our Schools*. New Haven, CT: Yale University Press, 2009.

Hochschild, Jennifer L., and Nahan Scovronick. "Democratic Education and the American Dream." In *Rediscovering the Democratic Purposes of Education*, edited by Lorraine M. McDonnell, P. Michael Timpane, and Roger Benjamin, 209–242. Lawrence: University Press of Kansas, 2000.

Hofstadter, Richard. *Anti-Intellectualism in American Life*. New York: Alfred A. Knopf, 1963.

Hutchins, Robert Maynard. *The Conflict in Education in a Democratic Society*. New York: Harper and Brothers, 1953.

———. *Education for Freedom*. Baton Rouge: Louisiana State University Press, 1943.

———. "Grammar, Rhetoric, and Mr. Dewey." In John Dewey, *Later Works*, vol. 11. Carbondale: Southern Illinois University Press, 2008.

———. *The Higher Learning in America*. New Haven, CT, and London: Yale University Press, 1936.

———. *The University of Utopia*. Chicago: University of Chicago Press, 1953.

Kaestle, Carl F. *Pillars of the Republic*. New York: Hill and Wang, 1983.

Kaestle, Carl, and Maris Vinovskis. *Education and Social Change in Nineteenth-Century Massachusetts*. Cambridge: Cambridge University Press, 1980.

Kammen, Michael. *A Machine That Would Go of Itself*. New York: Alfred A. Knopf, 1987.

Kozol, Jonathan. *Savage Inequalities*. New York: Crown, 1991.

———. *The Shame of the Nation*. New York: Three Rivers Press, 2005.

Kronman, Anthony. *Education's End: Why Our Colleges and Universities Have Given Up on the Meaning of Life*. New Haven, CT: Yale University Press, 2007.

Kymlicka, Will. *Politics in the Vernacular*. Oxford and New York: Oxford University Press, 2001.

Lasch, Christopher. *The True and Only Heaven*. New York: W. W. Norton, 1991.

Lepore, Jill. "Just the Facts, Ma'am: Fake Memoirs, Factual Fictions, and the History of History." *New Yorker*, 24 March 2008, 79–83.

Levine, Donald N. *Powers of the Mind: The Reinvention of Liberal Learning in America*. Chicago: University of Chicago Press, 2006.

Lewis, C. S. *The Screwtape Letters*. New York: New American Library, 1988.

Lincoln, Abraham. *Speeches and Writings, 1832–1858*. New York: Library of America, 1989.

Macedo, Stephen, ed. *Democracy at Risk*. Washington, DC: Brookings Institution, 2005.

———. *Diversity and Distrust*. Cambridge, MA: Harvard University Press, 2000.

Mann, Horace. "Against Fiction." The Horace Mann Papers I–V, Reel 2 of 40, at the Massachusetts Historical Society, Boston.

———. "Against Novels." The Horace Mann Papers I–V, Reel 2 of 40, at the Massachusetts Historical Society.

———. *Annual Reports* 1–12. Horace Mann League and the Hugh Birch–Horace Mann Fund of the National Education Association, 1947–1952.

———. "Answer to the 'Rejoinder' of Twenty-nine Boston Schoolmasters, Part of the Thirty-one Who Published 'Remarks' on the Seventh Annual Report of the Secretary of the Massachusetts Board of Education." Boston: William B. Fowle and Nahum Capen, 1845.

———. "The Common School Controversy; Consisting of Three Letters of the Secretary of the Board of Education of the State of Massachusetts, in Reply to Charges Preferred Against the Board, by the Editor of the *Christian Witness* and by Edward A. Newton, Esq. of Pittsfield, Once a Member of the Board; to Which Are Added Extracts from the *Daily Press* in Regard to the Controversy." Boston: J. N. Bradley and Co., 1844.

———. *A Few Thoughts for a Young Man*. Boston: Ticknor, Reed, and Fields, 1850.

———. *A Few Thoughts on the Powers and Duties of Women*. Syracuse, NY: Hall, Mills, 1852.

———. *Lectures on Education*. Boston: Lemuel N. Ide, 1850.

———. "Letter to the Rev. Matthew Hale Smith in Answer to His 'Reply' or 'Supplement.'" Boston: William B. Fowle, 1847.

———. *Life and Works*, vols. 2–5. Boston: Lee and Shepard, 1891.

———. "Reply to the Remarks of Thirty-one Boston Schoolmasters on the Seventh Annual Report of the Secretary of the Massachusetts Board of Education." Boston: William B. Fowle and Nahum Chapen, 1844.

———. "Sequel to the So Called Correspondence Between the Rev. M. H. Smith and Horace Mann, Surreptitiously Published by Mr. Smith; Containing a Letter from Mr. Mann, Suppressed by Mr. Smith, with the Reply Therein Promised." Boston: William B. Fowle, 1847.

———. *Slavery: Letters and Speeches*. Boston: B. B. Mussey, 1851.

———. *Twelve Sermons*. Boston: Ticknor and Fields, 1961.

Mann, Mary Peabody. *Life of Horace Mann*. Washington, DC: National Education Association of the United States, 1937.

Marshall, Megan. *The Peabody Sisters*. Boston and New York: Houghton Mifflin, 2005.

Marx, Karl, and Frederick Engels. *Selected Works*, vol. 1. Moscow: Progressive Publishers, 1977.

McCluskey, Neil Gerard. *Public Schools and Moral Education*. New York: Columbia University Press, 1958.

McConnell, Michael W. "Educational Disestablishment: Why Democratic Values Are Ill-Served by Democratic Control of Schooling." In *Nomos XLIII: Moral and Political Education*, edited by Stephen Macedo and Yael Tamir, 87–146. New York: NYU Press, 2002.

Messerli, Jonathan. *Horace Mann*. New York: Alfred A. Knopf, 1972.

Mill, John Stuart. *The Collected Works of John Stuart Mill*, vol. 21. Toronto: University of Toronto Press; London: Routledge and Kegan Paul, 1984.

Miller, Perry. *The Responsibility of Mind in a Civilization of Machines*. Amherst: University of Massachusetts Press, 1979.

Minow, Martha, Richard A. Shweder, and Hazel Rose Markus. *Just Schools: Pursuing Equality in Societies of Difference*. New York: Russell Sage Foundation, 2008.

Morgan, Edmund S. *American Heroes*. New York: W. W. Norton, 2009.

Morgan, Joy Elmer. *Horace Mann: His Ideas and Ideals*. Washington, DC: National Home Library Foundation, 1936.

———. *Horace Mann at Antioch*. Washington, DC: Horace Mann Centennial Fund, National Education Association, 1938.

Murphy, James Bernard. "Against Civic Schooling." *Social Philosophy and Policy* 21 (2004): 221–265.

Newman, John Henry. *The Idea of the University*. New Haven, CT: Yale University Press, 1996.

Nie, Norman, and D. Sunshine Hillygus. "Education and Democratic Citizenship." In *Making Good Citizens*, edited by Diane Ravitch and Joseph P. Viteritti, 30–57. New Haven, CT: Yale University Press, 2001.

Nie, Norman H., Jane Junn, and Kenneth Stehlik-Barry. *Education and Democratic Citizenship in America*. Chicago: University of Chicago Press, 1996.

Niemi, Richard, and Jane Junn. *Civic Education: What Makes Students Learn?* New Haven, CT: Yale University Press, 1998.

Plato. *The Republic*. New York: Basic Books, 1991.

Ravitch, Diane. *The Language Police: How Pressure Groups Restrict What Students Learn*. New York: Vintage Books, 2004.

Ravitch, Diane, and Joseph P. Viteritti, eds. *Making Good Citizens*. New Haven, CT: Yale University Press, 2001.

Reese, William J. *America's Public Schools*. Baltimore: Johns Hopkins University Press, 2005.

Reich, Rob. *Bridging Liberalism and Multiculturalism in American Education*. Chicago: University of Chicago Press, 2002.

———. "How and Why to Support Common Schooling and Educational Choice at the Same Time." *Journal of the Philosophy of Education* 41 (2007): 709–725.

Rosenblum, Nancy. "Pluralism and Democratic Education: Stopping Short by Stopping with Schools." In *Nomos XLIII: Moral and Political Education*, edited by Stephen Macedo and Yael Tamir, 147–169. New York: NYU Press, 2002.

Rousseau, Jean-Jacques. *Basic Political Writings*. Indianapolis and Cambridge: Hackett, 1987.

Ryan, Alan. "No Consensus in Sight." In Bruce A. Kimball, *The Condition of American Liberal Education*, edited by Robert Orrill, 244–249. New York: College Entrance Examination Board, 1995.

Scarry, Elaine. *On Beauty and Being Just*. Princeton, NJ: Princeton University Press, 1999.

Smith, Matthew Hale. "Horace Mann and M. Hale Smith." Boston, 30 April 1847.

———. "Reply to the Sequel of Hon. Horace Mann, Being a Supplement to the Bible, the Rod, and Religion, in Common Schools," 2nd ed. Boston: J. M. Wittemore, 1847.

Straker, Robert L. *Horace Mann and Others*. Yellow Springs, OH: Antioch Press, 1963.

———. *The Unseen Harvest: Horace Mann and Antioch College*. Yellow Springs, OH: Antioch Press, 1955.

Strauss, Leo. "Liberal Education and Mass Democracy." In *Higher Education and Modern Democracy: The Crisis of the Few and Many*, edited by Martin Meyerson and Robert A. Goldwin, 73–96. Chicago: Rand McNally, 1967.

Tarcov, Nathan. *Locke's Education for Liberty*. Chicago: University of Chicago Press, 1984.

Taylor, Bob Pepperman. *Citizenship and Democratic Doubt*. Lawrence: University Press of Kansas, 2004.

Tharp, Louise Hall. *Until Victory: Horace Mann and Mary Peabody*. Boston: Little, Brown, 1953.

Thoreau, Henry David. *Collected Essays and Poems*. New York: Library of America, 2001.

Tyack, David, and Elisabeth Hansot. *Managers of Virtue: Public School Leadership in America, 1820–1980*. New York: Basic Books, 1982.

Vinovskis, Maris A. *Education, Society, and Economic Opportunity*. New Haven, CT: Yale University Press, 1995.

Wallace, David Foster. *This Is Water*. New York: Little, Brown, 2009.

Walsh, Julie M. *The Intellectual Origins of Mass Parties and Mass Schools in the Jacksonian Period: Creating a Conformed Citizenry*. New York: Garland, 1998.

Webster, Noah. "On the Education of Youth in America." In *Essays on Education in the Early Republic*, edited by Frederick Rudolph, 41–77. Cambridge, MA: Harvard University Press, 1965.

Westbrook, Robert. *Democratic Hope*. Ithaca, NY: Cornell University Press, 2005.

Williams, E. I. F. *Horace Mann: Educational Statesman*. New York: Macmillan, 1937.

Wood, Gordon. *Revolutionary Characters*. New York: Penguin, 2006.

Woodruff, Paul. *First Democracy*. New York: Oxford University Press, 2005.

INDEX